Yellow Journalist

Dispatches from Asian America

William Wong

 TEMPLE UNIVERSITY PRESS
PHILADELPHIA

Temple University Press, Philadelphia 19122
Copyright © 2001 by Temple University
All rights reserved
Published 2001
Printed in the United States of America

⊗ The paper used in this publication meets the requirements of the American National
Standard for Information Sciences—Permanence of Paper for Printed Library Materials,
ANSI Z39.48-1984.

Library of Congress Cataloging-in-Publication Data

Wong, William, 1941 July 7–
    Yellow journalist : dispatches from Asian America / William Wong.
        p.   cm. — (Mapping racisms)
    ISBN 1-56639-829-0 (cloth : alk. paper) — ISBN 1-56639-830-4 (pbk. : alk. paper)
        1. Wong, William, 1941 July 7–   2. Asian Americans—Biography.   3. Asian
    Americans—Cultural assimilation.   4. Asian Americans—Social conditions—20th
    century.   5. United States—Race relations.   6. United States—Ethnic relations.
    7. Journalists—United States—Biography.   8. Oakland (Calif.)—Biography.
    I. Title.   II. Series.

    E184.O6 W66 2001
    305.895073'0092–dc21
        [B]   00-041196

For Joyce and Sam

Contents

Series Foreword

Darrell Y. Hamamoto

As an admirer of his work for many years, I had the opportunity at last to meet Bill Wong at a 1997 conference organized by Professor Ling-chi Wang of the University of California at Berkeley held at the Miyako Hotel in San Francisco's Japantown. The gathering had been called to ponder the implications of the so-called campaign finance scandal, which involved a host of well-placed Asian and Asian American donors and operatives who had been accused of strategically applying gobs of money where they thought it might be most effective within this system of government by plutocracy.

Momentarily suspending discussion of the issues raised by the most recent of periodic "Yellow Peril" moral panics, I asked Wong about a piece (included in the present collection) he recently had written that described his thirteen-year-old son's spontaneous hail-to-the-chief, President Bill Clinton. The Head Man himself (well before Fellatiogate) had appeared in Wong's hometown Oakland, California, at a political rally with about fifteen thousand people in attendance. Sam Mende-Wong, representing the Museum of Children's Art where he worked as a volunteer, seized the moment to exhort the crowd into calling for the president's reelection. Concluding his rousing cry of support, Sam then turned to the funky tenor sax-playing leader of the free world and gave him the thumbs up, shouting, "Rock on, Mr. President!" Thus did the paternal grandson of an immigrant from Guangdong province named Gee Seow Hong "make his mark" on a world shaped by his tenaciously resilient forebears.

As co-editor of the Temple University Press monograph series Mapping Racisms, I floated the idea past Wong that a collection of his essays would be an invaluable resource for those of us who needed a perceptive and empathetic intelligence to guide us over the tortuous terrain of contemporary politics, culture, and society. Wong said that he had been thinking along the same lines and I asked him to submit a proposal to produce an anthology of his writing. I left the conference buoyed in anticipation of hearing from the dean of Asian American journalists. But months were to pass with nary a word from Wong. Unlike those of us who have the good fortune of being kept on salary to think deep thoughts, I understood that a working freelance journalist such as he would need to keep producing salable new articles to keep rice on the table. The meticulously tedious job of preparing a manuscript suitable for publication would be onerous even if there were no other demands on his time and resources. Prospects for the project dimmed with the passing days.

Many months later, I did a guest shot in a segment on Asian American media depictions broadcast on KQED-FM, the San Francisco public radio station. I took the opportunity to pitch the necessity of an Asian American porno practice to counter attempts by The Man to contain Yellow people politically through the control of our sexuality. Among the listeners was one Bill Wong. Hearing my plans for producing Asian American erotica apparently was enough to rouse our man Wong into action. When I checked for e-mail the next day, a message from Wong awaited me. He had contacted me to inquire whether the offer to do a book still stood. It did. He promised to whip-up a proposal. After sending the proposal and a selection of his articles to a committee of outside reviewers—who voted unanimously in favor of publication—Temple University Press gave the project the green light. The result is the volume of essays before you.

In reviewing the passionate, reflective, and sometimes whimsical pieces in this collection, one is struck by how "right" Wong has been on questions that have been fiercely debated and contested by the best and brightest minds in policy circles, academia, and government. Affirmative action, the gender wars, race relations, sexuality, multiculturalism, and contemporary immigration are among the "hot button" issues that have fueled political discussion over the past decade. Wong even has managed to provide fresh perspectives on perennial questions of Asian American "identity," a topic that too often founders upon clichés, trite observations, and tired formulations.

Looking back on his writings, why is it that Wong so often has been proven correct in his observations and assessments? For the coherent thinking-through and making sense of complex historical events and issues *as they are unfolding* is a decidedly difficult task. There are several possible reasons for Wong's percipience. For starters, he evinces a profound humility in the face of vexing dilemmas that many of us have tried either to finesse or to conveniently ignore. In taking on the challenge of real-time sociocultural analysis, the author brings a deep appreciation and understanding of history to his work. Even as he delivers well-reasoned arguments, Wong takes care to consider all sides of a given controversy and is never judgmental except in his blanket condemnation of injustice. Importantly, he transcends the naive moralism of many social commentators by consistently pointing to the political-economic roots of the problems subjected to his critical scrutiny. Finally, in all its obvious erudition, there is an all-embracing humanism that animates Wong's life-work.

No innocent bystander, Wong on occasion has found himself at the center of history-in-process rather than simply reporting on it. After his having been invited by civil rights leaders Kweisi Mfume and Myrlie Evers-Williams to assist an NAACP-sponsored dialogue on race relations, the intrepid journalist had hopes of moving the discussion beyond the "Black-White narrative." But in finding that his goal of a truly multiracial, multicultural approach to the extirpation of America's original sin did not fully resonate with the NAACP leadership, Wong uses the experience to argue forcefully for a new model of race relations that includes all non-White peoples. The various pieces in this collection—tackling as they do persistent problems of media racism, criminality, interethnic tensions, and political marginalization—certainly make a strong case for the centrality of the Asian American historical experience in U.S. race relations.

It is only appropriate that this volume opens with an homage to the Oakland Chinatown of the author's childhood. For it was in this milieu that Wong lived the formative realities that shaped the sensibilities of an immigrant's son whose writing has become a guiding light to those of us groping through the darkness of duplicity, misinformation, and our own willful ignorance. From the world of the Great China restaurant operated by his family for eighteen years after its opening near the end of the robust war years, Wong early on absorbed the meaning of immigrant lived-experience, social justice, economic inequality, and the centrality of community struggle against the multiple forms of oppression. "China-man," Chinese American, Asian American; any way you slice it, Bill Wong is one straight-up righteous Yellow Man. We are fortunate to have him battling at our side armed with a keen intelligence that cuts through the rhetoric, lies, and evasions of our foes.

Acknowledgments

In addition to the individuals I name in the introduction as being influential on my writing career—high school teachers Blanche Hurd and George Stokes, editor Bob Maynard and his wife, Nancy Hicks, and editor Roy Aarons; editors Richard Springer and Patrick Andersen; publishers Gordon Lew and John Fang—many people have helped me, in one way or another, become a better writer and thinker. I have been blessed with friends, family, and colleagues who have been exquisitely generous and compassionate toward me. They include *Daily Californian* staff members Maggie Wilson, Janie Wood, Ron Bergman, Mike Berger, Josh Eppinger, Sandie North, and Pat Mar; college journalism professors Walter Gieber, Larry Pinkham, Melvin Mencher, Fred Friendly, and Frederick Yu; editors Harry Press and Paul Spindler; former *Wall Street Journal* colleagues Michael Gartner, Norman Pearlstein, Everett Groseclose, James Hyatt, Ralph Winter, Herb Lawson, A. Richard Immel, Dick Leger, Dick James, and Janice Simpson; former *Oakland Tribune* colleagues Roy Grimm, Eric Newton, Mary Ellen Butler, and Brenda Payton; *San Francisco Examiner* editors James Finefrock, Lynn Ludlow, and Lynn Myers Berger; and Ishmael Reed, the iconoclastic author and media critic.

One more person deserves special mention. He is Frank Chin, a brilliant and influential force in Asian American letters. Frank was a classmate at Lincoln School and Oakland High School. He went on to become a groundbreaking playwright, novelist, essayist and conscience of Asian American literature. His example and counsel have long been an inspiration to me.

I must express my deepest appreciation to Darrell Hamamoto, an Asian American studies professor at the University of California at Davis. I met

Darrell several years ago at a conference, and it was he who prodded me into pulling this book together and who introduced me to editors at Temple University Press. Without his invaluable guidance and assistance, this book would not have been possible.

My interaction with officials and editors at Temple University Press has been nothing short of respectful professionalism. I can't thank enough Doris Braendel, Tamika Hughes, Jennifer French, Gary Kramer, Ann-Marie Anderson, and Irene Imperio of the Press, Janet Greenwood of Berliner Inc., who oversaw production of this book, and Debby Stuart, who did a superb job of copy editing.

Finally, I am forever grateful to my late parents, Gee Seow Hong and Gee Suey Ting, who instilled in me and my sisters honorable values and who struggled on behalf of their seven children, always hoping for a better life in America for their children than they had. I also want to acknowledge my siblings—Li Hong Lew, Li Keng Wong, Lai Chop Webster, Nellie Wong, the late Leslie Yee, and Flo Oy Wong—and members of my extended family who have been wonderful in the love and respect they have paid me. And how can I possibly thank enough my spouse, Joyce, whose love, sense of humor, stellar ideas, and clear-eyed vision have kept me on this journey when there were times I wanted to stop; and my son, Sam, who is wise and mature beyond his years and who may have taught me more than I him.

Introduction

In 1948, when I was 7 years old, my family moved from our crowded rented house in Oakland's Chinatown to a spacious five-bedroom split-level house in a predominantly white neighborhood less than two miles away. I was still too young to be of significant help at my parents' restaurant, so I stayed home more than my older sisters, who were practically held hostage at the restaurant. A favorite pastime was to listen to the radio in our new home. (It wasn't until 1952 that our family bought our first television set, which was still a luxury for most households.) On autumn Saturday afternoons, my ears were glued to radio broadcasts of football games played by the University of California at Berkeley ("Cal" to locals). The late 1940s were the glory years of Cal football, whose coach, Pappy Waldorf, was a living legend. It didn't matter that I was a Chinese American kid whose immigrant parents spoke broken English and didn't know the first thing about American football. I became a football fanatic and by extension a sports nut who supplemented my radio listening with hours spent reading the stories and memorizing the statistics of my favorite teams and players in the sports pages of the local paper.

Kids don't immediately realize any limits. When I started high school in the ninth grade, I had the brilliant idea of trying out for the freshman basketball team. After all, I had spent years playing schoolyard football, baseball, and basketball. I was barely taller than five feet. As I joined other boys my age—but not necessarily my height—it became painfully obvious after one quick scrimmage that I was delusional. While my skills were about average, my height wasn't, so I was not invited back for the next tryout. I don't recall whether I was emotionally crushed by this rejection, but I turned to the next best thing—writing about sports for the school newspaper. Since I had absorbed by osmosis the sportswriting idiom—military analogies, action verbs, and colorful clichés—I felt confident I could chronicle the exploits of my high school's sports teams. So began my journalistic writing "career."

Sportswriting took a backseat in my senior year, however, because my journalism teacher, a slender, nervous woman in her fifties named Blanche Hurd, appointed me to be editor of the school's yearbook. I agonized over a decision since I really loved writing sports for the school newspaper, but Miss Hurd persuaded me to head up the yearbook staff. I'm not sure why I gave in, because she was not dealing from a position of strength. She had taken over my high school's journalism classes in my junior year, succeeding the exceedingly popular James Black. It took a long time for the mousy Miss Hurd to win any respect from her students, although I didn't have any animosity toward her. In fact, what I remember about her—other than her naming me yearbook editor—was some prescient advice that resonates with me even today.

One day during my senior year, Miss Hurd took me aside to talk about my future. I don't remember what I said, but I vividly recollect what she said. If I wanted to pursue journalism as a career, she said, I would have to be "twice as good" to succeed. I heard her words, but I did not fully grasp her meaning. Twice as good. I was 16 years old and while I thought I knew a great deal about myself and the world, I knew very little.

Miss Hurd was one of two high school teachers who were most significant in my development as a writer and thinker. The other was George Stokes, a history teacher. Mr. Stokes had only one arm; he wore a prosthetic for his other arm. He didn't let that disability bother him. More than any other teacher, he pushed me and my classmates to think for ourselves. His class lessons were filled with dates and important events, but he insisted that we think about dates and events and that we write critically in our essays. And he did it in an aggressive style that challenged us to do our best.

When I enrolled at Cal in 1958, I pursued my first love—sportswriting. Even before I registered for any classes, I signed up to be a sportswriter in the dungeon that was the office of the *Daily Californian* in Eshleman Hall. I had the good fortune of covering Cal's football team coached by Marv Levy before he became the successful head coach of the Buffalo Bills and the superb basketball teams under Coach Pete Newell. I saw Newell's team win a national championship, then lose it the next year. I even rose to the exalted position of sports editor in my sophomore year, a precocious rise for a Chinatown kid. Alas, my sports editorship was truncated by a political revolution at Cal, a precursor to the Free Speech Movement of 1964 that shook the world.

My Cal experience helped shape my political worldview. I was there a little more than ten years after the United States, as the leader of the Allied forces that defeated the fascist regimes of Germany, Japan, and Italy, emerged as a world power. Russia turned from friend to foe. The Cold War set in. Rabid anticommunism was in the air in Washington, D.C., and coursed through universities like Cal, where professors were forced to sign loyalty oaths and where nervous administrators tangled with student freethinkers.

I had only cursory knowledge of these irresistible forces from my cubicle at the *Daily Californian*. I was content to write a column, which I called "The Chinese Bandit," after the nickname given to the defensive unit of the Louisiana State University football team. As sports editor, however, I was a member of the editorial board of the *Daily Cal*, led by a quiet intellectual named Dan Silver. Silver and his news-side editors, all seniors and liberal to one degree or another, decided to endorse a set of candidates representing a leftist student group called Slate who were running for student government positions. I went along with the endorsement even though I was not fully invested in the ideological leanings of Silver and his top editors. It was not as though I were a political eunuch. I was simply less mature politically than the top editors of the paper, who were my elders.

Our endorsement of Slate was a giant no-no to the conservative administrators, who engineered a coup of the *Daily Cal's* editorial board, forcing us to resign. The administration replaced us with more compliant students from the fraternities and sororities. The *Daily Cal* staff went off campus and published a newspaper called *The Independent Californian* with the generous assistance of a veteran local journalist named Orr Kelly. We hawked our newly minted paper on the streets near the campus, but our enthusiasm wasn't sufficient to sustain our resource-poor efforts. Eventually, a deal was brokered, allowing some of the old *Daily Cal* staff to join the Greek-letter-society interlopers. Since I was the youngest of the editorial board members, I was named to a high news-side position—

managing editor—thus joining the ranks of the more serious news-side staff, and I haven't looked back since. In the last semester of my senior year, I took over as *Daily Cal* editor and led the staff back into a more liberal territory. The civil rights movement in the south was heating up, and I had friends who spent summers on freedom rides and otherwise lent their support to southern black people who fought to end legal segregation.

In the summer following my graduation from Cal, I got my first professional journalism job with the help of a Cal journalism professor—as a summer replacement reporter at the *San Francisco Chronicle*. I was only 21 years old, still wet-behind-the-ears. A veteran reporter told me at the time that I broke a color line, becoming the first Chinese American reporter on a daily newspaper in the city with the largest ethnic Chinese community in the United States. That summer job lasted only five months, but I was able to land two other jobs at Bay Area papers during the next year and a half. One was with the afternoon San Francisco paper at the time, a hybrid called the *News Call Bulletin*. There I continued my political education. One of the big stories I covered was the local civil rights protests at the famous Sheraton Palace Hotel, which didn't hire black people or other racial minorities.

With two years of journalism under my belt—and too many stories about five-alarm fires, petty crimes, and murders—I needed a break, so I signed up for the Peace Corps. I served three and one half years in the Philippines, which wasn't my specific choice. But since I wanted to go to Asia to get closer to my ethnic Chinese roots, the Philippines was a good alternative because it hosted a Peace Corps program, whereas China did not. With my unaccented American English and my Chinese face, I baffled ordinary Filipinos who thought Americans were white and blonde. As much as any experience of being a racial minority in the United States, my years as an *inchick* (the Tagalog word for Chinese) in the Philippines enriched my understanding of the sensitivities and pitfalls of interracial relationships.

Racial matters were never at the forefront of my early journalism career, which I resumed after the Peace Corps and a master's degree from the Columbia University Graduate School of Journalism. The *Wall Street Journal*'s hiring me in 1970 after my Columbia education was not because I was a racial minority. Newspapers in those days, like many other American institutions, did not have affirmative action programs.

Nonetheless, as I settled into a routine life as a staff reporter for the *Journal*, first in Cleveland, Ohio, then in San Francisco, a yearning to write about my racial roots and identity issues began to surface. The *Journal* was one of those rare major newspapers that encouraged young reporters to propose their own stories, especially for the three precious feature slots on its rigid front page. After President Nixon stunned the world by resuming relations with communist China, I wrote a front-page *Journal* story about how some Chinese Americans were being used as cultural "bridges" between the two societies. I profiled a new Chinese American civil rights group, Chinese for Affirmative Action of San Francisco. A year after the so-called fall of Saigon, I wrote a feature story about how newly arrived Vietnamese refugees were faring in their new home state of California. During Labor Day weekend of 1977, a San Francisco Chinatown gang shot up a busy restaurant in a spectacular revenge hit. Going beyond that criminal act, I wrote an in-depth front-page feature about how Chinatowns formed and why they incubate conditions that can lead to such acts of organized violence.

As prestigious as it was to work for one of the nation's finest newspapers, I ached to get closer to my community—both geographic and ethnic. When I heard that Robert C. Maynard was taking over the *Oakland Tribune* as its new editor in late 1979, I asked him for a job. I had met and conversed with Maynard before. He had a solid national reputation through his reporting, writing, and editorializing at the *Washington Post*. He quit the *Post*—and his wife Nancy Hicks had quit the *New York Times*—to launch an ambitious initiative to train more racial minority journalists to become staff members at more daily newspapers in the United States. This time, for me, race was a factor in my hiring. I had told Maynard I wanted a writing job. He replied that he wanted me to be business editor of the *Tribune*, taking advantage of my nine years at the *Wall Street Journal*. I had not given any thought before to an editing job, but I felt it was an opportunity I could not pass up. So began a seventeen-year association with the *Tribune*, the newspaper I grew up with but one I never thought was friendly to me or the neighborhood of my childhood, which happened to be in the shadow of the *Tribune* Tower.

The *Tribune* had its zenith under the ownership of the Knowland family, led by patriarch Joseph Knowland, a Congressman who happened to own a newspaper. Under the Knowlands, the *Tribune* ran Oakland, along with Henry J. Kaiser, the industrialist responsible for building dams and paving thousands of miles of highways throughout the western United States and building and repairing ships during World War II and whose legacy is the pioneering Kaiser Permanente health-maintenance organization.

Oakland was a different city before World War II than it was after it. Racial minorities such as African Americans, Mexican Americans, and Asian Americans were a relatively small presence before the war. But the Kaiser industrial complex needed workers for its shipyards, so thousands of black people from Texas, Louisiana, and other southern states migrated west for wartime jobs. Federal immigration restrictions kept the numbers of Asians low in Oakland and the rest of the United States. After the war, many African Americans stayed and immigration restrictions were loosened, allowing in more Asian and Latino immigrants. Meanwhile, flush with prosperity and a new hubris born of the war's triumphs, America was on the move internally. Suburbs blossomed everywhere, luring middle-class white families. The gritty industrial base began eroding too, leaving cities like Oakland to poorer racial minorities with fewer and fewer industrial jobs.

For about thirty years after the war, the *Tribune* managed to live off the wealth generated by its earlier successes. It was a powerhouse not only in Oakland but also in suburbs to its north, east, and south. Leadership at the *Tribune* shifted from the founding patriarch Joseph to his son William, who had been a conservative Republican United States Senator made famous by his staunch defense of the Nationalist Chinese regime that had escaped to Formosa, now called Taiwan, after losing to Mao Zedong's communists in 1949. William F. Knowland was apparently better as an anticommunist zealot than he was as a businessman, however. At a time when the suburbs were exploding, the *Tribune* inexplicably pulled back its resources and basically ceded that advertising-rich territory to two small chains—one owned by Dean Lesher, the other by Floyd Sparks—that later became prosperous at The Tribune's expense. By the time Robert C. Maynard took over as editor of the *Tribune* under the new ownership of The Gannett Corporation in 1979, the *Tribune* was a mere shadow of its former self.

Nonetheless, Maynard wanted to put his (or Gannett's) money where his mouth was, so he set out to hire qualified racial minority journalists to work at the *Tribune*, whose staff until then was predominantly white. I was among those he hired under his plan to further integrate the *Tribune*'s staff. Maynard gave me many wonderful opportunities. The most significant was the columnist job. First, I wrote a weekly column about journalism issues and ethics, when I was the *Tribune*'s first and only ombudsman in the mid-1980s. Then in 1988, I asked Maynard and Executive Editor Leroy F. Aarons if I could write a column on general issues for the paper's op-ed page. They agreed, with some reservations. Aarons was concerned I might not be able to sustain a column, especially one that occasionally focused on Asian American issues.

A few years earlier, I had begun writing columns for *East-West News*, a San Francisco Chinatown-based English language weekly run by Gordon Lew. Richard Springer, a white editor at *East-West*, had encouraged me to write a column. By the time I started my *Tribune* column, I had two outlets to voice opinions on a whole range of Asian American issues and, in the case of the *Tribune*, issues having nothing to do with my racial roots or identity. After *East-West* ceased publication in 1989, Patrick Andersen, editor at *Asian Week*, another San Francisco Chinatown-based English language publication, asked me to write my column for him. *Asian Week* was created by John Fang, a visionary businessman who, like the educator Gordon Lew, saw the value of a publication that wrote about Chinese American and Asian American issues.

Meanwhile, I continued to write columns for the *Tribune*, until March 22, 1996, when I was summarily fired at 3 P.M. and ordered out of the building without a chance to gather up my files. By then, the troubled *Tribune* had changed owners again—from Gannett in 1979 to Bob Maynard himself in 1983 to a chain owned by William Dean Singleton in 1992. The new editors under the Singleton regime didn't much like me, but they felt they needed me (and two prominent African American editorial page staff members) at the beginning of the transition from a Maynard-owned *Tribune* to one owned by a company notable in the newspaper business for its obsession with profits and its mostly white suburban markets. Oakland, a much-aligned appendage to world-famous San Francisco, was hardly a white suburb. Its population of close to four hundred thousand is approximately 70 percent non-white, and it was not politically smart for the new owners not to have prominent racial minority writers like me and columnist Brenda Payton, who is African American.

My firing ignited loud protests from local readers and supporters, who picketed the *Tribune* offices in a driving rainstorm demanding my reinstatement. That never happened. The official reason for my firing was "downsizing," but I was the only news-side employee downsized that day. And the way it was done—perfunctory notification by an immediate supervisor, then an order to leave the building immediately—left the distinct impression that I might be a deranged felon. To this day, I do not know the precise reason for my firing, but I suspect that the conservative white editors who took over the *Tribune* from Maynard did not like my politics and did not like my writing so often about Asian American issues. I thought the four other large newspapers in the San Francisco Bay Area— the *San Francisco Chronicle*, the *San Francisco Examiner*, the *San Jose Mercury News*, and the *Contra Costa Times* in Walnut Creek—might be interested in hiring me, but the best I could do was a freelance column twice a month from the *Examiner*. While the frequency of my columns is much less than what it was when I was at the *Tribune*, I continue to write journalistically, mostly on Asian American issues.

Why write about Asian American issues, and what exactly is "Asian America"? The Asian presence in the United States is both rich and mostly invisible. It is not my intention here to replay the 150 years of Asian American history except to note that Americans of Asian descent have until the past thirty years lived under second-rate (or worse) conditions and have mostly been worker bees—vilified ones at that during extended periods of economic difficulties. The legacies of exclusion and officially sanctioned discrimination are difficult to shed. The Asian American population grew enormously over the last one-third of the 20th century, and most Asian newcomers do not face the same overt conditions of segregation and discrimination. But even the most highly educated Asian immigrant professional sometimes discovers the ugly underbelly of the American experience—subtle (and not-so-subtle) discrimination based on race or ethnicity. Few of us have reached leadership roles on the national stage. Yet there is a great deal to be said about the Asian American experience that informs the complex American political, economic, and cultural landscape.

Which is why I have written this book, a compilation of stories, columns, essays and commentaries that range widely over a panoply of issues that touch Asian Americans and Americans in general. One of the great American stories of the late 20th century—and one that continues into the beginning of the 21st century—is the increasingly multiracial, multicultural aspect of the American experience. People of Asian descent have been a big part of that story, although the mainstream news and mass media have been slow to recognize our role in a changing America. Considering my background and politics and professional training, I saw the story developing almost from the time I resumed my journalism career some thirty years ago. I needed to find the appropriate forum to begin telling those stories within the story.

The stories, essays, analyses, and commentaries in this book cover many subjects, from the personal to policy, from the serious to the silly. A reader will learn some details of my cultural upbringing and my family's transformation from a poor rice-growing village in China to planting roots in the San Francisco Bay Area. A reader will also learn a little Asian American history and a lot about the nuances and intricacies of the contemporary Asian American experience. The overriding theme of this collection is the courage, forbearance, tenacity, survival skills, and humanity shown by people from east and southeast Asia who never allowed racism and hatred to deter them from winning a rightful place in the American sun.

1 Hometown

In the Shadow of San Francisco

American Dream, Chinatown Branch

East Bay Express, July 30, 1999

Walking along the west side of Webster Street between 7th and 8th Streets in Oakland's Chinatown, it's easy to miss the storefront in the middle of the block. Other stores catch your eye: the ones selling produce and fruits in boxes that bulge onto the sidewalk, another displaying roast ducks, chickens, and glistening maroon-colored strips of oven-roasted pork. At the 7th Street corner, strings of minilights showcase a refurbished Tin's Teahouse. On the 8th Street corner, a spacious window houses a bank.

The relatively unobtrusive storefront at 723 Webster, with its non-descript aluminum door and curtained window, is called the Happy Noodle House. From 1943 to 1961, it was the Great China cafe, the base of my universe for most of the first twenty years of my life. It is where several of my older sisters first lived when they came as children from China, and it's where my father ran two businesses, one of them legal, the other shady. The latter nearly cost him his life.

The Great China ("Aye Joong Wah," in our family's Chinese dialect) was owned and operated by my immigrant parents, Gee Seow Hong and Gee Theo Quee. My older sisters and I did hard labor there before going out into the world. With Chinatown today a veritable riot of economic activity, many of its current occupants, let alone outsiders, know little of the Chinatown of that era, when people like me were both of this society and outside it.

I think a lot about my Chinatown past, in part because memories are fading as middle age deepens. I want to hang onto the memory of a time and place that contrasts so sharply with today's version of the American Dream—anonymous suburbs where neighbors barely know one another and young people are bored to death, where multigenerational interactions are rare; where high technology makes a few of us obscenely rich and the rest of us neurotically insecure. And I wonder about the arc of development that brought my family from the poverty of precommunist China to the middle-class comforts of California today.

Occasionally I go to the Happy Noodle House and order a bowl of *chieu jow ho fun*, rice noodles in a hearty broth brimming with pieces of chicken, pork, fish balls, shrimps, kidneys, green onions, and bean sprouts. It's a soul-satisfying meal, especially when it is seasoned with droplets of Vietnamese red chili sauce. As I slurp the noodles and soup, breaking into a sweat, memories of my youth in this very space wash over me.

The Happy Noodle House uses the long, narrow space differently than my parents did a half-century ago. Tables for four line the walls on either side, with a big round table toward the back, on the left. Each table has a container of plastic chopsticks, a stack of small sauce dishes, and a tray to hold the chili and soy sauce. The kitchen is in the back; the menu is exclusively Chinese and Vietnamese.

The Great China had wooden double doors with windows; the doors were set back a few feet, creating a landing where I often sat as a toddler. Fifty-pound bags of rice were stacked inside the door. A counter ran along the length of the right side, curving like a reverse J into the wall at the front. Toward the back on the left side were three booths with bench seating. In the middle of the left wall, a staircase led to a second floor, which was filled with customers in the early days. Beneath the staircase, a rectangular table seated six. Our kitchen was also in the back; the menu contained an eclectic mix of Western and Chinese offerings.

At the first staircase landing, as it turns to go up to the second floor, a door opened into a tiny step-down office where my father kept his accounts and abacus. The office had a manual typewriter, which my sisters used to type the daily Western food specials. At my father's urging, I taught myself how to type, using a Gregg's textbook, when business was slow. After we typed the menu using a purple-ink ribbon, my dad would reproduce copies in a tray of gelatin.

Business was never slow in the early days of the Great China, during the last three years of World War II. Oakland's Chinatown prospered from the frenzied war machine that cranked into high gear after Japan bombed Pearl Harbor. I had been born exactly five months earlier in a house my parents rented at 725 Harrison Street, one block east of the Great China. Before starting the restaurant, my father and his oldest daughter, Li Hong, worked as welders in a shipyard a half mile from Chinatown. Once the restaurant got going, customers came, day and night, from the shipyards and surrounding neighborhoods. Jobs were plentiful, people had money, and rationing of basic ingredients discouraged home cooking.

Business was so good that my father was able to quickly repay the $3,000 he borrowed to open the Great China. In 1948, three years after the war ended, my parents paid $16,000 in cash for a five-bedroom house in the Cleveland neighborhood on the east side of Lake Merritt, less than two miles from Chinatown. It was a neighborhood that had once kept out Chinese and other racial minorities, but such restrictions faded in the postwar years. (Even into the mid-1950s, though, some Oakland neighborhoods did not welcome Chinese Americans, as one of my sisters discovered when she and her new husband went shopping for a home.) As an indication of the demographic changes Oakland has undergone since, the Cleveland neighborhood today is informally called "China Hill" because so many Chinese families moved there after the war.

Before the war, my parents struggled with a variety of small businesses while raising seven children. The war changed all that, launching us and other Chinese American families into the middle class. Yet often that existence was largely played out in an enclosed community.

And Chinatown was a true community, where we grew up surrounded by elders who watched over us if our parents could not. We hung out on busy commercial streets day and night. Some days, especially during the lunar New Year, the streets were festive, with Chinese opera music blaring from family association halls upstairs, accompanied by the distinctive clack of mah-jongg tiles. We practiced Old World customs while quickly adapting to American ways such as team and individual sports, social dancing, flirting, and listening to the radio. We did not have the opportunities that many American children today enjoy, but most of us managed to survive childhoods of constant manual labor and harsh opprobriums from barely educated immigrant parents.

The economic shot in the arm of the war years wore off in the fifties, and Oakland's Chinatown fell into a semicomatose state. The younger generation—my generation—went to college and worked outside of family businesses, which shrank or disappeared because there was no longer a war industry to supply customers. City people, especially the white middle class, moved to burgeoning suburbs, their exodus made easier by new freeways and inexpensive gasoline. Chinatown real estate was gobbled up for the Nimitz Freeway, Laney College, and the Bay Area Rapid Transit system.

By the time America veered sharply into a zesty era of youthful optimism with the presidential election of John F. Kennedy in 1960, the Great China was on its last legs. My father became ill, and in 1961, when I was at Cal enjoying life on the *Daily Californian* and ingesting the liberal idealism of the time, he died. So did the Great China.

Today's Chinatown has attracted big Asian money, enough to build the Pacific Renaissance Plaza on 9th Street between Webster and Franklin. The structure, which opened in 1993, is a Hong Kong–style multi-use development with parking underground, ground-floor retail shops, an open plaza in the middle, restaurants and offices on the second floor, the Asian branch of the Oakland Public Library, a cultural center, and multiple stories of condominiums and apartments.

More than that, where once Chinatown seemed to shrink, now its boundaries have expanded, first to Broadway on the west, and now even beyond Broadway. Core Chinatown in the old days stopped at 10th Street. The main commercial areas were concentrated on a few blocks along the axis of Webster Street between 7th and 9th Streets and 8th Street between Franklin and Harrison. Today, it reaches to 14th Street, with Korean-owned businesses dominating that stretch. Some folks say Chinatown should be called Asiatown.

Chinatown remains the heart of the immigrant Asian population of Oakland, and at some level, for the greater East Bay. Like other American Chinatowns, Oakland's began as a safe haven for sojourners and immigrants terrorized by anti-Chinese sentiments during the last half of the 19th century.

It is difficult to pinpoint when the first Chinese came to Oakland. Large numbers of Chinese people, mostly men, came to California as part of the Gold Rush of the mid-19th century. So, of course, did many others. Almost overnight, San Francisco mushroomed from a nothing town to a raucous sin city. On the east shore of the bay, three men—two from New York, the other from Connecticut—founded the town of Oakland, which incorporated in 1852.

Few seekers found gold. Many Chinese ended up in San Francisco after being driven out of the hills, but some found their way to Oakland. Says Beth Bagwell in her book *Oakland: The Story of a City*, Chinese "settled in the 1850s on the estuary in Oakland where they lived in poor shacks and fished for shrimp." Discriminatory laws forced the early Oakland Chinese to live only in "certain concentrated districts," among them the current Chinatown. Population figures for Chinese in Oakland in the last half of the 19th century are also hard to come by, but according to U.S. census figures of 1870 and 1880, the percentage of Chinese living in Alameda County showed a remarkable growth to about 8 percent. But by 1900, the percentage had dropped to only 1.6 percent, the stark effect of the Chinese Exclusion Act of 1882.

The reason for the precipitous fall was economic scapegoating. While dodging the hostility of white Oaklanders, early Oakland Chinese worked as farmers and produce peddlers and later as laundry operators because they could not find other work. Chinese workers had been recruited to build the western half of the transcontinental railroad, which was completed in 1869. Once the economy began to slump in the 1870s, competition for jobs grew stiff. White labor leaders in San Francisco organized a political movement, blaming Chinese laborers for the economic downturn. Oakland also had a strong anti-Chinese labor movement. This campaign led to the passage of the Chinese Exclusion Act in 1882, the single most influential law affecting Chinese American history.

My own family's journey from a remote Chinese rice-growing village to Oakland is inextricably linked to the Exclusion Act and its far-flung ramifications. While Chinese merchants, students, and diplomats could legally enter the United States, the measure excluded Chinese laborers. To get around restrictions, the Chinese devised elaborate fake-paper systems, the most notorious being the "paper son" scheme. Chinese American men would visit China and, upon returning, tell U.S. officials they had sons in China when they had not. The men sold the "paper son" slots to someone seeking to emigrate, thus legitimizing the newcomer's entry. The 1906 San Francisco earthquake and fire destroyed all birth records, including those of Chinese immigrants, which provided a golden opportunity to create fake documents that said many Chinese men were "sons of natives," making them U.S. citizens.

That is how my father, Gee Seow Hong, entered the United States on May 27, 1912, at the port of San Francisco aboard the SS *Manchuria*. He came through Angel Island Immigration Station, the main facility enforcing the Exclusion Act from 1910 to 1940. Immigration inspectors tried to trip up Chinese newcomers with detailed—and inane—trick questions about the immigrant's home village and family relationships. If members of the same family recalled details differently, that could be cause for deportation.

In documents I found at the National Archives regional office in San Bruno, my father's entry papers said he was born on May 26, 1896, in Goon Doo Hong village, Sun Ning district, China. That would make him 16 years old, but his papers said he was seventeen, perhaps reflecting the Chinese habit of saying a person is a year old at birth. His "alleged father" was identified as Gee Bing Fong, who swore he was born in San Francisco in 1870. My teenage father did not resemble Gee Bing Fong, but maybe immigration inspectors really thought that all Chinese look alike.

My father made four trips back to China, starting in 1919. Each time he returned, he told immigration inspectors quite a story. He said he was married twice, that both his wives had died in China, that he had fathered six children—three sons and three daughters. As far as my sisters and I know, he lied about the death of his second wife and the three sons. We speculate that he told the first lie to pave the way to get our mother into the United States, and the second to make money by selling the "paper son" slots.

The last time my father returned to China, he brought his wife and children to Oakland. According to documents, my father reentered the United States on November 27, 1933, accompanied by my mother and three oldest sisters. Since it was illegal at that time for an ethnic Chinese U.S. citizen to bring in a wife, my father told immigration authorities the adult woman accompanying him was his sister, the daughter of purportedly U.S. citizen Gee Bing Fong. That was a legal category for entry.

All these stories created difficulties down the line. The "sister" lie needed to be addressed when my mother, Gee Theo Quee, became pregnant in 1934. My parents' solution: Hire a guy named Wong Sheng to "marry" my mother, thus legitimizing the pregnancy. This Wong fellow never was my mother's husband, but the four children born in Oakland—Nellie, Leslie, Florence, and I—took the Wong surname, while the three older China-born sisters—Li Hong, Li Keng, and Lai Wah—kept the Gee surname. To this day, we retain this strange duality. Inside Chinatown, or what is left of it that remembers us, we are known as Gees. To the outside world, the four Oakland-born children are surnamed Wong.

Even before my parents opened the Great China cafe, 723 Webster Street played an important role in our family's history. Li Keng, who was 7 or 8 years old when she came to America, recalls living in the back of 723 for a few months after leaving Angel Island. In the mid-1930s, 723 Webster was a storefront, all right—with the emphasis on front. It was where my father operated a lottery, the favorite (if illegal) keno-like pastime in Chinatown in that era and the precursor of the California Lottery.

My father was by no means alone. Chinatown then had more than a dozen lottery companies, all operated by Chinese men but patronized by Oaklanders of all ethnicities. Each company issued different tickets daily, made up of eighty Chinese characters. Customers bought and marked tickets at various Chinatown businesses. Runners delivered marked tickets to headquarters and, twice a day, the winning numbers to the retail outlets. Each level of the lottery operation made money by raking off a fee.

The lottery business almost got my father killed. The story goes something like this: My father was treasurer of his company. One day, in 1939, the owners suspected someone had been siphoning off money, and somebody fingered my father. At the time, our family was struggling to make ends meet. A close family friend, also associated with the company, asked to meet with my father, presumably over nongambling business. My parents invited him to dinner at our Harrison Street home. My older sisters weren't home, but the three Oakland-born sisters, all quite young, were. After dinner, the two men repaired to the living room to smoke cigars, while my mother went to the kitchen. Suddenly four shots rang out. My mother screamed, "*Ah Bing Fook ah-uh bah! Bing Fook ah-uh bah!*" (Bing Fook shot your father!). Kicking off her cloppity slippers, my mother ran after the assailant. With the help of two bystanders, she detained Bing Fook several blocks away, at 9th and Webster. As she stood there, she reportedly screamed, "Since you killed my husband, why don't you shoot me?"

Miraculously, with transfusions and surgery, my father survived, though he bore permanent scars on his stomach. Lai Wah, the number three daughter, said, "Lots of people helped our family. They gave us credit for rice and food. Mom peeled shrimp to help make ends meet." To this day, my sisters do not believe my father had been dishonest. Nellie, the number four daughter, said: "I don't believe Pop cheated, and if he did, he did it to help us. I don't consider him a crook. Pop was so honest. He'd lend out money and never get it back. He tried to help his brethren."

Those days were over by the time I came along. My father was in his late forties, a slightly rotund figure with thinning hair who stood about five feet four inches tall. He was quick with a smile, a valued trait since he worked the front of the restaurant, while my mother, of sterner visage and demeanor, worked mostly in the kitchen as a sous chef. He often slipped us money and told us not to tell Mom. Sometimes she found out, but he'd give us money again. After a long day at the restaurant, he cooked himself a meal at home, eating by himself in the kitchen. Shots of whisky always washed down the food—and perhaps feelings of pain and suffering. He died of cirrhosis of the liver.

From the start, my father's life was characterized by hard work. He got some education at Lincoln School, and before he brought the family over in 1933, he sold vegetables to Cal fraternities and sororities, which often hired Chinese cooks. He also worked as a keno marker in Reno for a spell. Between 1933 and 1943, in addition to operating the lottery outlet and working in the shipyards, he ran a grocery store on San Pablo Avenue in Berkeley. As the war rolled on, he realized his shipyard job wouldn't last forever. With $3,000 dollars lent to him by a fellow Gee, my father opened the restaurant at 723 Webster—the right move at the right time.

By then, I was a toddler, the first real son born to Gee Seow Hong and Gee Theo Quee. "When you were born, Pop felt his luck had changed," sister Lai Wah told me. My parents were traditional enough to have wanted a son from the get-go, but instead they had five daughters. My father also had a daughter with his first wife, who really had died before he married my mother. My coming along brought great joy.

The kind of danger my father experienced in 1939 was the exception for us growing up. If anything, life was suffocatingly safe for us Chinatown kids. Most of us worked in family businesses and had little time to get into serious trouble. Not that we were goody two-shoes. At Chinese New Year, the boys sold firecrackers to outsiders who streamed into Chinatown hunting for illegal explosives. When cops came around, we hid our brown bags of firecrackers in the tire wells of parked cars. Sometimes we had fire-cracker wars on Webster, tossing lit packages across the street at each other.

I don't recall my parents' reaction to the firecracker mischief, but on most matters, they were not permissive. My mother would not let me ride a bicycle or roller-skate. But I could go to Lincoln Square, a concrete play-ground on the block next to Lincoln School, where all Chinatown kids went, day and night. The boys played baseball, football, and basketball, while the girls hung around the clubhouse. We had dances and parties there. It was a place to go to escape, for a little while at least, our chores at the family business.

And what chores those were. Our restaurant duties—as onerous as they were—taught me and my sisters the responsibility of work, even as they deprived us of a mirthful childhood. More than any house we lived in, the Great China was our home. During its eighteen-year lifetime, it opened variously in the early to late morning and closed at midnight at first and then earlier, when business slowed in the fifties. Each morning, around five o'clock, my father shopped for vegetables in the produce district between Chinatown and what today is Jack London Square. Sometimes I or one of my sisters went with him. Once he was almost killed when his car stalled on the railroad tracks near the produce district; he escaped just before a train rammed into the car.

While my father shopped, my mother opened the restaurant, and she and the chefs began preparing food for the day. From about 6 or 7 A.M., Mom worked straight through to just after dinnertime, seven days a week. Not only was she a sous chef but she waited on tables, wearing a crisp blue uniform. Having started his day early as well, Pop usually took a mid-afternoon break, tending to his garden or napping. Then he returned for the dinner trade and closed up after Mom had gone home. After the fran-tic war years, they decided to close the Great China one day a week, on Wednesdays. My parents used the time to go shopping or to a movie, but they always had the family over or took us out for lunch or dinner, even after some of their daughters had married and moved out.

The sights and smells of the restaurant are almost as fresh to me now, forty to fifty years later, as they were when I wandered the narrow con-fines of the Great China. I was given an easy task at first, washing water glasses. I filled sugar jars, salt and pepper shakers, napkin dispensers, and maple syrup and catsup bottles. I placed pats of butter onto small white plates. When I was about seven, my mother thought I was too skinny, so she force-fed me pats of butter straight from the refrigerator. Eventually, I helped myself. She wanted to fatten me up, since girth indicated good health to her. Surprisingly, I still like butter, but not as a pop-in-your-mouth snack.

Hanging out in the kitchen was a favorite pastime. The main chef was a man we called "How Chooey Goong"—*how chooey* meaning "head chef" and *goong* a term of respect for an older man. His family name was Gee, like my father's. He was a quiet, stoic man who had come to America from China sometime in the early part of the century, leaving his wife and children in a village not far from my father's. He was always kind to us kids, fixing special dishes if we requested it, to my mom's chagrin. Since he had few relatives here, he joined us on the Wednesday day-off expeditions and special holiday celebrations. Even in the years after the Great China closed, he was an occasional companion to my mother after my father's death. It is likely my father sold vegetables to How Chooey Goong when he was a chef at a Cal fraternity, which is where he learned to cook such typical American fare as mashed potatoes, biscuits, roasts, and stews.

In the mornings, the kitchen was the best place to be. Mom and How Chooey Goong chopped and sliced vegetables and prepared a beef rib roast and a loin of pork for the oven. They started the soup of the day, a stew, and brown gravy. Goong also baked wonderful biscuits and rolls. The kitchen smelled heavenly—redolent of beef and pork roasts, the richness of stew, the ineluctable aroma of fresh baked rolls.

While the lunch dishes were being prepared, breakfast customers needed to be tended to. Single men especially came for Mom's delicious pancakes, a stack of three with a butter pat and maple syrup, all for fifteen cents. A cup of coffee cost an additional dime.

The Great China made its own pastries as well, a chore mostly handled by a man we called Chel Goong. In contrast to How Chooey Goong's upstanding character, Chel Goong was a drug addict. I or one of my sisters was sent almost daily to wake him up in his nearby bachelor apartment. His eyes were heavily lidded, and he moved slowly, no doubt because of his opium addiction. But could he bake! He worked his magic in the little pastry room behind the kitchen. There he mixed pie and cake doughs on a dedicated countertop. While I didn't particularly care to be in Chel

Goong's company, watching him make apple and custard pies and strawberry and banana whipped cream cakes was still special, if for no other reason than to anticipate the delectable finished products. After his baking chores, Chel Goong helped Mom and How Chooey Goong in the kitchen.

Before my parents opened the Great China, my dad had a partnership with Harry Louie in a restaurant called Sam and Harry's Cafe, right next door to 723 Webster. That joint venture served up more Western food than Chinese. When my father had a business dispute with Harry and decided to open the Great China, he continued the culinary theme of mostly American food. Simple Chinese dishes (chow mein, fried rice, chop suey, egg foo yung, noodle and won ton soups, and deep-fried prawns) were an afterthought.

The American menu was most likely a response to supply and demand. In the 1930s and 1940s, there weren't enough Chinese people living in Oakland to support a lot of Chinese restaurants. This was well before Americans of all ethnicities embraced exotic "fusion" cuisines. The war years brought many customers to Chinatown, most of them not Chinese. Pragmatist that he was, my dad decided to feed the masses what they wanted: hearty American-style meals, greatly assisted by How Chooey Goong's cooking skills.

We are talking about a full-course lunch or dinner that consisted of a bowl of homemade soup (vegetable, split pea, clam chowder, tomato rice), a lettuce and tomato salad or coleslaw, two rolls with butter, an entree of fried halibut, hamburger steak, veal cutlets, beef stew, pork chops, chicken-fried steak, fried liver and onions, roast pork, or prime rib, served with a hot vegetable and either white rice or mashed potatoes. For dessert, a choice of vanilla, chocolate, or strawberry ice cream; Jell-O; or apple or egg custard pie. The price? From fifty cents to a little over a buck. Those prices changed little in the eighteen years of the Great China.

It is little wonder that crowds descended on our restaurant during the war years and into the late 1940s and early 1950s. After a languid breakfast business, Mom and How Chooey Goong placed the soup and prepared foods such as beef stew, cooked vegetables, and mashed potatoes into metal bins that fit into the stainless steel hot-tray counter that separated the public portion of the restaurant from the kitchen. We children helped our father brew coffee and put salads and desserts on plates. We placed the salads on counters next to one of the refrigerators and the cut-up pies along the back shelf running parallel to the customer counter. On another shelf toward the front of the restaurant, we kept coffee mugs, the cash register, and cigarettes and chewing gum that my dad bought at Hoy Chang, a candy and cigarette wholesaler on 8th Street.

Customers started coming in for lunch right at noon. They took counter seats, if they were alone, while small groups sat in one of the three back booths or at the larger rectangular table. The wait staff—my dad, my sisters and I, and for a while a lanky guy named Johnny Louie, who slicked down his hair with too much pomade and whose nose hairs were frightful—barked orders into the kitchen. The wait staff gave each customer a glass of water to start, then scooped up a bowl of soup from the pot and brought it to the table, along with a salad. Then out came the entrees along with the rolls. Finally, the dessert. Eating at the Great China was quite utilitarian. No leisure dining here.

By about 2 P.M., the lunch rush was over. My dad headed home for his daily break, and the dishwasher, a portly man we called Lo Wong Bock, got busy scraping uneaten food into a garbage can, then washing plates, cups, bowls, and silverware. With little time to rest, the kitchen crew got ready for the dinner crowd, which except for the busy war years was generally lighter than at lunch.

That was our routine for many years, with my sisters and me on duty when we weren't in school. Summer vacations or weekends away? Are you kidding? Even after some of my sisters got married and had moved out of the family home, they returned to help at the restaurant, especially during the noon rush. I can't honestly say that working in the restaurant was pleasurable, especially not during my teen years, when I just wanted to be out of there. Often, I negotiated with Flo, the sister just older than me, to trade shifts so I could go to a movie with friends. Sometimes she wanted out as much as I did.

Throughout the years, men of different ethnicities were our most loyal customers. For obvious reasons, they liked my sisters better than they liked me. Oakland cops also made our restaurant a regular stop. Flo remembers the industrialist Henry J. Kaiser eating at our restaurant. Among the most colorful of customers was a family of gypsies who ordered only bowls of rice or mashed potatoes with brown gravy, then poured on black pepper and catsup, which distressed my parents, who viewed them as a money-losing proposition.

No matter their standing or special tastes, customers came to the Great China because it had good food at cheap prices. Fewer and fewer came, however, as the fifties dragged on. The decrease in business gave me a chance to read, draw, and improve my English vocabulary, using a paperback guide. I scanned the baseball box scores in the daily newspaper to see how my favorite player, Hank Aaron, did the night before, and I calculated his batting average every day. I also followed the Cal football team, which I had grown to love by listening to its games on the radio. On menu paper, I sketched horses, football players, and western forts, influenced by TV and movie westerns like the Lone Ranger and Hopalong Cassidy epics. I read novels by A. J. Cronin (*The Keys of the Kingdom*, for one) without fully realizing the religious or literary significance.

These American and Western cultural forms were more influential than the Chinese language school I attended and the special Chinese tutoring my father provided me. The latter never stuck. I am the worst Chinese speaker among my siblings, all of whom retain some capability of speaking our village and other Chinese dialects.

My sisters and I occasionally wonder how the restaurant experience led to our various adult pursuits. Li Keng, the second oldest daughter born in China, was the first Chinese American teacher in the Decoto (now New Haven) school district in southern Alameda County. She retired in 1985 after thirty-five years of service. Lai Wah, the third daughter also born in China, raised two daughters in Sunnyvale and recently retired from working many years at a Silicon Valley company. Nellie, daughter number four and the first American-born child, is the San Francisco organizer for the Seattle-based Freedom Socialist Party and an accomplished poet with three volumes in print. She recently retired after working almost fifty years as a secretary and administrator in both the private and the public sectors. Florence, number six daughter, who now goes by Flo Oy Wong, is an installation artist and teacher who lives in Sunnyvale and travels all over the country on artist residencies. I have spent most of my professional life as a print journalist, writing for national and Bay Area newspapers and English-language Asian American publications.

Our parents did not have much time for literary or cultural arts, though despite his humble roots, my father was a fairly learned man. He read Chinese newspapers and wrote the language; his calligraphy was quite artful. My mother was largely unschooled, but she read a Chinese newspaper too and picked up English from working in the restaurant and watching television. Our family rarely engaged in what I would call intellectual dinner-table conversations. Quite the contrary. During restaurant days, we scarfed up our meals and got quickly back to work.

In reconstructing the ebb and flow of Chinatown's vitality over the past sixty years, I had always attributed its near death some forty years ago to suburbanization and the voracious urban projects that grabbed real estate and public money. But George Ong, who also grew up in Chinatown and is now one of its leaders, posited another key factor: a new law enacted in the mid-fifties that required a federal license to operate gambling establishments. "Prior to that, gambling was this type of crime," he says as he slaps his wrist. "Now you could get into trouble with the federal government and it could deport you. This really decimated Chinatown businesses. People no longer had reason to come into Chinatown and shop in the stores. When a white guy came into a Chinatown market to buy a lottery ticket, he'd pick up some milk or groceries. Now there was no added incentive to come into Chinatown because the [new federal law] dried up the gambling. Business just went down from there."

It has come way back—and then some. Chinatown slowly reawakened in the late sixties and seventies, and by the eighties, the renaissance was complete. After the devastation of World War II, Asia began its "miraculous" economic climb, thanks in part to U.S. generosity. Immigration laws changed in 1965 to grant more entry slots to Asians and Latin Americans, unifying families. The end of the Vietnam War in 1975 brought thousands of refugees to America, including Oakland Chinatown. Newcomers were determined to succeed in small businesses in spaces abandoned by children of the Chinatown business owners of the thirties and forties. Chinatown became less a place for the Pearl River Delta Chinese, and Chinese from other areas and other Asians found a home there. One can hear almost as much Mandarin spoken as Cantonese. My parents' village dialect, known as "see yip," is still heard but is not nearly as dominant as it was fifty years ago.

As though tethered by an invisible umbilical cord, I return to Chinatown frequently, mostly to shop for food and to eat. Very few of my generation own businesses or live there anymore. As thriving as it is today, business leaders are worried about increasing competition from suburban Asian shopping malls that have lots of free parking. But I can't resist the chaotic allure of Chinatown, despite parking headaches, dirty streets, and sometimes trenchant odors.

Will Oakland Chinatown be able to sustain its resurgence? Ted Dang also grew up in Chinatown and is now a successful real estate developer and manager. "Much of the Chinatown growth today is not from the Chinese or Asian community," he says, "but from growth in downtown and Jack London Square, the University of California president's office, EBMUD [the regional water utility that has its headquarters building in Chinatown], Old Oakland. We just have more people downtown now.

"[New housing projects nearby] will help Chinatown. Jack London Square is now thriving. I suspect some people go to Chinatown restaurants to eat before or after movies in Jack London Square. Immigration has not increased over the 1980s levels. The growth isn't coming in Chinatown itself. The future? Depends on immigration. If nothing changes there, Chinatown will continue to benefit even more from the growth in the rest of downtown Oakland. I see Chinatown in the future catering more to a tourist trade, catering to increased hotel occupancy, catering to the elderly."

It's an intriguing vision, one that mirrors in some ways the Chinatown of the World War II era, when it served outsiders who worked in the war industry. My family has moved on, having seen Oakland Chinatown as both a thriving and a sickly community. Now its well-being is beyond even the wildest imaginations of old-timers like me.

Two of my sisters, who spent much of their adult lives in the suburbs, talk about their lives as "straddling" or "bifurcating" cultures, one Chinese, the other American. These labels are difficult to define, let alone reconcile. You can bet that younger Chinese Americans are going through similar experiences. They too wonder whether they are Chinese or American. All I know is that I love watching NFL games on TV while devouring a plate of beef chow fun.

A "Manong" with Magical Hands

Filipinas, October 1998

Having one's hair cut is a very personal matter. It has psychological dimensions that are deeper than a bimonthly cut-and-snip might otherwise indicate. For most of us, a haircut may not have the gravity it did for the legendary Samson, who feared a trim because it would sap his other-worldly strength and virility. Choosing a barber (or hair stylist, in the upscale argot of our yuppie times) can be as significant as one's choice of an automobile, a place to live, or maybe even a partner in love.

As a boy growing up in Oakland, California's Chinatown, I had no choice. My parents sent me to a wisp of a Chinese woman everyone called "Fong Git Moo," or Mrs. Fong. She wasn't much taller than her young boy customers. Yet she was authoritative with her scissors and clips, peering through rimless glasses at the unruly mop of hair facing her. Her cuts were serviceable and clearly acceptable to our socially conservative immigrant parents. Nothing avant-garde, nothing razor cut, no "duck's ass" styles.

Those were the specialties of George A. Catambay, whose 7th Street "George's Movieland Barber Shop" was actually closer to our family's Webster Street restaurant than Fong Git Moo was. I had no idea then—in the mid- to late 1940s—why my parents eschewed George and chose Mrs. Fong instead. As I got older, I adopted the impression commonplace in Chinatown that George's was a place for fast and loose men who smoked cigarettes, drove fancy cars, and enjoyed the company of trophy girlfriends. They wanted the cool "feather-edge" (or layered) razor cut created by George Catambay, a Filipino immigrant. They wanted to impress their girl friends and their peers. World War II had ended, Americans yearned to forget the fighting in Europe and Asia, and America was on the march to unprecedented prosperity. It was an appropriate time for self-indulgence, and going to George's Movieland was a perfect way to be made over for men with a mission to live slightly dangerously.

That wasn't my mission—my parents saw to that—and my choice of barbers reflected a continuing conservative bent. Then I discovered the world of Filipino barbers. This was when I was in my mid-twenties, wearing the signature flat-top cut of quasi-nerds of the late 1950s and early 1960s. I was a Peace Corps volunteer living in Iligan City on the big southern island of Mindanao, where I was assigned as an English teacher.

The Iligan City barbershop I frequented was an air-conditioned oasis from the sticky humidity of the tropical island nation. And I had never experienced such a sensuous haircut. The barber took his time, even with my buzzcut, to meticulously trim all unnecessary facial hairs. He applied a hot facial towel, then gave me a shoulder and neck massage. After a close straight-razor trim of the edges of my hairline, he dashed on some sweet after-shave lotion. Time stood still. Guys hanging around the shop chattered away in Cebuano, the principal Filipino language of Iligan City and a language I studied during my Peace Corps training. But my ear and facility with the language weren't sufficient to catch the nuances of the chatter, some of which, I am sure, was aimed at me. All of this attention for less than a buck.

I never gave George Catambay much thought in all those years. In my years back in America, I followed the conventional hair trends—letting my hair grow long in the late 1960s style, eventually trimming it back to above the collar as I joined the cloistered world of the *Wall Street Journal* as a reporter in Cleveland, Ohio. Through the years, I changed barbers a lot, never having found anyone to be loyal to. I liked a young woman "hair stylist" at an Oakland athletic club I once belonged to. She was good. As she hopped from shop to shop, I followed her, but her cuts were getting expensive, $25 and up. She moved once too often, so I downsized to the SuperCuts chains then offering fifteen-minutes-and-out cuts for $8. I didn't know it at the time, but I was undergoing an identity crisis because of my capricious choices of cutters.

Then came my first (and only) son. When he needed his first professional cut, when he was about 3 or 4 years old, we found ourselves wandering around Oakland Chinatown. We saw George's Movieland Barber Shop, still on 7th Street, not nearly as busy as it was in the 1940s and 1950s. We peeked in, and next thing we knew, Sam, our son, was sitting atop a special chair that straddled the armrests of George's stolid antique swivel barber chairs, getting his first professional cut. George was cheerful and happy to cut even a fidgety 4-year-old boy's hair. That broke the ice for me. I began going to George for my own cuts. This was about a dozen years ago. George was already in his early eighties.

It was nothing for me to overcome the stereotypes I had formed about George serving only the fast crowd. There were no more "fast crowds." I felt, instead, as though I was coming home. Was I nuts, my wife asked, to subject myself to the physical risks of having an 80-something-year-old barber take a straight razor to my ear and neck areas? Maybe I was, but George never faltered, despite being hard of hearing and slower afoot than the vibrant man pictured in the ballroom-dancing photos plastered all over his 1940s-style shop. Faithfully, five or six times a year, I trekked on down to George's Movieland Barber Shop to get the wondrous George treatment, the closest thing to my Philippines experience I could get.

As he snipped away, I asked George about his life. He told me he came to America in the late 1920s from Tanay, Rizal province. He didn't say he worked a short time as a farm worker, a fact I got later from his children. He said his sweetheart from the Philippines, Catalina, came over to America at about the same time he did. I later learned they married about a year after both of them came, an unusual occurrence because most Filipino immigrants then were young men brought in for farm labor in Hawaii and California or to work in the fisheries in Washington state and Alaska.

George and Catalina settled in San Mateo just south of San Francisco about 1930, working as domestics for white families in San Mateo and Hillsborough. Their daughter, Lucy Bubenheim, remembers her parents taking in male Filipino boarders. "Mom was one of the few Filipinas around in those days. She cooked for these men. They missed Filipino cooking," she said. "It was close to communal living. They banded together for support." The men worked in San Mateo hotels. "Times were so hard. Food was so scarce," Bubenheim recalls, referring to the Great Depression. "These men would put eggs under their hats and take other food [from the hotel]. They contributed to seeing that Mom had enough food to cook for all of us."

Never complaining about their station in life, George and Catalina kept a dream alive—of working for themselves. In the Philippines, George had cut hair, even practicing on hairy pigs, he told his grandchildren. He couldn't cut hair in America without a license. So he commuted from San Mateo to San Francisco in the late 1930s to attend barbers' college to get his license. That done, George and Catalina, now with two children, Lucy and George R., moved to Oakland, where other Tanay immigrants had settled. George apprenticed for about a year with a Filipino immigrant barber whose house in Tanay was adjacent to Catalina's.

Oakland's cozy little Chinatown was bustling during the early 1940s, the teeth of World War II. Shipyards a half mile away were going great guns preparing and repairing floating instruments of war. Men and women who worked there flocked into Chinatown for cheap eats and great haircuts from barbers like George. Things were so good, in fact, that George opened his own shop and provided a place for other Filipino barbers. Then he opened a second shop, the current George's Movieland Barber Shop, sometime in the early 1940s. He recalled his opportunity to own his own shop was at the expense of a Japanese American barber, who was shipped away to an internment camp, like thousands of other ethnic Japanese on the West Coast. He said he paid the Japanese American barber $275 for his shop, "a lot of money then."

George's Movieland Barber Shop attracted men from far and wide, famous and anonymous. His son George, a dentist, recalls seeing actor Robert Stack, singer Tony Martin, and exercise guru Jack Lalanne getting their hair cut at his father's shop. Later on, Lionel Wilson, Oakland's first African American mayor, also went to George's for a trim. "Dad had a cross-section of customers from all over northern California," his son told me. "He had police officers, homicide detectives, longshoremen, pimps, robbers, millionaires. We'd see Cadillacs and Lincolns and hot rods parked outside. My dad was well liked in Chinatown. He was a hardworking, honest tradesman. He was able to bring all these different guys to China-town who would never otherwise go to Chinatown."

For almost sixty years, George Catambay cut hair. In the last few years, he reduced his schedule, working on Mondays only if he felt well enough, and most of the time he did. Seeing as how I had acquired the George habit late in his barbering years, I remained loyal to him and rearranged my Mondays to make sure I visited his shop for my bimonthly trim. Sitting in George's Movieland Barber Shop was a throwback to the 1940s and 1950s, but without the wartime energy. In old photos of his shop, six swivel barber chairs line the floor. The current George's Movieland Bar-ber Shop has three chairs and a wall that separates the space of the other three chairs. The wall also makes an inner room where George would rest between customers. Big round mirrors still face one another, giving cus-tomers a front and back view. Between the mirrors, photos of George ball-room dancing with a blond or redhead are hung, reminders of an era of gaiety and elegance that is all but a mist today. Almost at ceiling level is a shelf with trophies and mounted certificates from the Arthur Murray Dance Studio. George won three gold medals, one gold bar, one silver medal, and two bronze medals in Murray amateur dancing contests.

George took up ballroom dancing in the 1950s to soothe the loneliness after Catalina died. It was at a Murray studio that George met his second wife, Virginia. When not cutting hair or cutting the rug on the dance floor, George loved to fish in the delta region of the San Francisco Bay. His favorite spot was at Frank's Tract on Bethel Island, according to his son. "He was really good at it [fishing]. He knew what the fish wanted. He really knew about catching striped bass." When George moved to Alameda, an island city across the estuary from Oakland, he designed his deck so he could easily fish off of it, even catching a thirty-pound bass.

The last haircut I got from George was in March or April of this year. In early June, I called his home to make arrangements for my next cut. His stepdaughter told me George no longer cut hair. He was too ill. The last time he cut someone's hair, his hands were shaking. To me, he possessed magical hands, steady, reliable, precise. I expressed my sympathies and hoped George was feeling better.

He never got better. He died in the early morning of July 15, shortly after many of his children, grandchildren, and great grandchildren (who number thirty-six in all) had visited him. He was 93 years old.

George Catambay didn't have the visibility or heroic status in the Filipino American community of farm labor leaders Phillip Vera Cruz and Larry Itliong. But he was very much an exemplar of Filipino immigrant *manongs* who came to America for a better life and left his adopted country a better place.

"My dad was a real patriot," his son George said. "He ran a small business, taking hold of the American Dream. He hung onto it in the way of Asian immigrants of his day, and he brought to it a unique compassion."

Haircuts will never be the same for me again.

2 Family

From Agrarianism to Cyberspace

Finding Sacred Ground
November 1994

As I wander through Goon Doo Hong, a remote southeastern Chinese village where my father was born and where my mother gave birth to two of my sisters, I am overwhelmed by what I see, what I remember of my family's history, and what I imagine life was like here for my parents when they were young. It is like Shangri-la, a pristine place untouched by time. The water-laden fields with symmetrical rows of rice stalks glisten in the warm November sun. In the background are rolling hills in various shades of mint, beige, and gray—a real-life Chinese brush painting.

This village in Guangdong province seems like a dream to me, an overseas Chinese in search of family roots. But such a perspective is also an American middle-class conceit. I came here to Goon Doo Hong with some of my sisters to explore the generational and cultural gaps between us and our relatives in China, and, as it turned out, to experience subtle and sometimes wrenching differences among ourselves, a generation of siblings who have so much, yet so little, in common, who span preindustrial agrarianism and postindustrial cyberspace.

None of us on the American side really knew what to expect. What we found was a tiny dilapidated brick and tile-roofed hut, ravaged by time, weather, and natural disasters. But we found much more—distant cousins and a village life that was little changed from the time when my father first journeyed to the United States in 1912 and when he finally took his wife and three daughters with him in 1933.

Our family story, while not unique, illustrates the dynamic history of Chinese America and, by extension, the Chinese Diaspora. Some of my nuclear family was born in China, some in America, all within one generation. To think of the distances traveled—physically, culturally, emotionally—is to be humbled by the tenacity of the human spirit.

To us, of course, our journey of discovery was special. My five living sisters now range in age from the early seventies to mid-fifties, and I am in my early fifties. The time was right to reverse the journey my family made sixty-one years ago.

The journey began with our father, Gee Seow Hong, which was only one of his names. In the village he was known as Gee Bing Do. In the United States, he was first called Gee Ghee Geng, then later Gee Seow Hong. My father left Goon Doo Hong at the age of sixteen, pushed by his mother to find his fortune in *Gum Saan,* the Cantonese words (gold mountain) for the United States of America. My father's particular journey took place more than a half century after the discovery of gold in California. For the poor and ill-educated villagers in the Pearl River Delta of southeastern China, *Gum Saan* was a magical place to get rich, then retire back home.

My father settled in Oakland, California, amid a small, tight-knit community of Chinese from nearby villages. Over the next twenty years, he returned to Goon Doo Hong several times to father daughters, but he always returned to Oakland, to resume his prosaic American adventure. It's been thirty-three and twenty-one years, respectively, since my father and mother died in their adopted country. During those years the lives of their children grew complex, filled with their own children's lives and with their work and other pursuits, worlds apart from Goon Doo Hong. The strands of the close-knit Chinese American family stretched thin in the years after our parents had passed on.

Nonetheless, each of the siblings harbors a curiosity to one degree or another about where we came from. For me, the curiosity could be traced to a mixed cultural identity. I was born in 1941 into an immediate cultural environment of Chinese immigrants surrounded by white, black, and Mexican Americans. In the 1950s, there was no particular currency in flaunting one's Chinese-ness. My sisters, whether Chinese- or American-born, and I were developing dual identities.

Even as I made my way through college and a journalistic writing career, which at times took me far from my Chinatown roots, I could not—would not—shed part of my core existence, my Chinese-ness, whatever that was. I knew my American-ness—I lived it everyday. My Chinese-ness was elusive. It was with me, yet it was difficult to define, especially in a society that did not recognize or appreciate Chinese American culture. So I felt I had to travel to my parents' China village to better define my Chinese-ness.

Nellie, a published poet, a political activist, and the first American-born (and overall fourth) daughter, was the first of the younger siblings to visit the old village—in 1983, as part of an American women's writers group. There, she met a distant uncle who knew of my father's and my existence. "I was 'home,'" Nellie remembers.

In 1989, two of my sisters and I made plans to visit China. But the tumultuous spring of mass political demonstrations and the infamous crackdown in Tiananmen Square upset those plans. It wasn't until early 1994 that we decided to resume our roots search. This time Li Keng, the second oldest sister, was among those intending to make the trip. She had not been part of the 1989 plans. A retired schoolteacher in her late sixties who left the village when she was seven or eight, Li Keng has excellent recall of the physical layout of Goon Doo Hong. The rest of us felt her return was a special feature of our adventure.

The group that set out on our extended family's roots search consisted of three sisters (Li Keng, Lai Wah, and Florence), two brothers-in-law (Roger, Li Keng's husband; and Ed, Florence's husband), two nieces and a nephew (Allison, Lai Wah's daughter; and Felicia and Bradley, Flo and Ed's adult children), and me. Traveling on different schedules, we all met at the elegant White Swan Hotel in Guangzhou on Tuesday, November 8. Our goal was to find our village and Roger's, both of which are near the city of Toisan, about four hours by car southwest of Guangzhou.

Nellie's trip eleven years earlier provided us the barest of information about who might still be around. She had exchanged letters several times after her visit, but that correspondence ceased. None of us tried to resume contact. We simply took it on faith that we would find the village and that we might come upon someone related to us.

Our party of nine started off from the White Swan Hotel in a rented air-conditioned Mercedes Benz van in the mid-morning of Wednesday, November 9. It was a gorgeous day, warm but not too muggy. A hotel employee, in a neatly pressed white uniform, was our driver. Excited and anxious, we chattered away, reminiscing and retelling old family tales, trying to recreate the story of our parents' lives. But at times we fell into silence, lost in our own thoughts.

When we reached Som Bot, the market area not far from where we thought our parents' village was, we stopped at one roadside stand and asked a man, in the local dialect, whether he knew of a Goon Doo Hong. He said he did. Our excitement began to grow. Climbing into the van, he offered to show us the way. Before we could discuss the matter further, he was seated—and began negotiating a fee. We were skeptical, but he insisted he knew the way.

Lacking confidence in our newfound guide, who remained with us, we stopped again and asked a man driving two children on a motor scooter whether he knew of a Goon Doo Hong. He said he did! Now we were really excited. Revving up his motor scooter, he escorted us over bumpy dirt roads. A few minutes later, we stopped in a clearing in the middle of what seemed like nowhere. We alighted, our adrenaline pumping very fast. It was about two o'clock in the afternoon.

Li Keng led the way out of the van. She said she didn't recognize anything. The man who guided us to this point started walking down a dirt path bordered by trees on the left. Li Keng followed him. We followed her. Then I ran ahead of Li Keng so I could record these precious moments on my video camera. This was, after all, Li Keng's return to a village she left sixty-one years ago. At a clearing, she saw a pond where water buffaloes rested. She recognized it. We were "home."

Our short walk down the dirt path caused considerable commotion in this sleepy village. It was as though Martians had landed. All along the path people came out of their homes. They gawked at us while chattering among themselves. Through the confusion of a dozen voices speaking in machine-gun-like bursts of see yip, the local dialect, a man with a dark complexion and an older woman stepped forward. They said they remembered our father. Word spread quickly among us that we had found some distant cousins. This was more than we could have expected. We learned his name, Gee Fook Ying, and that he is the son of the uncle our sister Nellie met eleven years earlier. Fook Ying's father had died the year before, he told us. The older woman was his mother.

Villagers hovered around our large party. We heard, in the background, voices suggesting we donate money to repair the crumbling retaining wall of the village pond. After a few minutes of aimlessness, Fook Ying and his mother led us to our parents' home, up a narrow alley with houses on both sides. We turned right at a banana plant and emerged into a small clearing. A dilapidated structure stood partially hidden by wild brush. Li Keng remembered it. The doorway was covered by a heavy piece of cloth. There was no door. Surrounded by our milling party and some villagers, Li Keng stood in the courtyard, pointing inside to a small dark room that once had been a combination kitchen and living and dining room. Now, it shelters a water buffalo. A fresh pile of dung was in the corner. To the left were the remains of the bedroom, roofless and almost wall-less. Brush and other vegetation had overgrown the shattered walls. Trash was strewn about.

In a heightened daze, we wandered about the confined courtyard, asking questions of Fook Ying and his mother and other villagers. They in turn were trying to figure out who we were. They commented on how we looked and which ones of us appeared older or younger and how well we spoke *see yip*. We snapped away with our cameras. I spotted a shard of a rice bowl and instinctively picked it up. It had no value, except to me because it was a piece of my parents' old village home.

Fook Ying invited us to come to his home at the bottom of the narrow alley near the pond, but instead we followed Li Keng as she strolled to the edge of the pond and pointed out a low stone structure where, she said, villagers burned incense in homage to ancestors. This structure was next to a big banyan tree that provided shade and a center for village activity. A few curious villagers gazed at our alien party.

By the pond, we continued our clipped conversations. Fook Ying went back to his home and returned with a letter Nellie had written him eleven years before. It was crumpled but in good condition. Florence handed out photos to our newly found cousins and I thrust a photo of my son into Fook Ying's hand, awkwardly telling him my son's Chinese name.

My sisters and I had discussed in advance a plan to give *lay see* or *hoong bow* (red envelopes stuffed with money) to any relatives we found. Now the time was growing close to execute our plan, or to devise a new one on the spot. We talked in whispered English about how we would dispense our modest monetary goodies on Fook Ying and his mother. When I handed Fook Ying a *lay see* in as unobtrusive a manner as I could, he accepted in a similar fashion, without a fuss and without great surprise, almost as though he knew it was coming.

To keep to our schedule and get to Roger's family village before sunset, we had to cut short our visit. Almost as abruptly as we descended, we left. We might as well have been apparitions. We had spent no more than forty-five minutes in sporadic but intense interactions with strangers who were connected to us across continents and through generations of common ancestors and a common culture.

As my sisters slowly worked their way to the van amid vociferous thanks from our relatives, I broke off from the group and loped up the narrow alley to see my parents' home again. I wanted to videotape it in its humble and morose disrepair, without crowds. As I approached the house, I heard the voices of Ed and Brad. They too had returned to take pictures. Then I heard Felicia's voice behind me. Brad suggested he take a video of me standing in my parents' home.

I entered through some brush that had overgrown the broken-down wall of what had once been the bedroom and then went into the room that had been the kitchen-dining-living-room area. Brad stood in the courtyard looking into the room where I was standing. With the video camera running, I began a narrative. After a couple of sentences, I started to sob. The weight of several lifetimes' worth of family history crashed in on me. I regained my composure to begin again. Again, I cried. This was sacred ground and I couldn't hold back my emotions.

I managed to finish off a few sentences, fell silent, then quietly exited. Something else in the courtyard rubble caught my eye, a piece of bamboo with straw wrapping. It resembled a sheath. I picked it up to give to my son in America, who was just about to turn twelve and who loved knives and swords.

Because of their different travel arrangements, Li Keng, Roger, Lai Wah, and Allison never had a chance to revisit the village after the quick hit on November 9. Flo, Ed, Felicia, Bradley, and I, however, had greater flexibility and we decided to return for a longer, more leisurely visit the next day. This time we wanted to be better prepared, even though our return visit would be another surprise for our village relatives.

Early the next morning, on another clear, warm, beautiful day, before most of Toisan was stirring, Brad and I went shopping for goodies to bring to the village—to make amends for our appalling lack of social graces the day before when we brought nothing other than a couple of red envelopes. We came upon a block with outdoor vendors of candies, fruits, and other items that overseas Chinese purchased to take back to ancestral villages. Vendors could tell that we were a couple of *wah kue* (overseas Chinese). With good-natured prodding and suggestions from them, we bought candies, cookies, and oranges. Now we felt more prepared.

Our return visit at about 10 A.M. surprised the villagers. Lucky for us, Fook Ying and his mother were home. They were genuinely pleased we had come back. This time, we went inside Fook Ying's home, a plain high-ceilinged living room with a small entryway kitchen. Gazing around the humble abode, I noticed a wall hanging similar to one I had inherited from my parents that we use every Chinese New Year in California as an altar to pay homage to our deceased relatives. At Fook Ying's invitation, we sat around a low table and began to get to know one another better, in a more relaxed atmosphere than the rushed afternoon before. Fook Ying sent someone out to buy us soft drinks. Led by Flo, an artist and teacher whose command of the village dialect is better than mine, we talked about our newly discovered connections and about our shared past. Much of the awkwardly rendered conversation was about our ancestors and sketchy family history. But village kibitzers let it be known that we should contribute money to the village. No one directly asked us for money to repair our parents' broken-down home; that would come much later, long after we had gone back to America.

After about thirty minutes of conversation and some picture taking, Fook Ying and his mother suggested we go to my parents' house to burn incense in their memories. We were familiar with that simple ritual. We thought that was an excellent idea, so we went up the alley and entered our parents' house, now, to us, a rustic shrine. Flo quietly sobbed and Fook Ying's mother whispered to our deceased parents about how fortuitous it was for us to revisit our ancestral home. Fook Ying handed each of us clusters of incense sticks and arranged an offering of the candies and fruit we had brought. I went first, bowing three times with the lit incense cluster, then sticking it into the ground. Flo and her family followed suit. While still a little jittery from the roiling emotions inside me, I also felt a calm in our paying homage to our long-deceased parents.

Fook Ying next suggested we visit the hillside gravesites of our grandparents, so we trekked up a grassy trail. On a plateau overlooking the village, we again burned incense and funeral money at the graves of our grandparents. We took turns snapping pictures of the American and

Chinese cousins, interspersed with arms around each other's shoulders. We lingered for a few minutes to take in the breathtaking scenery. The vantage point from atop the hill gave us a sweeping view of the village and surrounding area. It was pastoral and pretty, totally unlike the cities and the new construction going on under Deng Xiaoping's economic modernizations near Guangzhou.

Once back in the village, Fook Ying urged us to take a walk along a dirt path that Li Keng once used to go to school. Feeling warm and satisfied with our incense ceremonies, we thought a walk around would be just fine, giving us more time to interact, however superficially, with Fook Ying, a lean, cigarette-smoking man in his early forties with a tanned, weathered face.

Our walk took us past a village shrine that had been banned under communist rule. We also saw several abandoned buildings, one of which used to be a small store. Fook Ying told us about a time in recent village life when food was scarce. Villagers had to forage for any edible parts of plants and trees. Another, more distant, cousin, Gee Gwok Gim, a slight, wiry man in his mid-fifties, accompanied us as well. Along the way, he explained to his American city-slicker cousins how rice is grown. He pulled up a stalk and separated the bud with his long pinkie fingernail. When Brad spotted a small snake in a dry creek bed, Gwok Gim seized it quickly, without fear, and with delight held it up to show us. Some of us were squeamish, and Gwok Gim laughed.

After three hours, it was time to go. Compared with the day before, when our visit was barely a blur, we felt much better about this sojourn. Our relatives invited us to stay for lunch, but we knew they weren't prepared for us since we had surprised them again. We also could see that while Fook Ying told us that times were better for them now, they had very little to share. As the five us of left the village for the second time in two days, we were drained but satisfied and happy we had made the extra effort. The first day's all-too-brief visit, full of riotous emotions and unresolved conflicts, was an unsatisfactory way to close our long journey to our parents' home. Fook Ying and his mother expressed gratitude for our second visit, saying we *yow sum* (had heart).

The momentous visits to my parents' village unleashed a welter of emotions and questions. Foremost was who we were. Perhaps this question of identity is peculiar to me, or to my generation of Chinese Americans.

I think not, however. I was born in Oakland, California, and have lived most of my life there, but I have been to Asia several times. Every time I cross the Pacific Ocean, I inevitably feel pangs of identity confusion.

As an ethnic Chinese born in the United States more than a half century ago and thus a product of dual cultures, with a family that in one generation spans the mind-boggling distance of preindustrial rural China to postindustrial high-technology America, it is understandable that I would feel anxiety and excitement on our roots journey. The identity question loomed large when at the beginning of our China trip I hooked up with members of my family in Guangzhou on Sunday, November 6, the night after I had landed in Hong Kong. I felt anxiety as I stepped off the Hong-Kong-to-Guangzhou train and found the Garden Hotel van at the teeming train station, where some beggar children confronted me and others as we headed out of the station toward the parking lot.

In the van, a young white woman spoke to her white male companion, who seemed to know China and spoke Mandarin. Listening in silence, I felt both jealousy and resentment because I, an ethnic Chinese, couldn't understand what two white foreigners were saying in a Chinese mother tongue. The white woman, now speaking in English, wondered whether the women and children beggars made themselves up to look dirty to win the sympathy of Western visitors. The man said simply, "Well, that's China."

That's China. The phrase stuck with me throughout my one-week China visit, the implication being that whatever happens in China is somehow fated to happen. In the West, we are so used to the idea of human beings controlling nature. Fate is too passive a concept in the Christianized, scientific West.

Some large metaphors played themselves out on our family roots search. My generation of siblings is split between three who were born in Goon Doo Hong and four who were born in Oakland. Almost twenty years, and an immeasurable cultural divide, separates the oldest, Li Hong, from the youngest, me, the only male. Two of the China-born sisters (Li Keng and Lai Wah) and two of the United States–born siblings (Flo and me) were on this trip. In general, the two China-born sisters, who have lived almost all their lives in the United States, are more passive than the American-born siblings. The distinctions are subtle but real.

One manifestation of this nuanced difference was in how long each of us spent in Goon Doo Hong. In the travel plans of Li Keng and Lai Wah, someone in their party arranged a group visa that limited their China portion. That meant they could visit the village only once. Flo and I, making separate and different arrangements, weren't under the same time constraints. We felt our older sisters should have pursued a change of plans more aggressively so they too could revisit the village.

Ultimately, their scheduling mix-up added a layer of mostly internalized tension between the older and younger siblings, in part because an extra van expense for the second day fell on Flo and me, but also because the forty-five-minute visit on Wednesday was so dissatisfying. It was difficult for me to fathom that we had come seven thousand miles for a discovery of roots that lasted less than an hour.

Those moments of flash frustration, however, weren't going to spoil my mission. Actually my mission had changed. Before the trip, I purposely did not view the visit as a way to explore unknown emotional territory of my own. In retrospect, that attitude was a rationalization to avoid confronting a scary Pandora's box of feelings related to identity, family, and cultural confusion. I was playing it emotionally safe. In my subconscious, I said, "This is not my trip home. This is Li Keng and Lai Wah's return home." I would merely be an observer. But once I got to China, once I experienced the bustle of Guangzhou, the hominess of Toisan, the tranquility and poverty of the villages, once I was transported back in time to a *see-yip* speaking universe that was like a womb, and once I stepped inside our parents' rundown house, the trip became mine. It engaged me emotionally and swelled me with pride and fear and a sense of mystery. Deeply unsettled by the fact that our first village visit was so hurried and ungracious, I was determined not to let our trip end so abruptly.

And so that first night, sitting in the lobby of our hotel in Toisan amid multiple layers of tensions after our whirlwind visit to Goon Doo Hong, the five of us—Ed, Flo, Felicia, Brad, and I—decided to stay in Toisan through at least the next afternoon even if it meant we had to hire another van at extra cost to take us back to Guangzhou, so we could return to the village in the morning.

That was the right move, validated by eerie coincidences. I am not a particularly superstitious person, but after our time in the village, I detected signs of an "other" force that made our trip memorable in unconventional ways. One was mundane. The room I got at our Toisan hotel was 1112. That happens to be my son's birth date (November 12) on the Western Gregorian calendar, not the Chinese lunar calendar. That fine distinction didn't bother me. It was a good omen.

As the nine of us drove away from Goon Doo Hong at about 3 P.M. after our hectic first visit, with the warm sun and dusty air of rural China choking us, the atmosphere inside the van grew tense and heavy. Suddenly, an otherwise innocuous request by Brad to his sister Felicia to share a snack exploded into a shouting match between the two of them, replete with profanities. Trapped in a confined space, our group was shocked into silence, including the usually voluble Flo, their mother. Finally, their father, Ed, sternly told them to stop.

My interpretation of this almost unheard-of outburst between a niece and a nephew who are easy going and loving people is that some outer force detected the inner tumultuous tensions of my siblings and me and funneled those feelings right through to a younger generation that is acculturated to dealing more openly with hurt and damaged feelings of the moment, rather than letting them stew, perhaps for decades, if not a lifetime. Even spookier is my feeling that because our village visit the first day was a mess and we really hadn't paid the proper respects to anyone there (even though we passed out a few *lay see*), someone or ones (our ancestors?) were angry, and their spirits roared disapproval in the form of Felicia and Brad's uncommon shouting match.

The two of them cleared the air at the hotel, then we gathered for dinner. But unresolved tensions hovered over the dinner. We might have discussed frankly what had transpired just hours earlier, but we held our tongues. Indeed, I felt that some of my siblings were being purposely polite, almost insincerely so, perhaps because we had a stranger (the van driver) in our midst or perhaps because they wanted simply to avoid any unpleasant confrontation. After the awkward dinner, Flo, her family, and I bid strained but cordial farewells to my older sisters and their families, who had to awake very early the next morning to be driven back to Guangzhou to make a morning train to Hong Kong to catch their flight home to America.

The five of us—Ed, Flo, Felicia, Brad, and I—chose to walk around Toisan before going to bed. We needed time to unwind, to let off some steam, to see something new, rather than to converge at the hotel to retell old and frustrating tales about our trip so far. It was well after nine o'clock, and the city near the restaurant and hotel was bustling. We looked into bakeries, beauty salons, and mom-and-pop groceries. We basked in the steady buzz of the *see yip* tongue that transported Flo and me back to our Oakland Chinatown childhoods.

As we rounded a dark corner, we came upon an elderly woman toking on an enormous bamboo pipe. Flo approached her and started a conversation. The woman, sitting outside a storefront, responded warmly. She said she was 98 years old. She said she had relatives who ran restaurants in San Francisco. She offered to fix Brad up with one of her granddaughters. Pointing to a tin can filled with dried leaves and a lighter, she asked us if we wanted to join her in taking a hit on her pipe. We all declined.

It was a magical moment for all of us, a great relief from the high-stress village visit and scheduling screw-up. For a few minutes we were enthralled by a vigorous, open-minded, and cheerful (what was she smoking?) old woman who instead of shooing us away welcomed our queries and shared a little of her life with us. Two younger women inside the store smiled and laughed as the old woman and Flo and I parried questions and answers. My *see yip* dialect is mostly a memory, but I managed to speak a few understandable phrases.

That the old woman toking on her pipe was 98 years old became noteworthy because Ed's mother and my father would have been 98 in the year of our visit. I was left to wonder whether this woman appeared to us on an anonymous street in a darkened Toisan as a living representation of our parents, to "approve" our plan to revisit their village.

Epilogue: Summer 1998

Thinking back more than three years after my roots visit, I vividly recall many moments, but sometimes it feels as though our trip was merely a dream. My reality, after all, is a rather conventional middle-class life in the East Bay area of the San Francisco region of northern California, one of the more favorable locales in the United States and, coincidentally, the informal capital of Chinese America and Asian America.

My siblings and I rarely talk about our China trip in 1994. Our daily routines of work, children, and recreational activities leave little room for idle reminiscences. My nephew Brad has taken a special interest in China. After our visit to Goon Doo Hong, Brad stayed on in China for a little while longer. Then he returned home to the San Francisco Bay Area and got a job as a reporter with a small northern California newspaper but quit within the year, feeling more wanderlust for China. So he returned to the homeland of his grandparents in early 1996 with only vague plans— to study more Mandarin, to try to get work as a freelance writer, to travel more around China.

He was based in Guangzhou with occasional forays into Hong Kong. He took time to revisit his grandparents' villages. His accounts of his revisits have had an odd effect on me. Once he visited when monsoon rains turned Goon Doo Hong into a muddy mess, a sharp contrast to the sunny warmth of our November 1994 visit. The conditions he described were a depressing reminder of the village's poverty and isolation. Our distant relatives would remind him of their needs and unsubtly suggest that we American cousins contribute money to rebuild our parents' old house.

I am not certain whether my vague feelings of disquiet in the years after our seminal roots visit are a result of naiveté. Before and during my November 1994 visit, I held a romantic notion of our journey to find our parents' humble little abode. Not that I ever thought the village residents were noble savages. Quite the contrary. They were the source of our family's experience. They were very much what our parents were like before they transformed their lives—and ours—by pulling up stakes and risking all to settle in *Gum Saan*.

Yet for second- and third-generation American descendants of Chinese villagers like my parents, life is far removed from the simplicity of a Goon Doo Hong. Immersed in a society and culture that is overrun with wealth and amenities, we have few material needs that aren't rather easily filled. We enjoy freedoms and liberties unheard of in China, especially in isolated villages like Goon Doo Hong. But our comfortable lifestyles and economic mobility have loosened family ties and have shaped identities that are a mishmash.

Perhaps I am uneasy about my Chinese roots visit because we children of struggling immigrant parents have lost that edge of hunger, of having

to strive for seemingly impossible goals, of battling unknown environmental and cultural elements the way my parents did to survive. Whatever the reasons, I sometimes feel slightly inauthentic, in part because of
my insecurities over my inability to speak fluently the village dialect or
Cantonese or Mandarin. My sisters and I, after all, aren't Chinese enough
to the Chinese living in China nor are we American enough to some
Americans who see us as perpetual foreigners.

Each of us on that November 1994 trip had our own reasons for going
and our own expectations of what we might find. I could more easily afford
my initial detached romanticism than, say, Li Keng, who was born in
Goon Doo Hong. It is possible to romanticize one's humble birthplace.
Given the impoverished conditions, however, one is more likely to want
to forget a downtrodden life and appreciate the obscene abundances of
Gum Saan.

My particular perspective may also be a function of my relative youth
among the siblings. As the youngest child, I am that much closer to a
wholly American cultural experience than the three China-born sisters,
even if they spent the bulk of their lives in America. This is not to say
that my three oldest sisters aren't American in the broadest terms of that
label. They certainly are. But I and my three Oakland-born sisters didn't
begin life in a rice-growing village in China and thus didn't have certain
seminal experiences of Chinese rural life. As one of the American-born
children, I was drenched in a genuinely Chinese American experience in
which the *see yip* dialect mingled with Cantonese and English, and mass
media such as radio, newspapers, movies, and television shaped our vision
of the world around us. As I matured, I wondered about my ethnic begin-
nings in a more desperate way than Li Keng did, perhaps, and all I could
do was imagine village life when she could conjure up a bona fide experience without making it up.

A deeper melancholy hangs over me long after our roots visit. When I
returned, I was enthusiastic in telling my wife and son about what I had
seen. Neither accompanied me because she had work commitments and
he was only eleven at the time, too young in my judgment to fully appreciate such a visit. Besides, he had started a new middle school only months
before and early November wasn't a natural school holiday period. I said
when I returned that we would all have to make a trip to the village when
he was older.

We will probably do that, but the romance has faded, and a nervous trepidation accompanies any prolonged thought about a future China trip with my wife and son. In part because of Brad's stories of villagers seeking help from us and the request by Fook Ying, our long-lost cousin whom we met, to sponsor his daughter in a proposed American education adventure, our relationship with our Goon Doo Hong relatives has taken on an air of obligation.

Obligation defines Chinese family relationships, so why should I be troubled by the obligatory nature of renewed connections with our village cousins? Any discomfort on my part has to do with a question about just how authentically Chinese is my family relationship now, decades after the passing of our parents, who embraced Chinese cultural values in ways that I or my sisters do not. The personal liberties we have enjoyed as Americans have eroded the sense of family duty, honor, and obligation we grew up with in Oakland's Chinatown. Eroded, but not erased. The continuing existence of these feelings of obligation is what is causing me mild anxieties about a return visit to China.

Would it be terribly selfish of me to simply incubate my unrealistically romantic feelings of November 1994—putting them in a psychological and emotional amber, to preserve forever—and never return? Or is it inevitable as a fulfillment of some time-honored family obligation to go back to Goon Doo Hong to advance whatever fledgling relationship we managed to resuscitate more than three years ago, even if it means we may take on greater financial responsibilities and even if it exposes my somewhat fragile emotional state to further jarring?

My sisters and I have not firmly established a time to return to Goon Doo Hong. Every once in a while, Flo and I will casually mention, in general terms, a return trip. Her fervor may be greater than mine at the moment.

My son, who is 15 years old and will be a sophomore in high school, has taken up studying Mandarin, in part as preparation for a trip to China. He knows that Mandarin is of limited or no use in the village of his paternal grandparents, but his effort is sincere and touching—and actually will be useful in broader terms in his bright future.

It is I who has doubts, and I have a feeling that whatever we do in the years ahead about a second China trip, those doubts—about family relationships and ethnic and cultural identities—will linger somewhere in the interiors of my psyche, finding companionship with those developed earlier in my life as a Chinese American kid growing up in Oakland's Chinatown during and after the World War II boom.

Traditions: Old and New

Asian Week, February 26, 1993

Having just hosted my family's Chinese New Year dinner for the twentieth year, I have tradition on my mind. Tradition can be an elusive or an antiprogressive concept. Tradition means you stick with something old.

I have no idea how the tradition of a formal sit-down Chinese banquet welcoming the new year came about. My family's is linked to how my parents observed the new year. I've had my extended family over for a Chinese New Year dinner ever since my mother passed away in 1973. When she was alive, she hosted the gathering of her seven children and their spouses and children. In her later years, after she moved from the five-bedroom house we had occupied in Oakland since 1948 to a one-bedroom apartment in Chinatown, these dinners were cramped.

Following tradition, I inherited the hosting duties because I am the only son. This tradition of patriarchy is certainly politically incorrect, but my sisters and I have an understanding about it.

Unlike my mother, who cooked everything, my sisters and I decided to each contribute a different dish. At first, some of the sisters would attempt elaborate concoctions, requiring cooking in our moderately sized kitchen. Things would get hectic as I or a sister would attempt stir-frying or steaming food for three or four tables of hungry and impatient relatives. We learned. Now, almost without exception, the potluck dishes come cooked. Warming up is all that's required.

In the early years, my wife and I needed more than cooking help. We didn't have enough rice bowls, soup spoons, chopsticks, serving dishes, chairs and tables to accommodate our expanding brood. So we potlucked those items too. Now we have enough.

At our peak, we'd have about thirty-five people for our sit-down dinner. Thirty-five people would be no problem at the Hearst Castle or Buckingham Palace, but we live in a modest three-bedroom house. We'd set up the dining room then put temporary tables in the hallway and in the living room. Once, we even had a set-up in the third bedroom (now an office) for the youngsters.

My sisters used to take a more active role in devising the multi-course menu. Now I handle the menu planning myself. Since it is tradition, though, there isn't much variation. Following tradition can be—dare I say it?—boring. But it's what we do. Actually, we're not all that persnickety traditional. We haven't always had whole fish, which is a hallmark of a traditional Chinese New Year dinner. The last couple of years, we did have whole fish, so we're leaning back toward tradition again.

Every year, we have *jai*, the so-called monk's dish, which consists of various Chinese vegetables, beans, and fungi. *Jai* has never been to my taste, but some of my sisters enjoy it. I usually assign this dish to Lai Wah, an older sister. Of course, we always have *bok-chit gai*, or boiled chicken, and a chicken-based soup. A brother-in-law, Roger, does these dishes expertly and by the time it gets to our house, the chickens are all cut up, and all we need to do is heat up the soup. The chickens started whole, so we adhere (sort of) to the tradition of having a whole chicken.

Other dishes that fill out our quasi-traditional menu are braised whole mushrooms, *sai fun* (Chinese vermicelli), *faw yook* (roast pork, which is purchased), and a more conventional vegetable dish (sometimes with meat). Then there's always the scrumptious chicken salad from my sister Nellie. She gets that assignment year in, year out. She got the recipe from *Sunset* magazine, of all places, but it is delicious and always a big hit. Several times, another sister, Flo, spiced up our usual Cantonese dishes with Szechwan peppers. Still Chinese, but not from our family's region. So was that breaking tradition, or merely stretching it?

Believe me, I've been tempted to radicalize our menus for the sake of differentness. But I'm stuck on tradition, so I don't fuss with the formula, which we're all used to. Where we have modified tradition is adding an appetizer, which doesn't have to be Chinese, and dessert, such as something gooey, along with fresh fruit. California wines and beer complement the meal, a local substitute for Chinese alcoholic beverages.

My mom and dad used to *bai sin*, or kowtow to ancestors, by burning incense and offering food at a makeshift altar. This ceremony has Buddhist roots, but we've always known it (since we come from peasant stock) as "ancestor worship." This may sound paganlike to Christians, but it's never bothered us.

If we adhered to strict tradition, only I would *bai sin,* since only sons did it, following the patriarchal, old-fashioned ways. But, given our modern, progressive outlook, we broke (or stretched) tradition long ago, after our mother died. My sisters now *bai sin* and so do our children, if they want. My son, who's now ten, is enthusiastic about lighting incense, bowing three times to the likenesses of his grandparents and a dead aunt, and placing the burning incense sticks into a container of sand. A few of my family members are born-again Christians so they stay away from the *bai sin* ceremony, which they don't believe in.

A big hit for me when I was growing up was getting *lay see,* or money-stuffed red envelopes. Kids got these from adults. We used to rake in quite a sum. Nowadays, third-generation kids don't hang around Chinatowns where there are lots of adults who give *lay see* to kids. The tradition continues but not in as bountiful a way. My son, for instance, gets from $15 to $20, a fraction of what I remember getting in much less inflationary times.

Over twenty years, things change. Life isn't static in a family. Relationships form then break up. Tragedies occur. So do joyous events like births of new babies. One tragedy was the death of a sister, Leslie, from lung cancer. A middle sister, she was one of the best liked of all the siblings, a person who listened well and dispensed sensible advice and love. Her death, in 1985, left a deep void for her three children and the rest of us.

The New Year dinner following her death was mournful and sullen. The following year, we had an exuberant celebration, as though spring had sprung. We still miss her, of course, but it's noteworthy how our collective mood can swing from down to up like that.

One year, we even marked an engagement between a family member and his betrothed. We invited his fiancée's family, so imagine the crush for space. Another year, we combined a wedding of a sister and a New Year celebration. This event featured the odd couple of firecrackers and rice tossing. Talk about bending tradition!

For some reason, this year, I wasn't enthusiastic about our Chinese New Year dinner. I'm not sure why. First, we had trouble settling on a date. That is always a problem with so many people involved. A few people couldn't make it. A couple of last-minute cancellations put a further damper on my mood. Then, I was out of firecrackers and didn't bother to ask around Chinatown for a secret stash. Stores in Chinatown used to sell firecrackers under the table but haven't done so in recent years. I've not nurtured the right connections. This year's dinner threatened to be dour without firecrackers scaring the evil spirits away. Instead, my son had us buy him boxes of "poppers," which explode (quite harmlessly) when thrown onto the pavement.

With all the absences, we had only twenty-four people spread over three tables, a manageable number. The food, traditional as always, was good, as always. My mood brightened. We had fun talking innocuously as only a family can about an assortment of mundane topics like Michael Jackson's famous TV interview with Oprah Winfrey and what we thought of the Oscar nominations and what our favorite TV shows are.

As my siblings and I are advancing in age, we no longer play mah jongg and poker late into the night, as we did when we were younger. Some of the nieces and nephews now have young children, and they can't stay out late anymore. But a hardcore group, some sisters and a nephew, my wife, and I, sat around till nearly midnight, talking and acting silly.

In a fast-paced America, we wonder sometimes about the viability of family and what family means. Family today has many different meanings, and Asian Americans can't find comfort in old stereotypes of "close-knit Asian families." My family reflects a fair share of life's many facets, of friendships among some family members and hostilities among others. We've had divorces and deaths, disappointments and delights.

We're no longer in constant, close touch with one another. But our Chinese New Year dinner serves a purpose beyond the symbolic welcoming of the new year. The *hoy nin* (or welcoming the new year) dinner, for us, is a reaffirmation of a connection that we seldom articulate but know in our hearts is fundamental to our existence and survival, through good times and bad.

Next year, I'll have to find a firecracker supplier.

"Rock On, Mr. President"

San Francisco Examiner, November 5, 1996

Journalists aren't supposed to get excited about events like presidential visits, but I shed my professional demeanor when President Clinton dropped by Oakland last Thursday night for one of his last public appearances before the election. I changed my attitude not for the president but for my 13-year-old son, Sam Mende-Wong.

He was one of two kids who presented the president an artistic "bridge to the future," evoking Clinton's campaign slogan of "Building a bridge to the 21st century." He was the kid who seized the microphone to rally the crowd to show their support for Clinton. And he was the kid who told Clinton to "rock on."

Sam wasn't very excited when he first heard he was being selected to present Clinton a gift. He had already made Halloween trick-or-treating plans with two old friends. Greeting the president would disrupt those plans. The Museum of Children's Art (MOCHA), where Sam has volunteered and worked before, was chosen to make a ceremonial gift for Clinton. Mary Marx, MOCHA's director, asked Sam to participate. Naturally, this prospect thrilled both his mom and me.

Clinton was only about thirty minutes late for the Jack London Square event. A crowd of 15,000 awaited him. Shortly after Clinton arrived, Sam and another youngster presented the bridge to Clinton. It was at that moment Sam seized the microphone when he wasn't supposed to and, in a manner that transcended his early teen years, warmed up the crowd.

"I have a few things to say," Sam said confidently into the microphone. "How many of you want President Clinton for four more years?" When he wasn't satisfied with the decibel level from the crowd, he implored, "I can't hear you!" The crowd responded with a louder roar. Next, he turned to Clinton, only a few feet away, "Rock on, Mr. President!" and gave him two thumbs up. This time, the crowd exploded, and Clinton threw back his head and laughed.

Smiling broadly, Clinton said a few words to Sam as they high-fived. Clinton told him, "Hey, kid. You're good at this. You should keep it up."

The rest of the evening was a blur and a crush. We caught up with Sam at the MOCHA offices a few blocks away. He told us he acted spontaneously and hadn't thought about what he was going to say. He was cool as a cucumber.

Of greatest concern to him wasn't his Big Moment with Bill Clinton. It was whether his two friends were still waiting for him to trick or treat. They were. So they went out into Halloween night.

Like other hyper-parents, I have mentioned to Sam I wanted him to "make a mark" in school. He had always scoffed at that idea. After his "Rock on, Mr. President" exhortation, Sam said, "Well, Dad, I just wanted to make my mark."

3 History

From Exclusion to Confusion

Conquering Frontiers and Barriers

San Francisco Examiner, May 7, 1998

Angel Island, a state park just across Raccoon Strait from Tiburon, pulsates with history beneath its natural beauty in San Francisco Bay. The immigration station at Point Simpton on the island's northeast corner once was a federal enforcement center for the Chinese Exclusion Act of 1882, the only piece of federal legislation targeting a specific ethnic group.

Several hundred thousand people were processed there starting in 1910, when the station was moved from San Francisco's waterfront. It was moved back when a fire in 1940 destroyed the administration building and other structures. After the fire, the army took over the station, renamed it the North Garrison, and turned it into a processing station for prisoners of war during World War II.

During the thirty-year period, almost 200,000 of the newcomers were detained, usually because of the Chinese Exclusion Act that barred Chinese laborers and women (including wives of U.S. citizens of Chinese descent) from permanent residence. The exclusion act was repealed in 1943, when China was a U.S. ally in World War II, but a quota of 105 Chinese immigrants per year wasn't abolished until 1965.

The detainees were crowded into open barracks. They dined while standing. Many were held for weeks, months, and, in a few cases, even years, often at the whim of the authorities, and many were forced to return to China. Of the detainees, an estimated 95 percent were Chinese. They included my mother and my three oldest sisters in 1933.

A refurbished Ellis Island Immigration Museum in New York has become a tourist attraction that memorializes the American immigration experience from Europe. It is time to lift the Angel Island Immigration Station to equal status to bring attention to the diverse and rich across-the-Pacific newcomer saga.

Becoming a National Historic Landmark is an important first step. Instrumental in getting the landmark designation were Daniel Quan and Felicia Lowe of San Francisco, president and vice president, respectively, of the Angel Island Immigration Station Foundation, and Philip Choy, a San Francisco architect and historian. Before them, Paul Chow was a courageous and visionary pioneer in the effort to save the dilapidated immigration station from destruction.

At the site is a stone monument, donated by the late Victor Bergeron in 1979, inscribed with a poem by Ngoot P. Chin in Chinese characters. The translation:

> Leaving their homes and villages, they crossed the ocean
> Only to endure confinement in these barracks.
> Conquering frontiers and barriers, they pioneered
> A new life by the Golden Gate.

The foundation, a nonprofit, all-volunteer group overseeing the station's preservation and restoration, is working on a plan its leaders hope will make the Angel Island site a nationally recognized center of West Coast immigration history. Over the past few months, Lowe said, that dream concept has come closer to reality with a serendipitous confluence of proposals.

One is proposed legislation by Senator Daniel Akaka, Democrat of Hawaii, to create a West Coast immigration museum and data bank. Another is the support of Brian O'Neill, superintendent of the Golden Gate National Recreation Area, a part of the National Park Service, who suggested that the immigration station become a West Coast bookend to Ellis Island as part of a National Genealogical Institute. A third is a $50,000 grant from the Gerbode Foundation to continue the group's work.

For Felicia Lowe, this is a labor of love. A former local TV journalist, Lowe is an independent documentary filmmaker whose work includes *China: Land of My Father, Carved in Silence* (which tells the story of the immigration station and its Chinese poems etched into the barracks walls), and *Chinatown,* a segment in KQED-TV's acclaimed series on San Francisco neighborhoods.

In a recent visit to Washington, D.C., Lowe told a friend that while she understood the ideas behind the Washington monument and the Jefferson and Lincoln memorials, she couldn't relate to them emotionally. With the immigration station, she can.

"This is really our institution," she said. "My father and grandfathers were detained there. Knowing that place exists and what it was help me appreciate American history in a different way. It makes me more secure about my place in America even though it draws on a sad experience. It gives me a greater appreciation of other immigrant stories."

Wong Is an American Name

Asian Week, April 30, 1998

A few weeks back, Yook Jim Wong went to Chinatown in Sacramento and, as was his custom, bought a Chinese-language newspaper, *Sai Gai Bo.* He turned to page two and was shocked to see his father's name in a headline. His father's name is Wong Kim Ark. Until then, Wong Kim Ark's name was known only to a small group of legal scholars, historians, and activists.

Wong Kim Ark is an important name in Chinese American and Asian American history. He was born in San Francisco in 1873. His China-born parents lived in San Francisco until 1890, when they returned to China. A teenager, Wong went to China that same year, presumably to visit his parents. When he returned not long afterward, he reentered the United States without incident. In 1894, he again went to China on a temporary visit, but when he came back in 1895, federal authorities barred his reentry on the ground he was not a U.S. citizen. This was just thirteen years after Congress passed the Chinese Exclusion Act to bar Chinese laborers from entering the United States.

Thus began a legal case that established that the Fourteenth Amendment to the U.S. Constitution applied to people of Chinese descent, and by extension to other non-white and non-black people born in the United States. The first sentence of the Fourteenth Amendment reads, "All persons born or naturalized in the United States, and subject to the jurisdiction thereof, are citizens of the United States and of the State wherein they reside."

The Wong Kim Ark case is relevant today. Civil rights advocates in the Asian American and Latino communities argue that the Wong case has bearing on contemporary political and legal issues, from attacks on immigrants to bilingual education programs, welfare dependency, immigration rates, and affirmative action programs.

From an Asian American perspective, the Wong Kim Ark case establishes that Chinese Americans were not passive about their victimization. In fact, legal scholars say the Wong case was one of almost a score of legal cases brought by Chinese Americans during the last half of the 19th century that set important precedents for citizenship rights of Asian Americans.

Few Asian Americans set out to become victims of racial, ethnic, or national-origins discrimination. It happens. When it does, we need to fight back. Wong Kim Ark fought back. He didn't fight back alone. He had the support of the Chinese Six Companies, which raised money to hire sympathetic white lawyers.

More important, the Wong Kim Ark case reminds newer ethnic Chinese and other Asian immigrants that our community has a history that goes back before 1965, when U.S. immigration laws were liberalized to allow greater numbers of Asian (and Latino) immigrants. Two-thirds of the people of Asian descent residing in the United States were born elsewhere, primarily in Asia.

This new immigrant class is incredibly diverse. Some are well educated and held professional jobs when they came. Others went to college or graduate school in the United States and stayed to contribute their skills in an expanding American economy. Many have done well. But how many of these relative newcomers realize the awful American history of Chinese, Japanese, and Filipino people in the 19th and early 20th centuries? The Wong Kim Ark case is one of the stories they should know in order to appreciate their rather privileged station in life, free of the virulent anti-Asianism that hit the young Wong squarely in the face when he tried to reenter the country of his birth in 1895.

The 100th anniversary observance of Wong's precedent-setting legal victory was the reason his name was in *Sai Gai Bo* and other newspapers, in both Chinese and English. That is how Yook Jim Wong came to see the name of his father resurrected in public. Yook Jim Wong had known about his father's legal case for many years, but he never shared it with his sons and daughters and their children. But after his father's name won a little media attention, he talked about it with his granddaughter, Alice Wong, a 19-year-old college student who lives in South San Francisco. "He really hadn't mentioned his father before," Alice Wong told me.

Someone told Alice about the National Archives and Records Administration regional office in San Bruno that houses 250,000 original Chinese immigration files, including that of Wong Kim Ark. Suddenly inspired to look into her family's history, Alice Wong went to San Bruno and spent ninety minutes perusing her great grandfather's immigration and legal files.

"I saw his court papers. I saw a paper of him getting arrested. I paid most attention to papers that had a photo of him on it. There were only five photos—from when he was 24 years old to when he was 62 years old. You could tell he was getting old," Alice Wong recalled. "I saw that he had signed his name in Chinese, and I was amazed because he was born in the United States."

Herself an immigrant from Hong Kong, Alice hadn't nurtured an interest in her family's history—until she discovered she was related to a meaningful figure. "When you find out about the history and culture of your family, it is so enriching and fulfilling," she said.

Yook Jim Wong was born in the Toisan area of Guangdong province in southeastern China in 1913. He had three older brothers, all of whom have passed on. When Yook Jim was 2 years old, his father, Wong Kim Ark, returned to America. It wasn't until eleven years later, in early 1926, that father and son met up again when the son emigrated to the United States. He remembers staying two to three weeks at the Angel Island Immigration Station, whose purpose was to keep out excludable Chinese immigrants.

When he got off the island, he stayed with his father for about six months at 875 Sacramento Street in San Francisco's Chinatown. Soon, he became homesick and went back to China, staying four years to finish high school. His father traveled to China again, but three months later, Yook Jim Wong returned to San Francisco. By this time, with the onset of an economic depression, Yook Jim had trouble finding work.

That began a worldwide odyssey as a Chinese restaurant waiter in Minneapolis, Chicago, and Sacramento, an inductee into the U.S. Army during World War II, switching over to the U.S. Marines but never seeing overseas duty, then working at a California naval shipyard, and eventually joining the Merchant Marines during the Korean War. He stayed twenty-five years with the Merchant Marines. "I liked the life," Wong said. "I went to Taiwan, Japan, the Philippines, Singapore, Malaysia, India, Pakistan. I went through the Panama Canal four or five times."

Yook Jim Wong learned of his father's legal case when he was very young. "I didn't know it was important. I didn't pay much attention." On one of his reentries to the United States, about 1946, he remembers an immigration officer telling him the historic importance of Wong Kim Ark's case. Again, Yook Jim Wong didn't pay much heed.

He learned of his father's death in a letter from village elders shortly after World War II. He said letters to and from his father didn't get through in the war years of the 1930s and 1940s, so he lost touch with him. When he heard about his father's death, he said, "I felt really bad." The last time he had seen his father was around 1930–31. He was with him less than three years, spread out over three separate periods. "I still think a lot about my father."

Aside from the intrinsic humanity of this story, it illustrates a truism: We all have unique stories that make up a grand American story, even though the political culture frequently restricts our rightful place in the American sun. Wong Kim Ark. Yook Jim Wong. Alice Wong. They are Chinese America—and the essence of America.

The "Forgotten Holocaust"

San Francisco Examiner, July 23, 1998

The photos and text of the "Forgotten Holocaust" exhibition at the Navy Library on Treasure Island could nauseate viewers, but that is the point. The exhibition wants visitors to know there were unspeakable atrocities perpetrated by the Japanese military in Asia from 1931 to 1945 that exhibition organizers believe haven't been accounted for and aren't well known in the West.

One photo shows the severed head of a Chinese man "displayed on a roadblock outside Nanking. A cigarette butt was inserted into the mouth by the killers as an exclamation point." The caption on a photo of a man named Chien Guei-Fa of Ning Po city looking skyward reads, "Two o'clock in the afternoon of Oct. 27, 1940, Japanese airplane flew in low altitude and dropped flour and fleas in Kai Ming Street. He started having fever on Nov. 1. Lymph node on both of his thighs swollen. Fortunately, he survived. But many people were not as lucky. Before they die they had convulsion [sic] and their bodies turned black." Testimony from a woman named Juanita Jamot, born November 12, 1924: "I want the Japanese soldiers who raped me to repent. I want to recover my dignity which was taken from me by the Japanese army."

Each example above represents the topics covered by the exhibition— the "Rape of Nanking" in which Japanese soldiers killed more than three hundred thousand Chinese; the workings of the Japanese biological and germ warfare operation known as Unit 731; and "comfort women," thousands of Asian women forced into prostitution by the Japanese military.

At ceremonies marking an extension of the exhibition, which has attracted more than eight thousand visitors over the past two weeks, local politicians, representatives of survivors' groups, and scholars all said, in one way or another, that cruel and inhumane acts of war must not be forgotten. Ignatius Y. Ding, an exhibition organizer with the Silicon Valley group Alliance for Preserving the Truth of Sino-Japanese War, reiterated the old saying that those who don't learn from history are condemned to repeat it. "We haven't learned anything in the past fifty years. Look at Bosnia, Croatia, Somalia, and Indonesia. We have to raise the awareness of past atrocities. We have to show the younger generation that justice will prevail and that good will triumph over evil."

When asked whether the exhibition was one that targets Japan, today an American ally, Ding said, "This could happen to anyone." Then he quickly added, "One reason we are bringing this out is that the Japanese government continues to distort and deny history." The introduction of the exhibition stated, "It should be emphasized that it's not our intention to stir up hatred between the Chinese and Japanese. Hatred-induced vicious cycles can only increase the suffering of these two people. We believe that both the Japanese and Chinese were victims of the Japanese militarists."

A fourth-generation Japanese American, Ian Kawata, visiting the exhibition with his Hong Kong–born woman friend, said World War II Japanese atrocities "need to be remembered the way the Holocaust against the Jews needs to be remembered." Kawata said he doesn't feel self-conscious about the exhibition targeting the homeland of his ancestors. "You have to make a clear distinction between Japanese and Japanese Americans." He noted that many Japanese Americans fought in the Allied military against the Axis powers and that Japanese attorneys today are working with ethnic Chinese to "resolve history to get the truth out."

Healing Wounds, or Opening Them?
Salon.com, August 3, 1999

The crowd of 250 gathered at Ming's of Palo Alto on a recent Sunday to honor Assemblyman Mike Honda, the liberal Democrat of San Jose, one of only two Asian Americans (both Japanese Americans) in the California legislature. At one table sat Ling-chi Wang, chair of the Ethnic Studies Department at the University of California at Berkeley and a long-time liberal Democratic San Francisco activist. What was he doing at a gathering organized by Lester Lee, who heads up a Silicon Valley high-tech company and, when he was a Republican-appointed University of California regent, supported Proposition 209, the anti–affirmative action initiative that Wang opposed? Wang was part of a mostly Democratic San Francisco Chinese American contingent that doesn't usually mingle with the more conservative Silicon Valley Chinese American high-tech entrepreneurial crowd. There were Chinese Americans who favor Taiwan and others who lean toward the People's Republic of China, two groups that usually seethe with hostility toward one another.

What's going on here? Assemblyman Honda's resolution demanding the Japanese government apologize and pay for World War II atrocities was what brought the mostly middle-aged, well-to-do but otherwise ideologically diverse Chinese American crowd together. The issue, however, is tearing apart Japanese Americans and Chinese Americans at a time when many of them are actively fighting the perception that they are foreigners and that their loyalties are suspect, as in the well-publicized alleged nuclear-spy case of Wen Ho Lee. At a personal level, it has caused a deep rift between Honda and Assemblyman George Nakano, a moderate Democrat from Torrance, two Japanese Americans who had been cordial colleagues now on opposite sides of an issue that involves the homeland of their ancestors.

Honda, in his second term, authored Assembly Joint Resolution 27 [which passed later that month]. In addition to its demands on Japan, the resolution calls on the U.S. Congress and the president "to take appropriate action to bring about a formal apology and reparations" by Japan. (AJR-27 closely resembles a Congressional resolution that died in the last session.)

Some analysts wonder why the Honda resolution is kicking up such a fuss. By their nature, resolutions are nonbinding, and they usually express the collective feelings of the lawmakers, but they are not laws themselves. After all, the California legislature has no power to order the Japanese government, or any other foreign entity, to do anything.

"People have criticized my timing on this resolution," Honda said, in an interview after the Sunday lunch. "There is never a good time. But now seemed to be as good a time as any. . . . This is my business. I am a public policy person. One of my jobs is to speak up. This is the right thing to do. It's consistent with my values and principles. But I didn't think it would cause such a ruckus." Earlier, to the lunch crowd, Honda said he is promoting the issue "so that historical amnesia will not occur. It's about healing. We want wounded relations between China, Japan, India, Korea, the Philippines to heal."

Nakano was not available for comment because he is on vacation, according to his Torrance office, but a friend, who asked for anonymity, explained the assemblyman's position. "George thinks the timing of Mike's resolution is poor. We are in this period of anti-Asian sentiments. It also brings on confusion over distinctions between Japanese and Japanese Americans, Chinese and Chinese Americans." This person added, "It's a mess. The situation has mushroomed into something intensely emotional on both sides."

People who know both men are chagrined at this internecine warfare between the only two Asian American Democratic lawmakers in the nation's most populous state where 40 percent of the Asian American population resides. Honda is a 58-year-old third-generation Japanese American (*sansei*) who before becoming an assemblyman was a Santa Clara County supervisor for six years. He describes himself as a 1960s liberal Democrat who helped establish the Ethnic Studies Department at San Jose State University. Nakano is a 64-year-old *sansei* too in his first term as an assemblyman representing a moderate-to-conservative district in southern California. He had been a Torrance city councilman for fourteen years and a teacher and school administrator before that. Both men, when very young, spent years in American internment camps for Japanese immigrants and Japanese Americans during World War II. Friends say the two men have worked together and helped each in the past, but one source pointed out that the two have different personalities. "Mike has always been a champion of civil rights and human rights. George takes a more methodical, moderate course. He is very analytical."

Whatever the personal stakes, the issue promoted by Honda and opposed by Nakano has shaken up Japanese Americans and Chinese Americans in California and across the nation. In the long and diverse Asian American history, those two groups have been most prominent in political activities among Asian ethnic groups. Two national scandals, however, have focused unwanted media and political attention on the evolving political development of Asian Americans. One was alleged illegal campaign contributions brokered by some Asian Americans, principally Chinese Americans, to the 1996 Clinton-Gore campaign and Democratic Party. The other is the so-called China spy case involving a Chinese American scientist. In both cases, the loyalties of Asian Americans have been challenged, and Asian American political activists have strenuously asserted the need for the national media and politicians to distinguish between Asians and Asian Americans.

"The Honda resolution is not a domestic issue. It does not belong in the California legislature. It perpetuates the myth we are foreign," said one California Asian American political activist, who asked for anonymity. "It compromises the battle that Asian Americans are fighting that we are loyal to our root Asian homelands." Some Japanese Americans are upset with Honda because they fear backlash from Americans who may consider them more Japanese than American. For many Japanese Americans, especially those who lived through the World War II internment experience, the matter of a distinct American identity has been crucial to persuade Americans they aren't loyal to Japan. Ironically, according to some sources, Japanese Americans who oppose the Honda resolution won't speak out publicly for fear their opposition will be interpreted as endorsing Japan's heinous acts half a century ago. "Some Japanese Americans are silenced on this issue," one observer noted.

To Honda supporters, ethnicity and nationality are irrelevant. "One shouldn't look at this issue in terms of ethnicity," said Iris Chang, the

Silicon Valley–based author of the internationally acclaimed book *The Rape of Nanking: The Forgotten Holocaust of World War II*. "It should be looked at from the perspective of human rights. When the focus is human rights, all other issues fall by the wayside. . . . Americans should care about this issue in the same way we care about the Holocaust. The rape of Nanking was an act of genocide." The "Rape of Nanking" refers to mass slaughter of hundreds of thousands of Chinese by the Japanese military in late 1937 and early 1938. Chang's book has brought widespread attention to the heretofore underexposed massacre.

UC-Berkeley's Ling-chi Wang sees no identity contradictions. "I see this issue as a kind of synthesizing of two experiences many of us have had. I have vivid childhood memories of Japanese atrocities in Amoy, near where I was born. But as an American, I feel the need to participate in the political process here. So supporting this measure is drawing upon my personal experiences and translating them to the American political arena. I see no contradiction."

For Gilbert Chang, a China-born retired computer programmer and founding president of a Silicon Valley–based group called Alliance for Preserving the Truth of Sino-Japanese War, the issue is deeply emotional. "Atrocity and war between Japan and China have been terrible for more than a century. This kind of hatred can't go on anymore. Wounds have to heal. To heal the wounds, to have a lasting peace, Japan has to acknowledge what it has done. It has to issue a meaningful apology and pay reparations."

In addition to Chang's alliance group, a new organization called the Rape of Nanking Redress and Reparations Committee has formed, co-chaired by San Francisco Superior Court Judge Lillian Sing and Dr. Clifford Uyeda, a former national president of the Japanese American Citizens League. "Ours is not a Chinese movement, but an American human rights organization," Sing said. Sensitive to the issue of Japan-bashing, Dr. Uyeda, a retired pediatrician, said, "You're not betraying the country of your parents or grandparents by criticizing it. We Americans criticize the U.S. government all the time."

In response, the Japanese consulate in San Francisco sent Assemblyman Honda a statement made on August 15, 1995, by former Japanese prime minister Tomiichi Murayama, who expressed "my feelings of deep remorse and state my heartfelt apologies" for the "tremendous damage and suffering

to the people of many countries, particularly to those of Asian nations."
The Japanese consulate response also includes a detailed breakout of Japanese history textbook treatments of the Rape of Nanking and other inhumane wartime actions such as a poison-gas unit and using Asian women as
prostitutes for Japanese military personnel. The textbook response was the
Japanese government's way of answering critics who accuse Japanese officials of ignoring or downplaying their World War II activities. Author Iris
Chang, for one, dismisses the responses. "Too vague. Not specific enough,
and nowhere near Germany's apology to its victims," she said.

Even though many Chinese Americans are pleased with Honda's resolution, others are not. The issue has driven a wedge in the ranks of the
Organization of Chinese Americans, or OCA, a 26-year-old national civil
rights group of primarily middle-class suburban Chinese immigrants. Last
year, the national OCA board voted not to support the Congressional
resolution similar to Honda's state resolution. It did so primarily because
the OCA constitution forbids the organization from getting involved in
foreign policy issues. But several OCA chapter presidents, arguing the
issue isn't foreign, are raising the issue again. Michael Lin, immediate past
national OCA president, explained the group's reluctance to support a call
for Japan to apologize and pay for atrocities in China. "If we go to Congress to advocate for our rights, we don't want anyone to question whose
rights we are speaking out for. We do not want to send out mixed messages. We stand as Americans for the rights of Chinese Americans and
Asian Americans."

The issue embodied in Honda's resolution clearly is vexing to many
Asian Americans. But some see a silver lining. One political operative said,
"Controversy is healthy. This shows we are growing up politically." UC-
Berkeley's Wang added, "What we saw at the Ming's lunch was a contin-
uing political maturity of the Chinese immigrant population."

The Price of Memories

Asian Week, April 16, 1998

When Guy P. Lee was 2 years old, his father was killed in an automobile
accident in San Francisco. In the seventy-six years since then, Lee never
knew what his father looked like. No family member had ever taken a

picture of Lee's father. A few months ago, Lee's niece told him about the National Archives and Records Administration office in San Bruno, just south of San Francisco, where thousands of original files are kept of Chinese immigrants during the late 19th century and through the first half of the 20th century, all victims of the 1882 Chinese Exclusion Act. Meticulous records were kept of Chinese immigrants to determine if they should be excluded from entry.

Lee and his 74-year-old wife, Rose, drove to San Bruno, hoping to find a photo of Lee's father. They struck pay dirt. With the help of an archives technician, they found the file of his father. For the first time in his life, Guy P. Lee saw what his father looked like, in two passport photographs. "I was so surprised, so happy," he said. Tears welled up in his eyes. "It was absolutely something. I've been looking all these years for a picture of my father."

The National Archives and Records Administration office in San Bruno is a treasure trove for Chinese Americans and other Americans curious about family history and the history of immigration through the West Coast. But that treasure trove may be threatened by bureaucratic belt-tightening. John Carlin, head of the National Archives and Records Administration, or NARA, has launched a "space planning" effort that could drastically change the status of San Bruno and other regional centers.

The agency's space-planning initiative suggests a predilection to store records electronically and on microfilm. Carlin's statement said the goal is to increase the quality and quantity of space used to store government records and reduce the cost of storage space. NARA hasn't yet decided whether to consolidate regional centers to save money, according to Lori Lisowski, assistant director for planning of NARA. About 45 percent of the agency's $200-million annual budget goes to rent for storage space. "Maintaining all of our buildings is expensive," she said.

The implications for the dozen or so NARA regional centers are uncertain. NARA will seek cheaper space or renegotiate rates with the General Services Administration, the agency's landlord. It is possible the agency will store temporary records of the vast federal bureaucracy in a place with cheap rental rates. But that is unlikely to happen to the historically valuable archival records such as Chinese immigration files, Lisowski said. The latter are permanent records, and they constitute only

2 to 3 percent of the paperwork generated by the federal bureaucracy. The other 97 percent are scheduled for eventual destruction.

Lisowski said she couldn't give a definitive answer about whether San Bruno's 250,000 Chinese immigrant files would stay or be moved. There is a fear among genealogists and scholars that these one-of-a-kind files may be made inaccessible to them.

All this talk within the National Archives and Records Administration about consolidating space, saving rent money, and going on-line should be a huge red flag for Chinese Americans and other Asian Americans. The San Bruno facility contains an incredibly detailed and irreplaceable record of pioneering Chinese immigrants. More than that, those records represent the essence of our community's tortured and inspiring history. We need to have easy and direct access to those files. Seeing a file on microfilm or on a computer screen is simply not good enough.

Historian Him Mark Lai helps run a "roots" program for young Chinese Americans descended from immigrants from the Pearl River Delta region in Guangdong province, where the earliest Chinese immigrants came from. Before they go to China, the young people visit the San Bruno facility to learn their family histories—leafing through files, finding sepia-tone photos, perhaps a fraying, folded-up map of their ancestor's village, the interrogation transcript of their long-gone relatives. These are living historical documents. "If you see that information on microfilm, it's just not the same," Lai said. "When you see the real thing, you can sense the real history, the background. Some things just don't project well on microfilm."

Original documents of Chinese immigrants, Japanese picture brides, and Filipino immigrants need to stay in San Bruno, or at the very least in the Bay Area somewhere, with knowledgeable archival experts helping people like Guy and Rose Lee learn about how their American lives began. How else would Guy Lee know what his father looked like? And what price can you put on a memory like that?

[After months of study and review, including holding public meetings around the country, the National Archives and Records Administration decided not to consolidate its popular regional centers.]

4 Immigration

Huddled Masses

Still Searching for Gold Mountain

Asian Week, June 18, 1993

The smuggling of Chinese nationals into the United States is a compli-cated story that embraces economic inequities across the Pacific Ocean, sophisticated criminality, American xenophobia, and confusion and anguish in Chinese American communities. One shouldn't blame the thousands who've endured appalling and unspeakable conditions in their naive quest for the American Dream

The Chinese smuggling phenomenon is a continuing drama in the great human search for economic (and, perhaps, political) betterment. China is undergoing astonishing economic growth. But with more than 1.2 billion people, China is still backwards compared with modern industrial standards. While capitalism is thriving in cities and regions along China's eastern and southeastern coastlines, the economic boom isn't reaching everyone.

The dangerous human-cargo trade is centered in Fujian province. Eco-nomic conditions are improving there, knowledgeable people tell me, but they are still dire compared with America's wealth and opportunities. For many years, Fujian immigrants have made the trip and ended up princi-pally in New York City. The costs are high for those doing it illegally—about $30,000, with $1,000 or so down, the rest a debt they work off over years in low-paying jobs in restaurants and garment sweatshops. For many of them, if not most, this paltry existence is better than what they left.

People who've been to China recently tell me they see the fruits of cap-italism blossoming, but not everyone is benefiting. The same folks who waved Mao's red book—the petty bureaucrats—are now figuratively waving Adam Smith's manifesto of capitalism. Corruption is a growth industry. Dirt-poor rural Chinese may be doing better in city jobs but are still earning little by Western standards, if they can find work.

So America's "gold mountain" appeal continues to beckon to people willing to risk life and limb to do better. Chinese and other Asian gangsters are more than willing to help them. These are the smugglers and enforcers who bribe government officials, in China, other Asian countries, and likely in Africa, Mexico, and Central America, to make the multinational illegal trade possible. Their greedy profiteering is easy to denounce but not easy to shut down, as corruption is rampant. The smugglers can play very rough if they don't get their money, either from the person being smuggled or from relatives who've promised to help.

It is a nasty business, and it's hard to imagine anyone outside the crime syndicates who wouldn't condemn such inhumane activities. Some civil rights activists are reluctant to denounce the smugglers because they occasionally serve a noble purpose: getting out people truly seeking refuge from political persecution. Smugglers exploiting naive economic refugees don't deserve our sympathy. Then there are other exploiters, employers who ask no questions about the next pool of very cheap labor. They too should be held accountable by the U.S. government.

There is no unanimity of views within Chinese American and other Asian American communities about the smuggling. Some deplore the inhumane treatment aboard the rickety ships. Some are confused and anguished over the seemingly never-ending supply and demand of the human-cargo trade.

As for the Fujianese themselves, some may be doing okay. Others can't find jobs because the recession has hit New York's Chinatown. They scatter to other Chinatowns in nearby states. Even exhortations from those who have come before and who have had a very rough time of it don't appear to stop others from coming. Some Chinatown observers theorize that's because previous Fujianese illegals want to save face, so they don't tell the whole truth about the harsh realities of an underground existence in America. Or maybe, the Fujianese villagers, desperate to make good somewhere, simply don't hear the negatives of American life and only can envision streets paved in gold.

Social-service agencies feel ambivalent and angry about the rush of illegals because, eventually, the demand for services increases without a concomitant increase in funding. Moreover, legal immigrants are feeling frustrated at seeing the illegals alight while documented immigrants wait patiently for years to bring over their relatives through legal channels.

Civil rights advocates are rightly concerned about whether the illegals are getting due process. While the immigrants are likely to ask for political asylum, coached to do so by the smugglers, their claims of fleeing persecution from either the 1989 Tiananmen Square crackdown or China's one-child policies seem far-fetched.

There certainly may be legitimate political asylum claims that can be ferreted out through an immigration hearing process. Unfortunately, the Immigration and Naturalization Service is overwhelmed right now. We need to be hard-eyed about this and admit that many, if not all, of this current group of illegals are probably economic refugees.

Ironically, right-wing elements in our society that pushed China's one-child policy are now complaining about the influx of illegal Chinese immigrants coming here claiming persecution from that policy. Moreover, a generous U.S. policy to grant asylum to those fleeing persecution because of the Tiananmen Square democracy demonstrations has also sent a signal to Chinese that they are welcome in America.

Law enforcement agencies like the INS and the Coast Guard have been the front-line U.S. government response, but a much higher level must become engaged to address this problem. Already, some politicians, shocked at the stories of inhumanity and deprivation told by the apprehended illegals, are talking about tougher measures to block undocumented immigration, including the power of "summary exclusion," or the sending back immediately of someone who's been determined on the spot not to have a legitimate political asylum claim.

That's typical political talk, pandering to xenophobic tendencies in America, but the difference is, the Chinese smuggling scandal has turned up the volume in Congress for "reform." What's troubling is that even as the smuggling of Chinese nationals has garnered extraordinary media attention, the number of Chinese illegals pales in comparison with the steady stream from Mexico and Central America. According to the INS, in 1991, the latest year for which statistics are available, 1.2 million illegal immigrants were detained. All but 70,000 came from Mexico. Only

6,000 came from China. It is probable the Chinese numbers are rising. But harsh government actions shouldn't be invoked only when the Chinese smuggling story is hot. That sends a distinctly hostile message to Chinese Americans and other Asian Americans.

I don't condone the exploitive smuggling of anyone, but we must be cognizant of the larger questions of economic inequities that drive this dastardly trade. And tightened-up policies ought not carry a tinge of racial bias.

In truth, the Chinese smuggling story exacerbates an already sensitive policy and political issue over immigration, legal and illegal. With the American economy still struggling, ordinary people and their elected leaders aren't in much of a mood to be generous or academic about a lot of poor yellow people washing ashore.

This story is far from over. It will continue to be buffeted by xenophobia and economic scape-goating, as America tries to figure out what kind of country it really wants to be, one that maintains its overwhelmingly large white majority or one that tolerates more racial, ethnic, cultural, and class diversity.

Second-Class Citizenship

San Francisco Examiner, September 27, 1996

The rush for citizenship has probably baffled and frustrated the folks who want to punish noncitizen legal immigrants under the new welfare-reform law. That law makes these perfectly legal residents ineligible for many public benefits. Cutting them off from services they are paying for is nasty. It means only one thing to them: America doesn't want you. It sends a clear message to anyone thinking about pulling up roots to settle here legally: Don't come.

Rather than take the abuse, thousands, if not millions, of "lawful permanent resident aliens," as the bureaucratese has it, are signing up for citizenship.

Extremists among the immigration restrictionists who promoted or supported the move against legal immigrants are fed up with the growing colorization of America. They don't like the different languages, the different cultural traditions, the different colors, religions, and cultures brought over by the millions who have come during the past twenty-five years, mostly from Mexico, Central and South America, and Asia and the Pacific Islands. They're ruining the country. They're stealing our jobs. Their children are gang-bangers. They don't speak English. They don't know our culture. Go back to where you came from.

Bear in mind many of these legal immigrants were encouraged to come here to fill jobs Americans either didn't want or couldn't do. Bear in mind many of these legal immigrants have revitalized small businesses in many cities. Bear in mind the children of some of these immigrants have boosted test scores and are beginning to work their way up the American ladder of success.

Even before they were told in no uncertain terms by Congress they were less than worthy, legal immigrants knew they didn't have the same rights and privileges of citizenship. The difference is more than simply the right to vote. Many states restrict certain jobs to citizens. Citizens also can't be deported, but legal residents can be for specific kinds of crimes.

In terms of immigration rights, citizens can petition for more kinds of relatives than legal residents can. For instance, citizens can sponsor parents, siblings, and married sons and daughters to enter the United States legally. Legal residents, however, can't petition for parents and siblings, but they can sponsor a spouse and unmarried sons and daughters, according to Bill Ong Hing, a legal scholar and an author of a book about Asian American immigration history.

"By dumping on legal immigrants, what the welfare reform law did was reemphasize how second class lawful residency status is. It says to them, 'You're second class anyway. We'll just take away another benefit from you,'" Hing said, adding he wasn't particularly surprised Congress targeted legal immigrants. What surprised him was the extension of benefits exclusion to those legal residents who first came to the United States as refugees. "We let refugees in because we're a great humanitarian country. I'm proud of that as an American," he said.

Refugees need public assistance. Many become lawful permanent residents but continue on welfare. Now they're being denied benefits under the welfare reform law. That, to Professor Hing, is like kicking dirt in their faces. Meanwhile, the legal residents signing up for citizenship in large numbers will soon be eligible to vote. Guess who they would like to dump from office?

Downsize Your SUV

San Francisco Examiner, March 11, 1998

Sierra Club members are engaged in a most intriguing vote at this time. Until mid-April, they can choose between staying out of the immigration debate and favoring a net reduction in U.S. immigration rates. The club's current position is no position on immigration. An Ohio chapter leader is pushing the club to call for a reduction in legal immigration rates.

The Sierra Club is barking up the wrong tree. Why should one of the most illustrious environmental organizations join immigrant-bashing ideologues like Pat Buchanan? Why go negative?

Some American environmentalists think that immigration is a major factor in escalating the use of natural resources and in polluting our natural surroundings. So they'd like to build higher barriers and maybe even a high security fence around U.S. borders to keep out all those polluting foreigners.

Some Sierra Clubbers are more rational than others. Club executive director Carl Pope and the board of directors see population growth as a global issue. Dissidents, however, are exhibiting scary nationalistic tendencies, contending that lowering U.S. immigration (and birth) rates will eventually save the U.S. environment, regardless of what happens everywhere else in the world.

Does this mean we blessed Americans are immune from acid rain and depletion of the ozone layer and oil spills?

Maybe I'm all wet, but I wouldn't rate immigration as a major environmental despoiler. I'd put American consumption at the top of anti-Earth list. So rather than scapegoat immigrants, Sierra Club members, why don't you stick to what you do best—push for sane environmental protection policies that focus on reducing just a little bit of our rather obscene extravagant life style? Here are a few ideas that the club already knows about:

- Go after sport utility vehicles. These favorite yuppie toys are selling almost as well as McDonald's hamburgers. And they are gas guzzlers—and dangerous to boot. Auto executives and marketers know they have sex appeal to the affluent American middle and upper-middle classes. Since they are selling so well and since they gobble up a lot more gasoline than regular old mid-sized sedans, the Sierra Club should make them a very high priority on its save-the-Earth agenda.

- Go after monster single-family homes. Do freestanding single-family homes—another component of the American Dream—have to be at least 2,500 square feet with front and back lawns and four bathrooms? Once, two Filipino women came to our modest 1,800 square-foot home for dinner. They were in awe that only my wife, son, and I lived there. After the 1991 fire destroyed homes in some upscale neighborhoods of Oakland, people who lost their homes used generous insurance settlements to rebuild homes more spacious than the ones that went up in flames. Ego palaces, I call them. Most Americans feel it is a divine right to have huge single-family homes, but if we reduced our living space only a little, we'd save a lot of flushing water and incandescent light bulb energy.
- Go after excessive food packaging. Food manufacturers like to market to a consuming public that includes a lot of single people. Plastic-wrapped small packages use a lot of energy and resources.

There are other ideas, like more and better mass transit systems, that the Sierra Club has worked on. It should continue doing so, rather than target immigrants, who are not the major villains in the environmental drama that engulfs us all.

[Sierra Club members voted to maintain the club's "no position" on immigration policy.]

Se Habla English

San Francisco Examiner, March 27, 1998

This has been a decade of cantankerousness toward California's growing multiculturalism. A solid majority of California voters has favored measures hostile to multiculturalism—Propositions 187, 209, and the upcoming 227, the Unz anti–bilingual education initiative.

Lurking behind the majority votes of the contrarians to multiculturalism is a fear that "our way of life" is in danger of being overrun by burrito trucks, sushi vendors, dim sum parlors, and vats of kimchee. And the cacophony of tongues! Doesn't anybody speak English anymore?

Guess what? Even the children of these brown, yellow, and black huddled masses yearning to breathe free prefer English to their native languages. This is according to a multi-year survey of adolescent children of immigrants by three Cuban immigrant scholars.

They interviewed 5,200 young people in southern Florida and the San Diego area in 1992, when the youths were eighth and ninth graders. Three and four years later, they found 82 percent of the youngsters and reinterviewed them. By then, the teenagers were mostly seniors in high school.

Almost 90 percent of them told the researchers they would rather speak English than the native language of their parents. They also said they believed the United States of America is the best country in which to live, despite personally experiencing some discrimination here.

"The findings suggest that the linguistic outcomes for the third generation—the grandchildren of the current wave of immigrants—will be no different than what has been the age-old pattern of American history: The grandchildren may learn a few foreign words and phrases as a quaint vestige of their ancestry, but they will most likely grow up speaking English only," said one of the researchers, Ruben G. Rumbaut of Michigan State University.

Rumbaut and two colleagues, Alejandro Portes of Princeton University and Lisandro Perez of Florida International University, also found that children of immigrants had higher grades and lower dropout rates than other American high school students.

There were differences among different ethnic and socioeconomic groups, but the overall findings are a loud rebuke to the idea that the current generation of immigrants seek to create linguistic and cultural fiefdoms that would Balkanize California irreparably.

What we have at work in this latest incarnation of the American Immigration Story isn't too far removed from earlier waves of European immigration. The Americanization process is very strong. I am not sure why some Americans have so little confidence in it.

What may appear to be a significant difference between today's immigrant experience and that of previous generations—the desire to retain some measure of their native identities in language and culture—isn't much of a difference after all. The progeny of immigrants, then and now, appears to want very much to be a part of the American mainstream, English language and all.

Children of immigrants realize at some point that they must be able to be as proficient as possible in English in order to avoid being ghettoized. If they are to compete in tomorrow's economic environment, they must do so in English. That doesn't mean they won't want to speak their native languages and exude their unique cultural ways. They may choose to live "inside out" or "outside in" lives, ethnic and American at the same time. And what's wrong with that?

5 Identity and Acculturation

A State of Mind

Filipinas, May 1999

Let's see. There's California and Hawaii and New York and Illinois and Texas and Florida and Washington—states with significant Asian American populations. But where is Asian America? In what state of the fifty that comprise the United States of America does Asian America reside?

Skeptics who say nowhere have persuasive evidence to support their case. Start with numbers. Asian Americans number about ten million, more or less, about 4 percent of the U.S. population, a sharp rise from less than 1 percent thirty years ago. Two-thirds of Asian Americans were born outside of the United States. That doesn't mean most are foreign to the core because some came to the America when they were quite young and grew up here, making them as American as, well, chop suey.

That is exhibit number one, buttressing the case of a nonexistent Asian America. There are a couple of million ethnic Chinese living in the United States. About the same number of Filipinos are spread throughout many states. Ethnic Japanese, Koreans, Vietnamese, Asian Indians, Cambodians, Laotians, Thai, Hawaiians, Samoans, Pakistanis, Burmese, Singaporeans—where do we put the Afghanis, Iranians, and others from western Asia?—make up the rest of what we call Asian America. Asian Americans trace our roots to many different places in Asia, stretching from the Bosporus to the Indian Ocean to the western edge of the Pacific Ocean.

Exhibit number two in the case against an Asian America is issues. What issues animate our psyches, move us to action, elevate our passions? Depends on whom you ask.

Among Filipino Americans, one issue of importance is justice for World War II Filipino American veterans who fought alongside American and Allied forces in defeating the Japanese Imperial military. Promises were made by U.S. presidents and Congress to grant citizenship and other benefits, but those promises have run false. Another Filipino American issue is cultural and historical identity. Are Filipinos Asians, Southeast Asians, or the Asian branch of Spanish imperialism?

The history of the Philippines is three hundred years of Catholicism under Spanish rule, fifty years of Hollywood under United States occupation, and independence for the past half century. Filipinos and Filipino Americans haven't worked through this mélange of historical and cultural traditions to settle on an overriding Filipino or Filipino American identity. Some regard themselves as part of a greater Asian American identity. Others prefer a separate Filipino American identity. Some Filipino Americans say they share more with Mexican Americans, another Spanish imperialistic victim, than they do with Chinese and Japanese Americans.

About the only thing that ethnic Chinese in the United States can safely agree on is that they are part of a Chinese Diaspora and that chopsticks are a principal eating implement. Affinity for the China run by the Communist Party or the Nationalists in Taiwan continue to split some Chinese Americans. A portion of Chinese America remains angry at Japan for World War II atrocities for which the Japanese government has yet to sufficiently apologize. Then there are Chinese Americans who couldn't care less about China-versus-Taiwan or Tibet-versus-China or about the Rape of Nanking, but, as native-born Americans, are imbued with vestiges of Chinese culture as transmitted to them by poor immigrant parents long before Mao Zedong and his followers made that long march.

Two hot-button issues that have garnered unusual national attention— the 1996 Democratic campaign financing scandal and the Los Alamos "spy" case—can be interpreted as "Chinese" because suspects have mostly been ethnic Chinese, either legal immigrants or naturalized U.S. citizens.

Because of their unique historical experiences, ethnic Japanese in the United States are the most Americanized of Asian Americans but not

necessarily by choice. Because of the geopolitics of the mid-20th century—Japan the enemy of the United States—Japanese Americans were
treated like the enemy within and locked away in camps without due con-
stitutional processes. That betrayal of their own government forced many
Japanese Americans to shed their overt Asian ethnicity and quickly assim-
ilate to an America dominated by white European cultural values.

An apology and reparations for the World War II internment experience have been accomplished. The issues that concern most Japanese
Americans today are far removed from those of Asian immigrants and
refugees like Vietnamese, Koreans, Filipinos, Chinese, and Cambodians.
For some Japanese Americans, outmarriages are a prime topic of intro-
spection, not something transplanted Southeast Asians worry about.

Speaking of the Vietnamese, passionate feelings over ideology continue
to divide some of them a quarter century after the end of the Vietnam War.
These passions play themselves out in Vietnamese American enclaves
such as Westminster, Orange County, and San Jose. The most recent manifestation of these divisions became a national story. A Vietnamese American video store operator in Westminster put up a poster of Communist
leader Ho Chi Minh. That set off prolonged protests from anticommunist
Vietnamese Americans in both southern and northern California.

Some Korean Americans have issues dealing with relations with African
Americans in inner cities where the former have set up shops and the latter are their principal customers. Like other Asian immigrant communities, the Korean American community has cultural adaptation issues that
separate parents from children.

In politics, there is no discernible Asian American pattern, despite the
desire of Asian American activists in both major parties to claim ownership over the potential resource- and vote-rich community. An ad hoc
group called 80/20, led by prominent Chinese Americans, hopes to mar-
shal 80 percent of the Asian American vote and contributions to support
the major-party presidential candidate in the year 2000 who agrees with
the group's goal of equitable appointments to the cabinet and federal agencies. It is a noble gesture, but it is doubtful that 80 percent of us will unify
behind any one candidate.

A decent case against Asian America, don't you think?

But wait ... One shouldn't be so one-sided on a matter as amorphous
as whether Asian America exists. If we are unable to cite a specific place,

location, nexus of Asian America, with well-defined borders, then such an entity could not possibly exist, right?

Asian America, as an entity, does exist—as a state of mind. It was conceived, gestated, then came alive during the 1960s civil rights movement, which spawned other liberation movements. The assertion of rights and ethnic pride called Asian America was a struggle fought primarily by ethnic Chinese, Japanese, and Filipinos, because those three groups were the main components of Asian America more than thirty years ago. They fought for ethnic studies at universities and colleges. They started health clinics and legal-aid services in urban Chinatowns. They led the battles to win equal-opportunity rights for Asian American workers and students. They protested anti-Asian violence, advocated the hiring of Asian Americans as cops and firefighters, and pushed for better media portrayals.

To many Asian Americans, that all may be ancient history—if they even know such activism took place on behalf of all Asian Americans, not just ones from their particular ethnic group. Ignorance is part of the baggage of Asian newcomers, who despite some awful conditions for refugees and uncertainty came to America when America was beginning to shed some of its political, cultural, and social segregation. Opportunities for people who look like us have expanded just as Asian America was growing exponentially. Many Asian Americans never had to live under the overt institutional racism that a minority of us have, so our respective psyches have been differently impacted.

It is not just for nostalgia's sake that I am arguing the existence of an Asian American state of mind. We are not out of the woods yet. We can easily become victims of overt racism, as appears to be what happened to Wen Ho Lee, the computer scientist suspected by some government officials of being a China spy. So while we cherish our individual Asian ethnic identity, let us think hard about those occasions when we should conjure up the state of mind called Asian America as a way of remembering our collective histories in this country and to honor those who have helped make it easier for the kind of yuppie upward mobility that many of us seem to embrace.

So That's Why I Can't Lose Weight

Oakland Tribune, January 30, 1989

J. Philippe Rushton has explained my life, and he knows all my deep dark secrets. Rushton, who teaches psychology at the University of Western Ontario, presented a paper on some of his research at the American Association for the Advancement of Science meeting in San Francisco. He said, in essence, that Asians—he called them "Orientals"—are superior to white and black people in intelligence and social organization and are less aggressive and less sexually promiscuous than other races.

His findings were hooted down by other scientists, who accused him of ignoring social factors that influence behavioral differences among races. He admitted that some financial backing for his work has come from a foundation that subsidizes racist academicians who seek to "prove" the intellectual inferiority of black people.

Rushton's theories strike me, a nonscientist, as silly, inflammatory, and, well, racist. Nonetheless, his unorthodox assertions regarding "Orientals" fascinate me, since I am one. Rushton claims that "Orientals" have bigger brains than other races—cranial capacity and brain weight.

That must be why I just can't lose any weight. Over the years, like other health-conscious Americans, I've tried to exercise and alter my diet to lose weight. Nothing seems to work. Here, I thought my girth had to do with all those noodles and fatty roast pork I so love. Wrong. It's my brain that's getting heavier, a weight gain that more than offsets any loss from my would-be svelte body.

No wonder too that my wife always complains about the weight of my head, whenever I want to rest it on her shoulders. "Bill," she'd say, with a sigh of weariness. "Do you realize how heavy your head is?" Now I do.

I am chastened, however, by the assertion by one of Rushton's many critics that the contemporary human brain (of whatever racial persuasion) is smaller than the Neanderthal brain. If so, does that mean "Orientals"—with the biggest and heaviest brain of all modern humans—are closer to the "missing link" than to a superior race?

My wife, who studied anthropology, has wondered about my shovel-shaped incisors and protruding brow ridges, features akin to the old Neanderthal man.

Then there's the matter of sex—my deepest, darkest secret! Rushton said that "Orientals" rank behind black and white people in the production of gametes (sperms and eggs). We "Orientals" also don't do as well in the age of first sexual intercourse, frequency of sexual fantasies, frequency of marital intercourse, and number of extramarital partners.

The big picture—not my personal life—suggests some anomalies to Rushton's findings. If "Orientals" don't do it as frequently as black or white people, how come there are so many of "us"? China's one billion plus people aren't an illusion, are they? What about all those Asian Indians?

The answer must rest somewhere with the superior "intelligence" of "Orientals." We "Orientals" are so smart that we know precisely when these reluctant eggs and sperm are ready to mate, and we just go madly about our business at the right moment. Maybe not frequent or fun sex, but very efficient sex.

I hope Deng Xiaoping, China's supreme leader, hears about Rushton's "Oriental" sex theories so that China's official policy of one child per family can be abandoned immediately. Why ban an activity—sex to have babies and not fun—that occurs so infrequently anyway?

Rushton also said that "Orientals" are less aggressive than black and white people. Hadn't he heard of Pol Pot, the Cambodian leader whose Khmer Rouge troops killed about a million of his fellow countrymen? Or Mao Zedong and Chiang Kai-shek, who waged bloody (and aggressive) civil war against each other? Or Japan's militarists during World War II? Or Bruce Lee? Or old Chinese women shopping in Chinatown?

Yellow Chic

Oakland Tribune, February 3, 1989

"Well, isn't that precious?" the patrician-looking woman said to her equally patrician-looking husband, as she scanned the *New York Times* over brunch in their sun-splashed breakfast nook in a palatial home in Pacific Heights, San Francisco.

"What's that, darling?"

"There's this mahvelous article about 'Asian chic,' about how Asians—whatever *happened* to 'Orientals,' anyway?—are bringing a cachet to Manhattan nightclubs."

"That's interesting, darling. Tell me more."

"It says that Asians are preferred customers. They're even being hired as hosts, waiters, waitresses, and bartenders to project an image of style and sophistication. They're said to look good, dress well, and spend money, and they're good tippers. One club owner said he hires them because he felt they were *incredibly* attractive people. He said Asian employees and customers lend an aura that he wants his place to project: a sense of style and fashion."

She paused. Her husband, looking reflective, puts down the *Wall Street Journal* and looks earnestly as his wife. He furrows his brow.

"You know, darling, that makes me think about our parties. I feel they've been lacking—oh, how should I put it?—a sense of style lately. The same old people, the same old chit-chat. Rather *boring*, don't you think? I'm afraid we're not chic anymore."

"Why, dear, I do my best. It isn't easy, you know, to bring together scintillating people *all* the time."

The man plays with his reading glasses. "That article gives me an idea. Why don't *we* hire some *Asians* for our next party? We'd be chic. We'd project a sense of style and sophistication!"

His wife shifts uncomfortably. She plays with the croissant crumbs on the Spode plate. "Dear, don't you remember we've hired Asians—we called them *Orientals* then—to work at our parties? They're so . . . so, oh, small and cute and hardworking. And don't you remember Ah So, our houseboy? He was wonderful, doing *everything* without so much as a *peep*. Too bad he had to go back to China, or wherever."

"I'm not talking about *those* kinds of Asians, darling. You always liked Ah So more than I did. He bowed too much and I couldn't stand it when he smiled. I couldn't see his eyes. I want some of these *stylish* Asians the *New York Times* is writing about!"

The woman rarely defied her husband. "As you wish, dear," she said, suppressing a pout. "But where am I to find these Asians? I doubt if any of our friends know any. Do you suppose the Yellow Pages—oh, my, isn't that a wonderful pun?—lists employment agencies that have *these* kinds of Asians."

"Finding them shouldn't be difficult. Biff and Muffy just went to the Orient, didn't they? Perhaps they'd have a thought. Or we could just to Chinatown. Isn't there a Little Tokyo? I heard of Little Saigons cropping up everywhere, and Koreatowns and Little Manilas too. Go to UC-Berkeley; they've got lots of them there, all young and I bet *very* stylish."

"Well, what should I offer to pay them?"

"Price is no object, darling. Didn't the *Times* say these Asians liked to pay their way into those clubs? We can do a club theme and charge them!"

"That's a wonderful idea, dear. Won't our friends be envious? I'll be sure to put on the invitation the kind of fashion we want for our Asian club theme evening. Let's see, what did the *Times* say was 'in' with these stylish Asians? Cropped haircuts, high-fashion clothes, and stylized accessories like large stovepipe felt hats and oversized sunglasses."

"Clever, those Asians, don't you think? First, they make all those cameras and TVs and stereo equipment and VCRs. Then they make all those cars, and you just can't get away from sushi and dim sum at any party these days. I never thought they'd ever become the latest in high-fashion trends, did you, darling?"

"No, dear, but I suppose it was inevitable because there are so many of them now. I do hope we're not too late with this trend, however. I'd hate not to be chic."

"Don't fret, darling. If we don't catch this Asian fad, we can start our own. Do you suppose Iranians will be 'in' someday?"

A Tumultuous World in Transition

Oakland Tribune, February 3, 1993

Phang Bun, a slight, stooped middle-aged woman with doleful eyes, reaches behind a mirror propped up on a low table in a bedroom once occupied by her 20-year-old son, Poch Seap. A likeness of Buddha and two containers holding burned incense sticks are on the table. She brings out a framed portrait of him, a picture that has run in local newspapers and on TV news shows because he was shot to death by one of two men who tried to steal his car and kidnap his sister on January 17 as he was delivering *Oakland Tribunes*.

She points to the portrait, a warm smile on an innocent face, then just as quickly puts it back behind the mirror. Tears well up in her eyes. She hasn't said a word. Even if she did, I wouldn't have understood. She speaks no English, I speak no Cambodian. But I understand.

The large Seap family is still mourning the loss of a young man who wanted to be an auto mechanic, in part to help support his parents and eight siblings. His newspaper-delivery job and whatever money he made repairing cars supplemented the income of a family dependent on public assistance. It's not the loss of money that Phang Bun weeps over.

The story of the Seap family is the story of a tumultuous world in transition. Phang Bun, 52, and her husband, Sauth Seap, 53, were rice farmers in the western province of Batambang. They and millions of other Cambodians became ensnared in the civil war between communist factions in Cambodia and neighboring Vietnam, complicated by French imperialism and American intervention. In 1979, the Seap family, then consisting of parents and six children, fled to Thailand by foot.

They stayed in a refugee camp for six years and eventually came to Oakland in 1985, sponsored by Cambodian cousins who had fled Southeast Asia several years earlier and settled in Chicago. "We didn't want to come here [America]," Samol Seap, the 22-year-old daughter who happened to witness her brother's horrifying death.

The family heard about settling in America in the Thai refugee camp and the parents "wanted us to get a good education." The family has relatives spread throughout the United States. Their four-room apartment is in a rugged flatlands neighborhood in the shadow of a freeway overpass. The parents don't speak English, and they don't have jobs. They pass their time watching TV, taking long walks to Chinatown, and picking up their younger children from school.

Samol and Eng, an 18-year-old daughter, attend community colleges in Oakland. Neither has been able to find work to help supplement welfare. "Poch was helping the two of us pay for college," Eng says.

Poch's violent death was the first untoward incident the family has faced in Oakland. Samol says about the early-morning trauma, "I'm just trying to forget it. He's gone. It's not safe here, but what can you do?"

Samol and Eng say their parents aren't happy in America because they can't speak English. "They're always talking about going back" when Cambodia stabilizes. The two daughters say they too would return, using their American educations to help their long-suffering country.

The effervescent Eng offers to show me Poch's things. She pulls out some compact discs Poch ordered through the mail: Elton John, The Fresh Prince, Vanilla Ice. "This came the day he died," Eng says of a CD soundtrack of *Boomerang*, the Eddie Murphy movie. Large posters of sports cars (Porsche, Lamborghini) cover his bedroom walls. Stacked along one wall are toolboxes he had just bought. Auto magazines line his bookshelf. Eng holds a worn copy of *Since 1900: A History of the United States*, which she says Poch read every night.

Eng points to the Buddhist altar. "We offer food and burn incense every night." Then, in her bubbly way, Eng says, "I'm staying in his room now. He's still with us. His spirit is still in the room."

"We Lost a Country"

Asian Week, May 5, 1995

This is a year of major anniversaries involving Asians, including the twentieth anniversary of the so-called fall of Saigon. The Vietnam War has been a bane for America. It was the war America lost.

I am torn about America's Vietnam experience, in part because I am an Asian American but not a Vietnamese American. I have no direct links to the Vietnam War. Like other Americans—including prominent ones like Bill Clinton and Newt Gingrich—I somehow evaded military service during the 1960s and 1970s.

I came close, but a minor physical condition lowered my draft eligibility. At the same time, the Peace Corps, established in 1961 by President Kennedy, became a viable option. Given my values and predilections, the Peace Corps was my first choice of government service even though Peace Corps duty wasn't a legal substitute for military service.

In the summer of 1964, when U.S. military involvement in Vietnam began to heat up, I was 23 years old—and on my way to Peace Corps training. As the Vietnam War raged on, I spent forty months serving my country as a volunteer teacher and editor in a country just southeast of the war zone. I thought a lot about this odd juxtaposition then, about how the powerful U.S. military forces were arrayed (again) against an Asian enemy, about how gut-wrenching a choice it must have been for Asian American soldiers to be serving their country battling Asian soldiers.

I knew very little about the respective histories of Vietnam and China and other East Asian and Southeast Asian countries, which have had interlocking and confrontational relationships for centuries. I was not sorry I never had to fight in Vietnam, although I harbored an odd kind of envy and guilt that the "real action" was in Vietnam, Cambodia, and Laos while I was sheltered in the relative tropical calm of the Philippines trying to do "good work." The Philippines didn't escape some Vietnam involvement. Major U.S. air and navy bases were in the Philippines as staging areas and rest-and-recreation sites for American fighting men.

True to my beliefs, I didn't support the escalation of U.S. military involvement in Vietnam. It struck me that perhaps the North Vietnamese and their Viet Cong brothers in the south were fighting a battle of national liberation, to be freed from the shackles of Western colonialism.

The Asian brotherhood portion of my anti–Vietnam War rationale is more complicated. Having grown up in a Chinese American environment surrounded by the dominant white society that exhibited overt and covert racism toward us, I naturally built up both a wall of resistance and a survival mechanism. I figured I had little choice, and the impetus in those days was to fit in, to become "American."

I gained a full appreciation of the complications of Asian American identity in the Philippines, where I learned quickly that "American" meant white, preferably blonde. By being a Chinese American, I confused Filipinos. I was "American" in every sense, but the Filipino stereotype was that Americans had to be white. Besides, Filipinos weren't especially fond of ethnic Chinese, who dominated local economies. Even Filipino leaders with Chinese ancestry didn't advertise that fact.

Despite these internal identity wars percolating within me, I couldn't accept the morality of America pushing its way onto an Asian landmass, even if it were at the purported behest of other Asians (the discredited and corrupt South Vietnamese leadership). My response was to stay away. In the years since, in reading Vietnam War books, in viewing serious Vietnam War films, this confused mix of feelings always came back. Who should I cheer for?

Visiting the Vietnam War Memorial in Washington, D.C., some years ago, I couldn't stop tears welling up as my wife and I descended the pathway. This despite the fact I didn't think I knew anyone personally whose name was chiseled on the black granite. Despite my ambivalent feelings about the American effort in the war, I couldn't extinguish the American in me.

Yet, I chafed at the selfish American perspective of the war. Where are the Vietnamese perspectives? They are background fodder, so many body counts, a cardboard one-dimensional enemy. Can we even fathom what it means to lose 3 million people in warfare, when "our" losses were 58,000? Can we imagine the heartache, pain, and suffering of the families of the 3 million, to say nothing of the entire country that had defoliants sprayed and exploded on it, that had its women defiled and its livelihoods uprooted and dreams snuffed and humanity smothered?

These thoughts are back, as America and Vietnam remember the "fall of Saigon" twenty years ago. They hit home when I picked up my phone. A Vietnamese American friend, Thai Nguyen-Khoa, wanted me to read a commentary he had written about his thoughts on the twentieth anniversary. A writer and teacher who lives in Oakland, Thai said he still suffers from what he calls the Vietnam Syndrome, a man split asunder by his country of birth and his adopted country.

His essay is eloquent, an elegy to a lost land. He laments the lack of a Vietnamese voice in the years of the war, and even now, as his root country rushes into a market economy, as though the struggle over ideology or nationalism was a prelude to the real war of Coke versus Pepsi. "America may have lost a war, but we lost a country," Thai wrote.

I told Thai about a Vietnam War–related media conference in Oakland sponsored by the Freedom Forum. When I entered the lunchroom at the conference, I discovered he had already sparked a passionate debate as he listened to former star American journalists tell Vietnam War stories. He interrupted the nostalgia with his lament about the muted Vietnamese voice in all the retellings of the war, tales of American soldiers returning to the scenes of their devastation, sorrowful now after wondering what they had fought for, especially after their civilian leader, former Defense Secretary Robert McNamara admitted how wrong he was in pimping the American war effort a generation ago.

Bernard Kalb, who covered the war for CBS News, took the opportunity as luncheon speaker to respond to Thai's remarks. Kalb said he understood Thai's perspective but judged it "extreme" at a conference devoted to a media retrospective. That was a dissonant response, I felt, another case of American media arrogance or misunderstanding of an Asian point of view.

After lunch, two Vietnamese Americans had their say. In a voice barely louder than a whisper, Phuong Tran, an Oakland high school student, related how she loves to write and has found a vehicle for her writing in journalism. She said her parents won't talk about their experiences, leaving her to learn about the country she left when she was two from secondary sources like the media. She also said she was the only Vietnamese American student at her high school working on her school newspaper, of which she is the editor. She told a familiar Asian American story, of how parents pressure their children into "safe" callings like science, medicine, and engineering because journalism isn't a prestigious vocation.

In a controlled, passionate tone, Mai Hoang, a reporter with the *Hayward Daily Review,* told the conference she was quitting her job to take "the most important trip of my life," a planned June departure for Vietnam to reunite with her parents and to write about her experience. She said she had deeply mixed emotions. "I'm looking forward to it, yet I'm dreading it. It will be rewarding but also scary."

Hoang criticized the heavily American slant of Vietnam War retrospectives. "They ignore two million Vietnamese soldiers and one million Vietnamese civilians who died.... There are three hundred thousand Vietnamese MIAs [missing in action], compared with two thousand American MIAs." She called this kind of American arrogance a "great injustice."

Like many of her generation, she too has hazy memories of Vietnam, memories she holds dear. "My knowledge of Vietnam comes from my research in college. I had to search for myself. Many of my generation are returning as seekers of their cultural birthright."

I am wondering whether Americans who wallow in their defeat twenty years ago can begin to understand the emotional yearnings of Thai Nguyen-Khoa, Phuong Tran, and Mai Hoang. If and when they do, you can mark it as progress much the way the Pentagon toted up its daily body count in Indochina.

Who's a Bonehead Now?

Asian Week, May 14, 1998

Thinking about the Unz Initiative, the California antibilingual education measure on the June 2 ballot, has dredged up embarrassing memories. As a 17-year-old freshman at the University of California at Berkeley in 1958,

I had to take "bonehead English." Its nickname says it all—bonehead, dumb-o, dunce. It was for freshmen who couldn't pass an English language exam. It was remedial English. How could this be?

I wasn't some F.O.B. ("fresh off the boat"). I was an A.B.C. ("American-born Chinese"). I spoke, read, and wrote English far better than I did Chinese. I was almost a straight-A student in my high school, where English was the only language of instruction except in foreign-language courses. I wrote sports articles for the school newspaper and was editor of the yearbook, by golly!

But when I got accepted by Cal, why was I shunted into bonehead English? And what does that have to do with the Unz Initiative?

Let me explain. English is not my first language even though I was born in Oakland, California. The part of Oakland where I was born, however, was very Chinese. My first language was *see yip*, a dialect spoken in the Toisan region, Guangdong province, China. Since my family was plunked down into a larger English-speaking environment, we were in a "dual immersion" language situation: *see yip* mixed with English, sometimes all *see yip*, sometimes all English.

Gradually, English dominated. It wasn't anything my parents did. Buddha knows they wanted me and my older sisters to retain *see yip* and to read and write Chinese. We went to Chinese school after "American school." I even got a special tutor for high Cantonese and fine Chinese literature. Didn't work. English overwhelmed Chinese. We heard it all the time at school from teachers and classmates, from our customers at our family's restaurant, on the radio and TV.

We thought little about this transformation. No one really had to say anything. We Chinatown kids knew implicitly that if we were to "succeed" in the world outside, we had to know English. No one said to us Chinatown kids, "Oh, it's okay if you retain your native language and culture too."

What I gained in my ability to read, write, speak, and think in English was the demise of my parent's culture. I can barely speak *see yip* now, and I have no literacy in Chinese. That is why the Unz Initiative is potentially harmful to millions of California children who come from backgrounds similar to mine, and I do not mean just ethnic Chinese youngsters.

One of the lesser-discussed aspects of the debate over bilingual education is the question of cultural identity and what it means to be an

American. The Unz Initiative, or Proposition 227, if approved by California voters, would eliminate bilingual education programs in California public schools and require newly arrived immigrant children who aren't proficient in English to take an "immersion English" class for up to one year. During that year, the children would not study other subjects like math, science, and social studies. Then they will move into classrooms where English is the only language of instruction.

Ron Unz, a Silicon Valley millionaire software entrepreneur, says bilingual education programs have failed to teach limited-English-proficient children English by using too much of an immigrant child's native language in those classes. I do not defend all bilingual education programs. Some have worked; others haven't. I do think the Unz method is simplistic and overly rigid and doesn't tolerate primary-language support for immigrant children who are not English proficient.

For many of these kids, the Unz prescription is going to be a rough road because linguists say it takes a lot longer than a year for non-English proficient children to acquire English well enough to handle subjects taught in English. The classroom scenario under Unz is scary, and I can see a lot of immigrant children being discouraged if they can't keep up in their schoolwork because their English skills aren't up to par. This could potentially hurt immigrant children from relatively poor backgrounds the most. In addition, the Unz approach will force immigrant children to make a difficult choice: Immerse yourself in English at the expense of who you were, a person born into a language and culture that isn't English. They are already doing this, with or without bilingual education.

The Unz Initiative doesn't celebrate bilingualism, or the ability to speak, read, write, and think in two languages. Helen Joe-Lew, a San Francisco bilingual teacher for the past twenty-five years, asks, "Why is it that we as a language minority are asked to give up something, and middle-class white parents put their kids into Spanish or Mandarin immersion classes, and they see value in learning a second language? Why are we [Chinese speakers] asked to strip ourselves of our native language and culture in order to learn English?"

Lily Wong Fillmore, an education professor at the University of California at Berkeley specializing in language and literacy, said many Asian American students in the California state university system (one tier down from the University of California system) do not pass their English placement exams. "The majority of students in remedial English in the California state universities are Asian," she said.

For many American-born Asians like me, she said, "You lost your mother tongue. What you may have forfeited was a close relationship, an easy loving relationship, with your parents. My children couldn't talk to their grandmother [who spoke very little English]. There are other things that count too besides learning English well, and that is family relationships."

Fillmore is correct about my loss. My relationship with my parents suffered because we spoke two different languages. I learned English well enough to earn a living using it, but I gave up something dear.

Paradise Lost

Asian Week, January 15, 1993

My first visit to Hawaii in the fall of 1964 wasn't a vacation. It was Peace Corps training in a simulated village in the gorgeous, but rugged Waipio Valley on the big island of Hawaii. Rural Hawaii was quite enough to give me a flavor of the awesome natural beauty of Hawaii, which had become the fiftieth state only five years earlier. But questions of statehood or political empowerment of Hawaiians weren't part of my conscience then.

They are now, as I am discovering, through Hawaiians living on the mainland, the so-called sovereignty movement bubbling up in Hawaii like a latent volcano. The discovery is triggered by the 100th anniversary of the overthrow of Hawaii's last monarch, Queen Lili'oukalani on January 17. The overthrow is one of those pieces of history that hasn't been well circulated in the mainland. This lack of knowledge helps mainlanders relegate Hawaii to its bittersweet status as island paradise resort. Hawaiians who live on the mainland say they never learned their own history. In this regard, they echo the lament of Asian Americans and other formerly subjugated peoples of America who've been severed from their ethnic roots.

The overthrow of Queen Lili'oukalani has strong symbolic value to today's Hawaiians. It reminds them of their profound loss and it inspires them to envision a better future. The first significant Western contact in Hawaii was in 1778 when Captain James Cook of the British Navy landed.

Cook didn't immediately impose Western forms of government. Starting in 1820, another event occurred that was destined to change Hawaii forever—the arrival of white Christian missionaries.

Nonetheless, for about a hundred years—from 1795 to 1893—the islands were unified under one monarch. In 1887, in the thirteenth year of King Kalakaua's reign, white residents, both Hawaii-born and from the United States, forced the king to accept a new constitution that took away some of the king's powers. According to a *Honolulu Advertiser* historical account, "Haole [white] merchants and planters defended the 1887 constitution as a means of recognizing equal rights of all races—meaning Hawaiians, Americans and Europeans qualified to vote. They wanted to protect their estimated $50 million investment in Hawaii."

King Kalakaua died in January 1891, succeeded by his sister, Lili'oukalani. The *Advertiser* describes her as a strong-willed woman who believed in the monarchy. Even though she swore allegiance to the 1887 constitution that weakened the monarchy, once on the throne, she worked to restore the lost power. This didn't please the white missionaries and merchants, and they engineered the bloodless coup on January 17, 1893, that Hawaiians today want never to forget. The overthrow, carried out by U.S. Marines in what is widely thought to be an illegal action, set off a chain of events that first led to U.S. annexation, then statehood in 1959, and inevitably, tourism.

The Hawaiian sovereignty movement has been building for years. The 100th anniversary of Lili'oukalani's fall, however, gives Hawaiian activists a perfect opportunity to take their case national. Two scenarios have emerged from the sovereignty movement. One is independence through secession and possibly a restoration of the monarchy. Another is a "nation within a nation" concept akin to what Native Americans have on set-aside lands. The more moderate "nation within a nation" idea is apparently more popular among Hawaiians, many of whom are tethered to Hawaii's $9-billion tourism industry.

For mainland Hawaiians, the sovereignty movement arouses deep emotions—anger, pain, reawakening, and hope. Paul Kealoha Blake says he's "insistent" on using his Hawaiian middle name. He notes that Hawaiian youths who move to the mainland try to "melt into" the mostly Eurocentric mainland culture. "It's important for youth to have community leaders with whom they can identify as Hawaiian. Without this modeling, there's less of a chance of Hawaiian children who are willing to identify themselves as Hawaiians."

Just what is a Hawaiian is a matter of some dispute, but the people I talked with regarded anyone as Hawaiian who has some blood lineage to the indigenous people of Hawaii, or who identify themselves as Hawaiian. A more precise genetic definition (at least 50 percent Hawaiian) has been required of Hawaiians seeking the right to lease lands from the Hawaii Home Lands granted Hawaiians in 1921.

Blake grew up in Hana, Maui, and is Hawaiian on his mother's side. He is president of the East Bay Media Center, a nonprofit production and post-production facility. "I grew up in a social structure where being Hawaiian wasn't a good thing to be," he says. "My mother was adamant that I not use my middle name." He describes what happened to him and other Hawaiian children as "ethnocide" because the public schools banned the Hawaiian language and didn't teach Hawaiian history. "If you spoke Hawaiian in school, you were reprimanded. . . . Destruction of language is one of the main [weapons] imperialistic cultures use to subvert other cultures."

In post–World War II Hawaii, Blake remembers, the tug of white middle-class values was strong. "The goal of adults [in Hawaii] was to be measured by white middle-class terms." Blake says it is "difficult for Hawaiians to face the sovereignty issue. There's lots of pain, anger, and rage, in direct conflict with the aloha spirit."

The issue also splits families. Blake says he and an uncle who's an executive with one of Hawaii's big companies haven't talked in years because of differences over sovereignty and tourism. Blake says he isn't against tourism per se but thinks that a tourist industry based on less exploitation of Hawaii's beautiful, precious, but finite resources would be better than the helter-skelter development favored by American, Japanese, and European interests.

Rena Nelson describes herself as a "volunteer activist" in the scattered Bay Area Hawaiian community, which numbers an estimated 20,000 in the nine-county region. She and her husband, George, have been Bay Area residents for almost thirty-five years, but she maintains ties to her state of birth. She is half-Hawaiian, and part Chinese, Portuguese, and English. They came to California for economic opportunity, and she has retired from her Pacific Telephone job and devotes her time to Hawaiian social and political causes. Her monthly radio show on KPFA makes her an unofficial communications link for Bay Area Hawaiians. She says she was ignorant of much of Hawaiian history until five years ago. She believes it's now important for her and other Hawaiians to educate young Hawaiians about their history.

Sharon Lumho is an artist who left Hawaii in 1975 but like other Bay Area Hawaiians learned of Hawaiian history only recently. She is one-quarter Hawaiian on her father's side. She says the sovereignty movement and what it represents "affects my self image" and "it affects me because our language was taken away. I grew up with no knowledge of this part of my history." It wasn't until she came to California in 1991 that she learned of Hawaiian history. "Queen Lili'oukalani wasn't mentioned in my history book. That's not surprising. I grew up with 'See Dick and Jane run through the snow.'" Now, she says, she identifies as a Hawaiian. "I'm one of the few Hawaiians who grew up with a pretty good image of Hawaiians. My grandparents said they were proud to be Hawaiians. They were landowners. They could afford to be proud."

J. Kehaulani Kauanui grew up in Los Angeles, graduated recently from the University of California at Berkeley but identifies also with Hawaii. Her father is Hawaiian. She hopes to attend graduate school at the University of Hawaii to study the history of the Pacific islands. She spends her time now studying and educating people about the current sovereignty movement. She believes Native Hawaiians should control what happens on the lands that are already set aside for Native Hawaiians, about one-third of the state.

The trouble is, the U.S. military occupies some of that land. "The military will definitely have to leave," she asserts. She would like to see Hawaiians make the decisions on how revenues generated on lands set aside for Hawaiians are to be used—for education and health care, for instance. Because there were so few Hawaiians at Cal, she says she feels a kinship with Native Americans and other indigenous peoples.

Carolyn Lau, a poet, writer, and teacher, laments most the loss of the Hawaiian language. Lau's mother is Chinese and her father is half Hawaiian, and part Chinese and English. She says the Hawaiian language was outlawed from 1829 to 1978. That loss, she says, meant "we didn't have access to metaphors" to understand what it is to be Hawaiian.

"We were never encouraged to look at Hawaiian history. I never thought of myself as being colonized. . . . When my father's friends visited, they spoke Hawaiian outside the house, never inside. My mother was compulsive about speaking English without an accent. We went to English-language schools. We wanted to be Americans." Lau says she now feels an "immense loss" of culture.

The next time we vacation in Hawaii, we should think about this loss too.

Minnesota Chow Mein

East-West News, July 21, 1988

"I'm from Minnesota," the man told the San Francisco radio talk-show host, "and I miss Chinese chow mein the way they fix it there. Can you tell me where I can get chow mein like that here?"

Within seconds, I lapsed into a minor culture shock. The host said Chinese cuisine in the San Francisco Bay Area is sophisticated, and the man from Minnesota was probably out of luck if he wanted Minnesota-style chow mein.

I have no idea what Minnesota-style chow mein is, but I can imagine: lots of bean sprouts, some sliced celery and onions, glopped together in a corn-starchy sauce laced with soy sauce and topped with a few shreds of *cha sieu* (Chinese-style barbecued pork), all sitting on a bed of pan-fried or crispy deep fried noodles.

The man's question triggered a complex set of, pardon the phrase, sweet and sour reactions. I have long been fascinated by "Chinese" food and how Chinese Americans are both embraced and trapped by it. The chow mein I described was one I experienced at my parents' restaurant in Oakland's Chinatown. At the risk of offending my late parents' reputation, I must say our restaurant's chow mein was disgraceful when compared with what one finds today in most big-city Chinese restaurants. Today's chow mein is usually hearty servings of pan-fried noodles mixed in with generous portions of a meat and some vegetables in a lighter sauce. You won't find many bean sprouts bulking up the dish, unless you specifically ask for them.

At its most basic level, so-called Chinese food is *our* food—that is, the food that ethnic Chinese people eat. Chinese people don't call it "Chinese food." We call it by the proper name of the dish.

In the United States, however, because Chinese America is so small, most people call it "Chinese" food. Which is why, in parts of America (New York City, for instance), you get people saying, "Let's eat Chinese," or a slang version that is a slur against the Chinese. If you say, "Let's eat Chinese," that means it's a diversionary meal. Hamburgers, meat loaf, pizza, fried chicken, or *moo goo gai pan*. You won't hear any self-respecting Chinese American say, "Let's eat Chinese." We'd more likely say, in guttural Toisanese, "*Heck fahn*" ("Eat rice," literally, but meaning, "Let's eat").

Even though "Chinese" food has been around almost 5,000 years, it's only become popular in the United States over the past ten to fifteen years. It took off in the mid-1970s, after President Richard Nixon's resumed relations with China. Chinese food became trendy. Woks were in. Suburban matrons all bought cleavers. They discovered fresh ginger and coriander. At the same time, Americans became exposed to a variety of Chinese cuisine, not the old faux Cantonese slop (see Minnesota chow mein). Hunan. Szechwan. Hakka. Chieu Jow. This was even a liberating time for some Chinese Americans like me who grew in Cantonese Chinatowns where our food was humble home-style offerings like salted-fish steamed pork patty and winter-melon soup.

When the Chinese food explosion hit the Bloomingdale's crowd, I felt alienated. Suddenly, people got apoplectic over chopsticks, woks, and peanut oil, staples of most Chinese American households. I felt cultural appropriation taking place. An offshoot of this phenomenon has been non-Chinese Chinese-food "experts"—primarily white folks who "discovered" Chinese cuisine and started hawking it to America, under the guise of its being the hottest trend.

My reaction was not simply ethnocentrism. One does not have to be Chinese to appreciate Chinese food. What I find offensive are non-Chinese Chinese-food "experts" who lecture ethnic Chinese on how to cook our food. In the food-hip Bay Area, foodies are creating all sorts of hybrid cuisine, many including Asian inflections. Lots of this hybridization is pretentious poppycock. For many food groupies, being on the cutting edge is better than eating the food itself.

This transient trendiness aside, there are actually some fascinating goings-on regarding Chinese food as the Chinese American and Asian American population increases. For instance, Chinese restaurants in the

Bay Area and other areas with significant Asian American populations fall into two broad categories: old and new. The old feature Minnesota-style chow mein and other staples like iridescent red sweet and sour pork and the aforementioned *moo goo gai pan*. Comfort food for white tourists, mainly.

The most interesting stuff is happening in the new Chinese restaurants. They include authentic Cantonese houses patterned after Hong Kong establishments that feature fresh seafood, fresh produce, and meats in light sauces. Their cuisine is honest and uncompromising. Ethnic Chinese families eat at these places, where round tables are ubiquitous. Other new Chinese restaurants highlight cuisine from other Chinese regions such as Shanghai, Hunan, Szechwan, and Hakka.

The key to the growth of these new Chinese eating places is the growth of the Chinese American and Asian American populations. The old places didn't have a large Chinese-Asian customer base. They had to compromise their cuisine to make them palatable to white and other tastes.

Mr. Minnesota need not fret. Despite the growth of more authentic Chinese restaurants, he can probably still find his favorite chow mein in some suburban restaurants and perhaps in lonely outposts where the Chinese American population is minuscule.

Whenever I travel outside the San Francisco Bay Area, I hunt for Chinese restaurants. When I lived in Cleveland, my wife and I went to a Chinese joint that served white bread and butter with the so-called Chinese food. Even in Minneapolis, I found a place that looked "authentic." Its front window displayed what I thought was a roast duck. My heart jumped a beat. I trekked on over to that place, where, in my fractured Toisanese, I ordered a couple of dishes not on the menu, which had the usual suspects (fried rice, chow mein, sweet and sour pork, etc.).

When my salted-fish steamed pork patty and stir-fried bok choy came, I was ready to dive into this Chinese soul food meal. Alas, I was disappointed. This place undoubtedly didn't get much of a call for the dishes I ordered. The choy was overcooked, and the pork patty was tasteless and undercooked. I probably should have ordered the chow mein.

Best Friend or Best Meal?
Oakland Tribune, March 24, 1989

Dogs are among America's favorite pets, so killing one for food is a huge no-no in our society. Two male Cambodian refugees in Long Beach did just that and were caught. The two went on trial in Long Beach Municipal Court for misdemeanor cruelty to animals, an offense that could have cost them each a year in jail and a $2,000 fine.

The judge dismissed the case for lack of evidence that the men inflicted unusual pain on the four-month-old German shepherd puppy. Killing a dog for food isn't a crime. Killing a dog for any purpose in a cruel and inhumane way is a crime.

This case illuminates a culture clash that emerges as America absorbs newcomers from different lands. It raises the question whether America is flexible enough to incorporate some different customs or whether Americans will insist that newcomers adapt to dominant cultural norms.

Because America has long been a nation of immigrants and refugees, different cultural customs and practices have been woven into the country's complex multicultural fabric. This is especially true in food, music, and fashion.

There is less acceptance for deeper, more substantive aspects, such as religious, political, and economic systems. American culture remains mostly a reflection and adaptation of European-derived Western civilization based on a Judeo-Christian value system.

Since the large influx of Southeast Asian refugees, reports have cropped up about some refugees killing dogs and cats for food. The Long Beach case was the first to be brought to trial. It would be arrogant to condemn the two Cambodian men for their actions without knowing the cultural impulses that motivated them.

They offended prevailing American cultural sensibilities, which hold that killing dogs for food, if not technically illegal, is morally repugnant. The two Cambodian refugees, however, were doing something they had done before in their homeland, not knowing it would offend many Americans.

Vegetarians and animal-rights activists aside, the killing of animals for food is as American as Kentucky Fried Chicken. Human beings are the ultimate predator, destroying other animal species for food. Most

Americans don't oppose the killing of cows, pigs, chickens, lamb, ducks, and rabbits for food.

One shouldn't assume that all Cambodian refugees eat dogs. According to Touch Sim, a community mental health worker with Oakland's Asian Community Mental Health Services, Cambodians turned to eating dogs and cats for food in large numbers after the Pol Pot regime launched its deadly genocide campaign in the mid-1970s. That campaign radically disrupted Cambodian society, and Cambodians desperate for food started killing dogs and cats for survival.

Some Cambodians ate dogs and cats for medicinal purposes before the Pol Pot–led madness, Sim said. Black dogs were the special prey of Cambodians seeking an antidote to certain ailments, such as chilled extremities. Dog meat, in these cases, restored vigor to the body's circulation, Sim said.

Dog eating was introduced to Cambodians by Vietnamese-Chinese, Sim said. In addition, dog eating in Cambodia before the Pol Pot era was looked down upon by many Cambodians. "People who ate dogs were considered inferior and low class," Sim said.

Violating the Crustacean Creed

San Francisco Examiner, May 8, 1997

Christopher, a San Francisco crustacean, was in a, uh, crabby mood. Scrunched on all sides, claws entangled, legs poking into him from above and below, Christopher was fit to be tied. His tank mate, Fred, noticed Christopher's foul mood.

"What's wrong, mate?" Fred asked cheerfully.

Even though the water was murky, Fred could feel Christopher's laser-like glare.

"You know those humans who say they love all animals? Some just don't know anything about us crabs," Christopher asserted.

"What are you talking about?" Fred said, puzzled by his friend's vehemence.

"Hadn't you heard? One of those human 'animal-rights activists' said it's harder to prove cruelty against us than against other animals."

"Where'd you hear that?"

"Where've you been? It's been all over the *Crustacean Gazette* and the Internet (www.crabs.org). This human, a lawyer named Baron Miller, told this human group, the San Francisco Board of Supervisors, the reason he and his animal-rights clients didn't sue these other humans, merchants in Fisherman's Wharf, for 'cruelty to animals' was because it was harder to prove cruelty to us than it is to frogs and turtles. Can you imagine that human's stupidity?"

Fred was slow to catch on. Unlike Christopher and other crustaceans jammed together in the water tank, Fred didn't read the *Crustacean Gazette,* nor was he adept at surfing the net. He rather enjoyed just lying around, surrounded in close quarters by fellow crabs.

Christopher noticed Fred's blank expression. "Our supposed friends, the human animal-rights activists, have been trying to save our butts. They don't like those Chinese merchants selling us and frogs and chickens and fish live so other humans can kill us for food. Frankly, I'm resigned to my fate. No one said life was fair. No one told me I would live forever. But, hey, if those human animal-rights activists want to try to save us, let them."

Fred was now paying attention. He found Christopher's story fascinating.

"So we're safe then? We won't be killed for food?" Fred asked innocently.

"No, not at all," snapped Christopher, impatience building in his voice. "It's just that humans selling us live to be killed later for food aren't going to be targets of our animal-rights friends. They are going after only those human Chinese who also sell live frogs, turtles, chicken, and fish for fresh food."

"That doesn't seem fair," Fred offered.

"No, it isn't," Christopher replied. "What our supposed friends, the animal-rights activists, are doing violates the Crustacean Creed of treating every animal equally. I'm especially incensed that Baron Miller is saying cruelty to us is harder to prove than cruelty to frogs, turtles, fish, and chickens."

"I see what you mean," Fred said. "I know we crabs accept our fate. We're born, we grow up swimming around without a care in the world. We know there's a chance we'll get harvested and put into tanks to await the day we become some human's meal.

"Now that you mention it, I too am offended that this Miller fellow implies we're somehow immune to pain and suffering. Has he ever been put into a pot of boiling water? Has he ever been chopped up, then had his meat sucked out of his shell? Has he ever been dunked into a yucky mayonnaise sauce? I'd put that kind of cruelty up against any that our frog or turtle friends have to endure."

Christopher was taken aback by Fred's sudden militancy. But he was pleased to convert a heretofore slacker crab into an activist.

Parenting, Chinese Style

Asian Week, October 5, 1990

A well-publicized case in the San Francisco Bay Area of a missing Chinese American teenager who, at first, was thought to have been kidnapped is a perfect opportunity to discuss parenting and pressure on Asian American children to excel. It turned out that she ran away from home temporarily, fed up with her China-born father's rigid, authoritarian ways.

Heavy-handed parenting is a throwback to another era, even though it is still practiced today. The contrast is the laissez-faire methods of some American parents: Let the kids do what they want. Provide them with plenty of material goods and opportunities. Don't pressure them. The result sometimes are "overindulged and undermotivated" children.

Such is now the paradigm for American children reared under these hands-off methods. Some feel American kids are lazy, ill prepared academically, without hunger to do well. Asian American kids, on the other hand, reared under the Damocles-sword methods of threatening parents, are driven to success, rigidly conformist, and well behaved but not terribly creative. That at least is a prevailing stereotype with more than a grain of truth.

The story of the missing Chinese American teenager illustrates some parenting dilemmas. I choose not to name the people involved, to protect their privacy now since the "public" nature of their story has long since passed. The story became public when the parents—Chinese Americans who live in Berkeley—reported their 15-year-old daughter missing. She was last seen waiting at a bus stop on a Saturday morning at a well-traveled corner in north Oakland. She was reportedly going to pick up new eyeglasses.

Both parents pleaded on television for the public's help to locate their missing daughter, who was a rising tennis star in high school. The father's plea was directed at the putative kidnapper: Return my daughter, we won't press charges, we won't identify you. The mother's plea differed in target and tone: Come home, daughter. We love you.

This story made major news for a few days in the Bay Area. Then journalists learned from police sources that the teenage girl probably wasn't abducted but had run away to avoid her father's oppressive parenting methods.

A few days after the story became public, I called the father. The story intrigued me because it involved an Asian American family and it could be a prime example of the catastrophic extremes of the "model minority" myth so many Asian Americans are saddled with. At first, the father didn't want to talk. When I told him I was interested in the story because of its cross-cultural implications and how it might define different parenting methods, he started talking, almost nonstop for almost two hours. What he said was, to put it mildly, fascinatingly bizarre. Several times in our conversation, he volunteered, "I'm a strange guy, not your run-of-the-mill person."

He told me he was born in Shanghai and spent time in Japan, Hong Kong, and Taiwan before coming to the United States as a teenager in 1957. He went to public schools in San Francisco, got his bachelor's degree at the University of California at Berkeley, a master's degree at the California Institute of Technology, and a Ph.D. at Columbia University in nuclear engineering. "I got a full dose of an American education," he said.

Tragedy hit his family hard. He and his wife lost two boys when they were infants. The teenage girl is their only surviving child. Perhaps because of this almost unfathomable loss, the girl, in her father's words, "was almost raised in a glass jar." He said she was "pampered all her life, totally protected," especially by her mother, who understandably was devastated by the loss of two sons. "Her mother babied her," he said.

(I wanted to talk with both the mother and daughter, but at the time this story was public, the mother and daughter were in seclusion away from the father. I asked the father to convey my request to the mother and daughter, but they declined. The daughter had returned to her mother after her brief sojourn to Connecticut.)

Given his obsessive personality, the father sought to train his daughter in a sport. First, he tried ping pong, a sport he excelled in. She didn't. "She was too slow," he said. He chose tennis for her, a sport she's been playing for five years. "I wanted to give her a gift—a healthy body," he said. So he devised what he described as a tennis style unique to her. He called it "body tennis for the physically weak." He designed a regimen that excluded all influences except his. "She had to play with me or against the wall— 'shadow' tennis. Our game [emphasizes] speed. We play with two hands, even on the serve."

His daughter, under this rigid training, began to make a mark. "She was by far the best female tennis player" in her high school, the father said. Had she continued, she would have developed "the best return of serve" of any player, he boasted. (Her running away obviously interrupted her budding tennis career.) "I agree that I was exerting pressure on her," he continued. "Anyone who plays competitive sports will say that you have to push people to the limit."

Take the case of one of his training routines. "[She] was such a perfect girl, good girl. She did everything we asked of her. So in the department of mental toughness, I asked her to run home from school while swinging a racquet. It took her an hour." They lived in the Berkeley hills. Her school was in the flatlands. The vertical rise from school to home over a stretch of distance was 1,500 feet.

"I tried to create an artificial adverse environment. I had to go the other way—to embarrass her" to toughen her up mentally for tennis, he said. "Were the other kids going to laugh at her, or were they going to be inspired by her example? It did embarrass her."

The girl's sudden break from home was undoubtedly a reaction to her totalitarian upbringing. The humiliation of her running home from school swinging a tennis racquet was one thing. Spanking was another. "I do believe in spanking," the father said. "I spanked her when she was younger. In tennis practice, we'd practice some shots. She wouldn't do it [the way I asked]—intrinsically, she's timid. I'd say, 'Let's arrange for some spanking.' I'd spank her. It was effective. She'd cry. I told her to hold back her tears." He told me he's been arrested by police for incidents involving spanking of his daughter, especially for disturbing the peace when he and his wife would argue loudly about his disciplinary methods.

Upon her return, the father discovered a different person. "She said to me, 'We're in America.' I would normally say, 'We'll do it the Chinese way.'" Before her bolt from home, "she was totally without imagination. She was slow, totally straightforward. Now she's all pepped up. She took a risky adventure. She had to go through with it. Now she's full of imagination. She's so honest, it's ridiculous."

Generalizing from the particulars of one story would, of course, be hazardous. But it contains elements of one vision of parenting, the kind that tends to produce automatons, or "model minority" children. Is it typical? Who knows? Yet, I hear too many stories from Asian American young people about the unrelenting pressure they get from their parents to excel in school. One Chinese American parent told me recently that he's heard parents say to their children, "Get all A's or don't come home. Win the match or don't come home."

The father of the teenage tennis player said his parenting methods stem from his belief that "American" parenting is much too lax. He feels (white) American children are being let down by their parents, who "appease" their children. He feels the same about (white) American teachers who, in his eyes, seek to win a "popularity" contest rather than pressure students into learning.

Is there a right and wrong? You tell me. All I know is that we parents should be exploring humane, caring ways of bringing up our children while still channeling their natural gifts toward productive and happy lives.

The American Nightmare
Asian Week, July 15, 1994

The Palomares Hills development sits high in the eastern hills of Castro Valley, a middle-to-upper-middle-class suburb southeast of Oakland. Families move to places like Castro Valley to get away from cities like Oakland, where crime and substandard schools are always a worry.

John, Mei-Lian, Rhoda, and Jennifer Lin were just such a family, close-knit, hardworking, law abiding, anonymous. Until Friday, May 28, the start of Memorial Day weekend. Sometime between 5:15 P.M. and 6:45 P.M., someone entered the Lin's four-bedroom, 3,400 square-foot home on Pineville Circle and stabbed to death Jennifer, who only three days earlier had celebrated her fourteenth birthday. John came home from his job as director of computer services at the Federal Reserve Bank in San Francisco to make the horrifying discovery in the upstairs master bathroom.

And so evaporated the Lins' American Dream, just like that, without warning, without rational explanation.

The Lins are not the first, nor will they be the last, family of Asian descent who are inexplicable victims of violent crime in America. But theirs is a melancholic tale of hope, happiness, and now abject horror, a caution for Asian Americans who dream of "mainstreaming" and acceptance in this seemingly limitless land of opportunity. The irony is, John and Mei-Lian made a conscious decision to remain in the United States rather than return to their native Taiwan, just so their daughters would have better opportunities for a bright future.

John and Mei-Lian Lin came to America in 1973 to pursue their own educational dreams. John had graduated from Chiao Tung University in Hsinchu, while Mei-Lian finished undergraduate work at National Taiwan University in Taipei. "I wasn't that crazy about coming to this country," John told me from the living room of his Palomares Hills home that now has become a memorial to the slain Jennifer. Blue ribbons are pinned to a tree out front. Another is pinned onto the front door. John, 45 years old, and Mei-Lian, 43, wear blue ribbons and buttons with a likeness of Jennifer. "I was an electrical engineering major, and electronics was beginning to take off in Taiwan at that time. I'm sure that if I had stayed in Taiwan, I would have had a good future."

Besides, students from Chiao Tung University (one of the two best science and engineering schools in Taiwan, John Lin says) didn't have the same tradition as students from National Taiwan University, that of going to America for graduate studies. "It was Mei-Lian who was much more committed to coming here to study," John says.

John enrolled at the University of Rhode Island in computer science, and Mei-Lian got into the biochemistry program at the University of Pennsylvania. They were engaged to be married at the time, and the distance between their schools forced them into a commuter relationship. They married a year after they got to America, and a year later had their first daughter, Rhoda. Even after they married, they were separated by their respective educational pursuits. "We thought that was our hardest time," Mei-Lian says, barely above a whisper, the wistfulness in her voice lingering in the air.

In his mind, John Lin thought he'd get his master's degree in computer science, then return to Taiwan. But Rhoda's birth in 1975 changed his perspective. John and Mei-Lian asked themselves two questions: "Which would be a better place for our kids to get a good education for a better future? What place has a better environment for them to enjoy their lives—such things as open space, good schools, the attention to children?"

Mei-Lian explains, "Education is very tough for kids in Taiwan. They have entrance exams for junior high and high school, and there's major competition to get into the best universities. This can burn a kid out." How well a student does on those exams could very well determine his or her future.

So the answer to their two questions wasn't hard to reach: Stay in America. The Lins adjusted to a nurturing life in Rhode Island. The university is in a small town called Kingston. Hardly any people of Chinese descent live there. Townsfolk "wanted to take care of us," John remembers fondly. "We got a lot of attention and care." Three neighboring families in particular were close to the Lins. Even though families lived on large spreads of land (fifteen to twenty acres), they thought nothing of dropping by to visit one another. "We established some deep friendships" with those families, John says. One family "took me shopping and taught John how to drive," Mei-Lian says. A second family "totally adopted us. . . . Our kids still call them Nanna and Grandpa."

Despite the warmth of these relationships, the New England winters were unforgiving. "There was a blizzard in 1978, and I got tired of shoveling snow," John says. Besides, baby Rhoda was "constantly sick" the winter before, and her doctor recommended the Lins move to a warmer climate. California was a natural choice. Besides its fabled warm weather, it was closer to Taiwan than Rhode Island is, and the Lins, with relatives still there, visit Taiwan periodically.

Having spent their American life in a small-town environment, the Lins knew almost nothing about housing in the bustling San Francisco Bay Area. John had applied for and gotten a computer programming job at the Federal Reserve Bank of San Francisco. A Realtor recommended Castro Valley because of its sunny weather and good schools.

In 1979, they bought a home in Castro Valley. Jennifer was born a year later. The next year, the Lins bought another home in Castro Valley and stayed there ten years before moving into the "more prestigious" Palomares Hills development in the fall of 1991. "We wanted a bigger house," Mei-Lian says. Their second Castro Valley home was nice but had only 2,200 square feet and four bedrooms, not quite spacious enough for the times friends of their daughters visited.

"My husband and I were chased to our bedroom" during these visits, and they "felt like intruders" when they crossed the space occupied by their daughters and their friends, Mei-Lian says. The Palomares Hills home has as many bedrooms, but it also has a game room, where teenagers could gather without forcing the parents into bedroom isolation.

You couldn't ask for a better embodiment of the American Dream than Palomares Hills. The homes on Pineville Circle are higher than other Palomares Hills homes and are spacious, many with three-car garages. The street is quiet, giving a sense of safety and security. "This place is as far and remote from crime as possible," John says, with a tone of disbelief.

The apparent serene environment didn't calm all of Mei-Lian's worries about her younger daughter. When Rhoda was still in high school, the two sisters would be companions at home after school while their parents worked. But Rhoda went away last fall to college, so Jennifer was home alone during weekday afternoons after school.

At first, the school bus dropped children off more than a half mile down the hill. But the Lins and other parents lobbied the school board to get the bus to drop students up the hill. That assuaged Mei-Lian's latent fears, as did the fact that Jennifer walked from the bus with several other children who lived along Pineville Circle. Mei-Lian remembers Jennifer chiding her about her motherly worries. "You're over worried," Mei-Lian says Jennifer said. "This is a safe community."

The still unsolved murder has shocked the Lins, their relatives and friends, and the neighborhood. The Alameda County Sheriff's Office still has no solid leads, spawning speculation as to motive. Nothing was stolen from the Lins' residence, so robbery wasn't a likely reason. The killer could have approached the house from the open field behind the home and broken in through an unlocked sliding glass door.

By all accounts, Jennifer had no enemies. To the contrary, her family and friends say she was popular, bright, engaging, talented. Understandably,

John and Mei-Lian Lin can't talk about their slain daughter without tears and awkward pauses. But their pride in her is undeniable. "She got straight A's in her six semesters of middle school. She was very mature, responsible, considerate," her father says. "She did nothing to hurt anyone's feelings. She cared a lot about us." Mei-Lian interjects, "She told us she wanted to buy a home nearby, to be close to us." Her father adds, "She had good organizational skills, a good personality. She was people-oriented, friendly. She lit up the room when she entered."

Who, then, would want to murder such a promising child, and why? In an almost plaintive wail, John Lin expounds, "No one can match our profile with a serious crime situation, not in a million years. We're both full-time employees. We haven't had a lot of time to socialize with anyone. [On weekends], we take our children to Chinese school [in Walnut Creek] and we do chores. Sometimes we work on weekends."

Could this be the work of a serial killer or a hate crime? There's been no evidence of a hate crime. A few years ago, a Chinese American father and son and a Korean American young man were beaten up by a small group of white hooligans, some of whom shouted racial epithets, in a Castro Valley strip mall.

After Jennifer's murder, someone told the Lins about a Chinese American boy getting beaten up on a Castro Valley basketball court. John says, "We've heard stories about hate crimes against Chinese [and Asians], but we've never experienced any problems. People have always treated us well."

Before I leave, Mei-Lian wants to show me recent photographs of Jennifer. She brings out a small album filled with photos of Jenny's spring cruise to Ensenada, Mexico, with the Castro Valley Chamber Orchestra, of which she was a violist. When Mei-Lian comes to the last photo, showing Jennifer with her, her husband, and their older daughter, Rhoda, quiet sobs break the silence. John braces his head in his hands, hiding his face from me. I can feel the strain and the pain.

"Americans have a hard time understanding how close Chinese families are," John says, reverting to the confusion of mixing ethnic and national identities. At another point, when discussing the possibility of this being a hate crime, John volunteers that he and his wife consider themselves more "American" than "Chinese" and that their daughters are or were thoroughly "American" with friends of many different racial, ethnic, and cultural backgrounds.

"We save all our moments for our children. We took them with us on vacations," John says. "Our kids thought we were too unromantic, so on our anniversary, they kicked us out [of the house] to have a romantic dinner. We drove around not knowing where to go and ended up at a Red Lobster restaurant in Fremont. While we were there, all we could talk about was what Rhoda would have liked to have eaten, or what Jenny would like. We even brought food home for them. We never thought of not having our kids with us. Lots of Chinese families feel the same way. We were closely bonded, the four of us. This is our life. We lived for our kids. Now one of the two is gone, so half of our life is gone."

A Buddhist shrine now sits in the Lins' living room, next to a piano that's covered with photos and mementos of Jenny. "We're trying to look for comfort in religion," John says.

[The crime remains unsolved.]

6 Anti-Asian Racism

Forever Foreigners

"The Boat People Own Everything"
Asian Week, October 18, 1989

Nine months ago, Patrick Edward Purdy went to Cleveland Elementary School in Stockton, California, and opened fire at a school yard filled with children and teachers. California Attorney General John Van de Kamp has issued a report on the shooting and possibly why it occurred.

The report has generated additional heat in this much-discussed case. Many Asian Americans are gratified that a state official has focused on anti-Asian violence. Others, however, particularly people in Stockton, are incensed that the case has once again become a subject of public scrutiny. They would like the case to fade away.

Asian American community leaders in San Francisco (Ling-chi Wang, Henry Der, and Dale Minami, particularly) asked Van de Kamp to investigate the circumstances surrounding the case because of suspected racial motivations of the killer.

Purdy's extraordinary deed—spraying 105 rounds of ammunition from his semiautomatic AK-47 assault rifle into a crowd of elementary-school students, killing five of them and wounding thirty others plus a teacher—horrified everyone. But Asian Americans felt a deeper chill because all those killed and most of those wounded were Southeast Asians. Many Asian Americans I talked with in the days following the incident instinctively felt that a racial motive was a factor in Purdy's desperate behavior.

Speculation at the time—January 17 and the days immediately following—included the possibility of race hatred by Purdy against Southeast

Asians. An acquaintance of Purdy's was quoted in some news accounts as saying that Purdy resented Southeast Asians for taking away jobs from him and other white Americans. Stockton police officials quickly put a lid on a possible racial motive by saying that Purdy hated everyone. They closed the case because the killer had killed himself and police could find no specific evidence that directly tied his shooting spree with any hostile feelings toward Asians.

Van de Kamp's report deepens our understanding into the possible motives of Patrick Edward Purdy, a troubled individual who, according to the report, received little love and affection when he was a child and who, since the age of thirteen, was essentially on his own. He had problems with alcohol and drug abuse as a teenager and had difficulties holding onto jobs. He drifted, on the tawdry edges of society, and found a fascination with weapons and toy soldiers and a hatred of all racial and ethnic minorities.

The attorney general's investigators couldn't find any direct evidence that linked the shooting to Purdy's attitudes, but they unearthed plenty of circumstantial evidence that strongly suggested a racial motive. Van de Kamp called Purdy's act "premeditated murder, carefully planned over the course of a month. And the choice of victims was not random." The attorney general continued, "Purdy attacked Southeast Asian immigrants out of a festering sense of racial resentment and hatred. And he attacked children out of his own insecurity and cowardice."

Purdy spoke "openly and often of his resentment toward Southeast Asian immigrants," Van de Kamp said. "He told friends and co-workers both in Oregon and in Stockton of his dislike for Vietnamese, Indians, Pakistanis and others. He believed they were getting money and jobs that he wasn't getting. He also believed many of the immigrants were communists and that they would overrun the country."

State investigators learned that Purdy, two weeks before the shooting, spoke about the power of rapid-fire weapons such as his AK-47 and his resentment of Southeast Asian "boat people." Purdy was seen watching the Cleveland Elementary School playground one morning, then watching a Stockton high school where a large number of Cambodian refugees attend. "We believe he was scouting the two schools as targets for his assault."

On the morning of January 17, before he took off for Cleveland School, Purdy told someone at a motel where the two of them stayed, "The damn

Hindus and boat people own everything." Those were possibly the last words Purdy said to anyone.

In the aftermath of the Van de Kamp report, questions are being asked as to the value of recounting the Purdy case. An editorial in the *Stockton Record* expresses one school of thought. "It is simply irresponsible to conclude on the basis of one mentally deranged person's actions, horrible as they were, that a new threat of violence to Asian Americans exists in California," the editorial on October 10 stated. It was written partially in response to a statement made at the Van de Kamp news conference on October 6 by Dale Minami, a San Francisco civil rights attorney and chair of the attorney general's Asian and Pacific Islander Advisory Committee. Minami had said, "Patrick Purdy's attitude toward Asian Pacific Americans is not a simple aberration but more a frightening omen of what could become a theme—a dominant theme—in California over the next decade."

Minami, in a subsequent conversation with me, said he was pleased with the attorney general's report. He called it "balanced" and said that it didn't conclude that race was Purdy's only motivation because humans are complex beings and they act on the basis of multiple motives. But, Minami said, the conclusion is "inescapable that race was a factor." He added that it is easy for people who aren't potential targets of race hatred to ignore signs of growing anti-Asian sentiments in California and elsewhere in the United States. "Asian Pacific Americans can't ignore it because we are possible victims" of race hatred.

Van de Kamp's Purdy report recommended steps that can be taken by educational, law-enforcement, and political institutions to combat hate crime, such as multicultural curricula, adequately funded human-relations commissions, hate-crime reporting mechanisms, and enhanced-penalty provisions of criminal statutes.

People in Stockton are divided on the Van de Kamp report. A white parent objected to the report's focus on anti-Asian sentiments, according to the *Stockton Record*. "My son is white and he was hit," said Debra Copeland, whose 10-year-old son was wounded in the shooting. Copeland told the *Record* that she is "sick and tired of everyone just talking about the Southeast Asians. They weren't the only ones hurt." Other non-Asian parents in Stockton felt that the news media were sensationalizing the report. "I am not interested in the report," Debbie Smith told the *Record*.

"I think we all know the guy is pretty well nuts. How many ways do we need to hear it?"

Stockton police officials declined comment on the Van de Kamp report because of some damage complaints filed against the city by parents of the victims. Stockton City Attorney Tom Harris, who said he hadn't yet reviewed the report, said that if Purdy were partially motivated by racial animosities, "I don't know whether that indicates the city could have done anything differently" in response to the incident.

At least one Stockton Cambodian parent, however, said that the Van de Kamp report's finding that Purdy hated Southeast Asians wasn't a surprise. Sam Chit Koy, a 33-year-old mother of three boys who attend Cleveland School but who weren't directly involved in the Purdy shooting, said she has talked with other Cambodian parents who all felt that Purdy was a racist and that "he hated us."

"The Cambodian people here in Stockton weren't surprised [by the Van de Kamp report]," Koy said. Some in the Cambodian community are fearful that they could still be targeted because of racism, she indicated.

Learning from the Vincent Chin Case

Asian Week, October 6, 1989

When the Jim (Ming Hai) Loo killing came to light two months ago, it was inevitable that it would be compared with the Vincent Chin case seven years ago. In some respects, comparisons are apt. In others, they aren't. Nonetheless, the Loo case is quickly becoming a cause célèbre in the Asian American community because it's the latest and most extreme reminder to Asian Americans that they run the risk of being targeted for racist hatred in this country.

The killing of Jim (Ming Hai) Loo in late July in Raleigh, North Carolina, has eerie echoes of the Vincent Chin killing in June 1982, in Detroit. Both had clear racial overtones. Both involved cases of mistaken ethnic identifications. But the two cases differ in important respects, particularly in how the Asian American community, national news media, and criminal-justice system have reacted. The response to the Loo killing at all levels except national news-media coverage can be traced to lessons learned from the Chin case.

Loo was killed after a pool-hall argument. Chin was killed after a dispute in a seedy topless club. Loo's accused killer and his brother were heard to express anti-Vietnamese sentiments; Loo himself was ethnic Chinese who came to the United States thirteen years ago from China. Chin's killers were heard to explicitly imply that Chin was of Japanese descent and somehow responsible for the American auto industry's problems. Loo was hit in the head with a pistol, causing him to fall to the ground where his face smashed into a beer bottle that shattered glass into his eye socket. Those injuries led to his death two days later. Chin was repeatedly hit in the head by a baseball bat.

From the perspective of the criminal justice system, the two cases diverge. Chin's killers—Ronald Ebens and Michael Nitz, both of whom worked in the auto industry in the Detroit area—were found guilty of manslaughter but given a probationary sentence and light fines. Ebens, the man who swung the bat, also beat federal civil rights charges on a technicality. The result was that Vincent Chin's killers never spent a day in jail for their crime. The criminal justice system failed the family of Vincent Chin, and by extension, the Asian American community.

Robert Piche, 35 years old, has been indicted on a second-degree murder charge, along with four lesser charges, for which he is currently serving a two-year sentence for one of them (disorderly conduct). His 29 year-old brother, Lloyd Piche, has been sentenced to six months in jail for disorderly conduct and simple assault in connection with the pool-hall attack (but not specifically for the assault on Loo).

For two men, Po Chan and Jim Tso, the Loo case has become a turning point in their lives. Chan is a 53-year-old toxicologist with the National Institutes of Health in the Raleigh area. Chan's previous political involvement had been limited to serving as the president of the Triangle Area's Organization of Chinese Americans chapter.

Chan says he read about the case in the local papers. The account of the killing quoted police as saying the killing had racial overtones. "After reading the paper, it didn't occur to me that I should react," Chan says. But then something told him to attend the funeral a few days later.

The funeral of Jim (Ming Hai) Loo attracted the mayor of Raleigh and a representative of the area's Congressman, David Price. The representative of the Loo family who had organized the funeral felt it would be appropriate for a Chinese American community spokesman to make remarks to the mourners. Po Chan reluctantly stepped into that role—and since then, he's been in the middle of the coalition trying to bring justice to Loo's killers. The case "was bigger than I imagined" at first, he says. "I didn't realize at the beginning that it would draw the attention of so many people."

Unlike the Chin case in its early days, the Loo case has already attracted widespread attention from Asian Americans across the country. The Chin case didn't seep into the national Asian American conscience until sometime in 1983, after the local courts had basically let Ebens and Nitz off. But the Loo case became known to different Asian American communities across the country relatively quickly.

Such a quick exposure is due in large part to the legacy of the Chin killing, which has taken on mythic proportions in the Asian American community. Today, Asian Americans in general are much more sensitive to, and much more willing to speak out on, the issue of race hatred aimed at them. The network of Asian American groups all over the country is also much better developed than it was in the early 1980s.

The Chin case got a lot of national news-media exposure after the Detroit Asian American community, which had organized a broad coalition of sympathetic Detroiters, protested the light sentences against Ebens and Nitz. The Loo case has barely been heard of in the national news media.

Jim Tso, the coalition's general counsel, says that thus far, national news-media exposure isn't a high priority for the coalition. The coalition is concentrating on making sure the criminal-justice system handles the case fairly and prosecutes the accused killer vigorously. Tso indicates that the time for national news-media exposure will come later.

Tso learned of the Loo killing about three weeks after it happened when he received a mailing from the Organization of Chinese Americans. With previous organizing experience and the ghost of the Vincent Chin case haunting him, Tso sprung into action. He went down to the Raleigh area and met with the Jim Loo Coalition. He then volunteered his services and has traveled frequently to Raleigh, spending countless hours in his Fairfax, Virginia, practice on aspects of the case. The Loo case has become his cause. "We want to win this one, we want to win it bad," he says. That is why he has advised the coalition to adopt a "moderated, measured" approach in its legal strategy.

For both Chan and Tso, the Loo case symbolizes the current status of Asian America. Chan, a scientist by training and inclination, has no regrets for getting involved because "this [the killing of an Asian American] can happen to me or my kids."

Tso wants the Loo case to be remembered for its potential victories. Tso says the Chin case "destroyed the feeling of the Asian American community. It reinforced our sense of lack of empowerment. [The Loo case] is all about giving our people empowerment."

Robert Piche was convicted and sentenced to thirty-five years for second-degree murder and two years for assault with a deadly weapon.

Escaping Racism: No Way Out
Asian Week, April 21, 1995

These past few weeks haven't been kind to Japanese American and Chinese American men. It's easy enough for yellow men to become paranoid in this society. Mostly, we're invisible or ignored. But when you have a phenomenon as consuming as the O. J. Simpson case that includes Asian American men, then, inevitably, the Asian American men will be swept up in the intense public scrutiny.

Judge Lance Ito is now famous since he's a central player in the long-running Simpson drama that is getting extraordinary worldwide media coverage. Being famous doesn't always mean good things. What it means is that you can't escape the often ugly glare of the public spotlight. Dennis Fung, however, is just a supporting player, having been in the spotlight only in recent weeks.

Both have taken their hits. Not that they should be immune to legitimate criticism. Their very public performances, as part of the continuing Simpson saga, should be evaluated, the way the media and public have had their say on how the prosecutors, defense attorneys, and defendant are doing. Some of the hits, though, have been clearly racist. These latest examples of anti-Asian bigotry confirm what we've known all along, that no matter how accomplished an Asian American is in this society, he or she can't fully escape racism.

The most blatant instance of racism against Ito was generated by New York Republican Senator Alfonse D'Amato, who mocked Ito on a syndicated talk radio show hosted by Don Imus. D'Amato expressed frustration at the fact that the Simpson trial is consuming inordinate media attention, so much so that Whitewater hearings D'Amato hopes to conduct would probably not get the kind of coverage he believes they should.

Rather than offer a straightforward comment, D'Amato chose a phony Japanese accent to criticize Ito for allegedly dragging out the Simpson trial. This is part of what D'Amato said, "Forever and ever, because Judge Ito will never let it end . . . Judge Ito loves the limelight. He is making a disgrace of the judicial system. Little Judge Ito. For God's sake, get them in there for twelve hours; get this thing over. I mean, this is a disgrace. Judge Ito with the wet nose. And then he's going to have a hung jury. Judge Ito will keep us from getting television for the next year."

It didn't take long for Japanese Americans and others to strike back. This quick and effective national counterpunch is a silver lining for Asian Americans in this sorry episode of high-level insensitivity. Congressman Norman Mineta, a Democrat from San Jose, responded on national TV news shows in understandably emotional terms. Several Japanese American Citizens League officials lashed out at D'Amato on national news-media outlets. In addition, Stanley Mark of the Asian American Legal Defense and Education Fund of New York called for D'Amato to apologize. Asian American critics were joined by the Anti-Defamation League of B'nai Brith and the National Association for the Advancement of Colored People.

D'Amato first issued a nonapology apology. "If I offended anyone, I'm sorry. I was making fun of the pomposity of the judge and the manner in which he's dragging the trial out." The heat continued, so D'Amato was forced to be more sincerely contrite on the floor of the Senate. A *New York Times* story said, "In barely audible tones, a chastened and visibly nervous Senator Alfonse D'Amato delivered a rare apology on the Senate floor today, calling his heavily accented remarks about the Japanese-American judge in the O. J. Simpson case 'totally wrong and inappropriate.'"

Less than a week later, D'Amato was admitted to a Long Island hospital with chest pains. He had had a rough week.

The most curious aspect of D'Amato's mockery of Ito was why he chose a racist vehicle, the phony Japanese accent, to comment on Ito's conduct as a judge. This is a frequent pattern for Asian Americans. If anyone notices us at all and we do something someone disagrees with, more often than not you'll hear that critic use a racist slur rather than a substantive comment.

In other words, all some people see of us is not what we've done or said but what we look like. There's no denying Lance Ito is of Japanese descent. But he's a Japanese American who speaks English without a Japanese (or any other kind of) accent. It defies logic why D'Amato engaged a badly done Japanese accent to criticize Ito's courtroom conduct.

Dennis Fung fell victim to the same kind of racism. Fung is a Los Angeles Police Department technician who collects crime-scene evidence. His role in the Simpson case is important because he was responsible for collecting blood samples and the bloody glove from the site of the killings of Nicole Brown Simpson and Ronald L. Goldman, whom O. J. Simpson stands accused of murdering.

Barry Scheck, one of Simpson's lawyers, grilled Fung relentlessly, practically accusing him of lying and being part of a police conspiracy to frame the former football star and actor. While it could be argued Fung didn't do his job very well, it was more the style of the cross-examination and Fung's response that struck a sensitive nerve with Asian American men. Scheck's courtroom manner was aggressive. His questions were rapid fire. He was in Fung's face every chance he got. He asked a lot of hypothetical questions in a convoluted way to try to elicit as incriminating a response from Fung as he could.

Fung didn't help his own cause when he seemed evasive and hesitant. He was caught in some contradictory testimony and overall he seemed a beaten witness. In terms of his style, Fung played into the stereotype of Asian males as stoic, reserved, and passive. News highlights I saw weren't flattering to Fung, from the stylistic perspective.

Some Asian Americans were upset at Fung's performance because it reinforced the stereotype that Asian Americans are passive. Was this a true reflection of Fung's personality? Was he intimidated or merely incompetent? I don't know about the first question, but many commentators and observers felt Fung did badly on the stand.

David Margolick of the *New York Times* wrote, "In the four days they have cross-examined Mr. Fung, Mr. Simpson's lawyers have laid at his feet a dazzling array of mistakes, inconsistencies and deceptions, an assault that prosecutors left Mr. Fung poorly prepared to handle. Mr. Fung has made matters worse for himself by appearing evasive, picking foolish fights and steadfastly refusing to criticize his colleagues."

Dennis Fung and, for that matter, Lance Ito have to stand or fall on the basis of what they do. To rub it in against the hapless Fung, Simpson's lawyers engaged in racist bantering themselves, a sign of incredible hubris and arrogance given the kind of racial politics they have played in this sensational case.

After Fung's ill-fated week, Robert Shapiro, one of Simpson's lawyers, passed out fortune cookies to some writers and said they were from the "Hang Fung" restaurant. Ha, ha, very funny, Shapiro. There is no such restaurant in Los Angeles. It was also reported that Johnnie L. Cochran, another Simpson lawyer, was heard to chortle, "We're having Fung," a play on the criminalist's Chinese name. Shapiro said Cochran didn't say that about Fung.

Here again is an example of racializing comments about Asian Americans when racial comments aren't germane. Shapiro and Cochran didn't simply state how incompetent they thought Fung was, or more appropriately, crow about how much he had hurt the prosecution's case and helped theirs. Whether we like it or not, that would have been fair comment based on Fung's courtroom performance and the defense's version of his crime-scene competence. No, they chose instead to make fun of Fung's Chinese heritage and name when neither had anything to do with what Fung did at the crime scene and testified to in court.

After a long weekend, Shapiro sort of apologized. He said he apologized to Fung, then in a statement to the news media, he said, "My heart has been heavy all weekend if even one person has been offended, and for that I sincerely apologize." Apologies aside, Shapiro turned Fung into a martyr. Had Shapiro shut his expensive trap, Fung would have remained a badly wounded supporting player on the basis of substance. Now he's a victim of racism who's gained the sympathy of many Asian Americans and, I hope, other fair-minded people.

The Golden State of Bigotry

Asian Week, October 22, 1993

As capital of one of the most ethnically and culturally diverse states, Sacramento, one might think, would be free of racism. That would be a naive assumption about any American city. Racism thrives everywhere in America. We who belong to groups that have been excluded, in one form or another, know that. American history teaches us that lesson, and now we are relearning it almost daily.

California's Golden State reputation is built on ossified Hollywood images. The nation's most populous state has a long history of anti-Asian racism that began in the 1850s, when large numbers of Chinese workers and miners first started coming to America. This is not to say that California hasn't also afforded golden opportunities to all people to try to achieve the American Dream. It has, but this state hasn't been a multicultural panacea either.

Sacramento made big news because it had five firebombings, two against Asian American targets. The firebombings, dating back to July, form an apparent pattern of racial violence. A heretofore unknown group called the Aryan Liberation Front has claimed credit for the attacks.

That racial attacks occurred in Sacramento is a sign of our times. Some Americans are frustrated about economic sluggishness, jobs lost and jobs threatened. Some Americans don't particularly like the rising numbers of nonwhite newcomers. America has been a violent society, reveling in a gun culture and a tough-guy posture that no amount of "sensitivity training" is going to overcome.

For Asian Americans, the Sacramento attacks reinforce feelings of insecurity about our place in society. The Asian American targets of the Sacramento firebombings—the Japanese American Citizens League (JACL) and City Councilman Jimmie Yee—are maintaining stiff upper lips, but underneath the resolve, there resides an edginess and a sadness.

In the long history of the JACL, even through the days of World War II, the civil rights group has never had an office firebombed. "Many of our offices have been threatened and received hate mail, and a couple have been vandalized, but nothing this serious," said Carole Hayashino, acting director of the national organization.

The Sacramento office of the JACL was hit with a so-called Molotov cocktail thrown through the front window at about 1:45 A.M. Saturday, October 2. The explosive ignited a fire that destroyed the group's office equipment. Three days later, at almost the same early-morning hour, the home of Councilman Yee was firebombed. Luckily, the Molotov cocktail did relatively minor damage to a bedroom that only weeks earlier had been occupied by a 28-year-old son.

These two attacks followed two in July, an incendiary device tossed into the office of the National Association for the Advancement of Colored People (July 27) and a similar incident at the Congregation B'nai Israel Synagogue (July 25). After Councilman Yee's home was hit, a state office was similarly targeted about a week later—the Fair Employment and Housing Commission, which investigates discrimination and hate crimes.

Law-enforcement authorities and officials of civil rights organizations that monitor hate crimes say they've never heard of the Aryan Liberation Front.

The attack on Councilman Yee's home was particularly egregious. Not that firebombings of a synagogue and offices aren't outrageous enough. But targeting a home endangers its occupants more so than an office or building that is empty in early-morning hours.

Jimmie Yee never thought he'd be the object of racial hatred when he decided to run for the city council last year. The 59-year-old native of Sacramento said he was never particularly interested in running for public office, despite many years of community service in the Chinese and Asian American communities. Yee is the youngest of six children. His parents emigrated from Toisan, Guangdong province, China, his dad in the early 1920s, his mom in the late 1920s. His father eventually owned a grocery store and his mother worked in a laundry, then a cannery.

Yee earned a bachelor of science degree at the University of California at Berkeley, Class of 1956, and went back home to Sacramento to settle into a comfortable professional life as a structural engineering consultant. Among other extracurricular activities, Yee has been a member of the Chinese American Council of Sacramento and he organized the first Asian bone-marrow drive.

"The farthest thing from my mind was politics," Yee told me. It was his friend Tom Chin who talked him into running for city council. Chin had been on the city council for nine years after serving twelve years on the city's school board.

Yee was able to win his first public office in a district that has a 20 percent Asian population (and, undoubtedly, a lower percentage of Asian voters) against a white candidate. A conservative Democrat who's been in office about a year, Yee said he sometimes gives people the impression he's a Republican.

One natural question is whether Yee has been doing or saying anything that would inspire the ire of white supremacists. Nothing he can identify, he said. Yee said he led a campaign against cars "cruising" along a main Sacramento street, something young Latinos might have reason to be angry at him for. But Yee said he doesn't believe they would retaliate against him for that stance. He also said he has spoken out against a mural painted by high school students. The mural pictures, among other things, the burning of an American flag. "I hold the American flag in high esteem," Yee said. "But it wasn't students" who firebombed his home. "I feel this was a racial hate crime," Yee stated without hesitation.

He said his home received a phone call about ninety minutes before the Molotov cocktail was tossed. He characterized it as a "crank call." His wife of thirty-nine years answered the call (he was asleep). The caller said he wanted to speak with Yee. His wife asked who was calling. The caller asked whether this was Yee's home and hung up.

Neither he nor his wife heard the window being broken by the firebomb. A smoke alarm awoke them. A neighbor, up late watching TV, heard some commotion and came to Yee's aid. The neighbor saw a white car drive off.

Ironically, the attack on his home came hours before Yee was scheduled to speak at a news conference to denounce the firebombing of the JACL office. So when Yee showed up at the news conference, the incident at his home superseded the earlier attack. He was greeted with applause and wide support. Yee said police are giving him some extra protection, "but I'm not going let the incident change my life." He said he's become "more alert. . . . My main concern is my wife. . . . I'm away so much."

More than a week after the attack, Yee said, "I still can't believe it happened." When I mentioned how jovial he seemed to be, he answered, "That's just me. I have to maintain some humor. I'm not going to crawl into a shell. I'm not going to pout about it. I will joke about it to my friends."

He admitted the attack, however, has "affected my nerves, but I can't let it intimidate me. I'm not at the point that I'm going to kowtow to these guys." He said the "tremendous support" he's gotten is "the real Sacramento. The firebombings are a little aberration. They aren't the real Sacramento." Yee doesn't believe the firebombings are because of the economic downturn or resentment at immigrants. "It's racial hatred, taught within a family or group of white supremacists."

Others aren't shy about citing a growing mood of anti-immigrant bashing for the Sacramento attacks. The city's mayor, Joe Serna, for instance, is indirectly quoted in the *Sacramento Bee* as criticizing "certain politicians" for encouraging hate crimes by making immigration a divisive issue. California Governor Pete Wilson has been the principal politician fanning the flames of anti-immigrant resentment. He denies doing so and he has spoken out against the racial firebombings.

Until politicians start talking seriously about the economic imperatives of illegal immigration, no amount of law enforcement is going to "solve" the problem. But then, politicians are interested in reelection, so they will resort to pandering and pointing fingers at disenfranchised people like the undocumented and therefore figuratively toss additional fuel onto Molotov cocktails that are heaved into the offices and homes of people who look "different" from the Aryan Superman that a handful of sickies want America to be populated with.

Swastikas in the Sunset

San Francisco Examiner, March 28, 1997

San Francisco mythology got a sobering dose of reality when graffiti vandals recently slashed swastikas onto some businesses owned by Asian Americans in the city's Sunset District. The city's mythmakers don't usually include hatemongers among their poster children of interracial harmony in Everybody's Favorite City. San Franciscans of all ethnic backgrounds helped clean up the swastikas. The spirit that moved them reflected the kind of tolerance San Franciscans should be proud of.

Nonetheless, fear and hate of "others" in San Francisco have long been a reality. The most significant "other" groups are those of Asian descent who are now one-third of the city's population. Hateful racial anecdotes that don't make front-page news have been discussed among San Francisco's Chinese Americans and other Asian Americans for years—anti-Asian graffiti or insults in the Richmond and other districts outside of Chinatown. There was private grumbling about these disquieting greetings, but little official political action. One major difference now in the response to such incidents is the presence of Asian American politicians like Supervisors Mabel Teng and Leland Yee, who led protests against the Sunset hate messages.

The Sunset swastikas are a local manifestation of a resurgence of anti-Asian sentiments on a national scale. The Democratic fundraising scandal has unfortunate anti-Asian aspects that include the provocative idea (among others) that the communist Chinese government sought to buy influence with the Clinton administration through laundered campaign contributions. An ominous subtext of this anti-Asian phenomenon is that China looms large as the next Evil Empire. It's the Yellow Peril all over again, and it's also a sickening replay of "We All Look Alike, Don't We?"

The latter stereotype has been revived in the March 24 *National Review*, the conservative periodical. Its cover caricature shows President and Mrs. Clinton in elaborate "Oriental" garb and facial characteristics and Vice President Al Gore Jr. in a Buddhist monk outfit, a reference to his presence at a questionable fund raiser at a Buddhist temple in the Los Angeles area last year.

Asian Americans across the nation protested the *National Review* cover, and the frustration level is at a fever pitch that press coverage of the fundraising scandal has unfairly tainted many Asian Americans when only a few may have been involved in any possible wrongdoing. For whatever reason, the popular culture and mass media have difficulties distinguishing between Americans of Asian descent and Asian nationals. That was the case in early 1942 when thousands of U.S. citizens of Japanese descent were unconstitutionally imprisoned because U.S. government and military officials determined they might be spies for the evil Japanese empire at the time.

The assumption that people of Asian descent are too different and unassimilable has deep historical roots. Historian Stuart Creighton Miller, in his study *The Unwelcome Immigrant: The American Image of the Chinese, 1785–1882*, found convincing evidence that American anti-Chinese attitudes were national and predated a heavy Chinese presence in California and the west in the last half of the 19th century.

There has certainly been progress in interracial-interethnic relations in San Francisco and the nation. But the Sunset swastikas here and the shadowy "Asian connection" allegations in Washington demonstrate a stubborn streak in our culture of intolerance for Asian-related issues. Since Asian Americans aren't going away, the question is how San Francisco and America will deal with their confoundingly complex ethnic relations. It might be too naive to think the spirit of coming together in the Sunset to clean up the graffiti will prevail without more resistance on the part of some people who fear "otherness" in their midst.

Un-American Christians

San Francisco Examiner, August 24, 1999

One of my in-laws is a Chinese American postal worker who works in the Los Angeles area. My sister said that when she first saw TV-news pictures of the mass shootings by Buford Furrow in the Los Angeles region, she immediately thought of our in-law, because a "non-white" postal worker was shot and killed.

Our in-law of course was not a victim of Furrow's. Nonetheless, that moment of worry is part of a deeper emotional response on my part, and perhaps that of many other Americans who do not qualify as acceptable to Furrow and others who think like him.

Furrow reportedly told authorities he saw postal worker Joseph Ileto, a Filipino American, as a "target of opportunity" because he was "non-white" and a federal government worker. Furrow, who has a history of mental disturbances, is a white supremacist who despises "non-whites" and government employees. He also hates Jews. He stands accused of gunning down Ileto for no other reason than Ileto's ethnic background and of spraying shots inside a Jewish community center, wounding an adult, a teenager, and three children.

My queasiness isn't related to just Furrow's madness. Other recent hate crimes—the arson fires of some Sacramento synagogues, Benjamin Smith's shooting spree of African Americans and Asian Americans in the midwest—weigh heavily on me too. They are a reminder that no matter how American I may feel, there are some Americans who will not see beyond my so-called non-white features. They see me and others like me and African Americans and Latinos and even "white" people who are Jews and "white" people who are gays and lesbians as inferior or unworthy. They see us as targets of opportunity—to kill, to maim.

I know that the vast majority of white Christian Americans—that is, the vast majority of Americans—are not sick in the way that Buford Furrow is. But white supremacists do not believe in democratic principles. In the aggregate, they may amount to a relatively small number, but as Furrow and Smith have shown, they strike with deadly force, almost anywhere, anytime. That is what is so scary for a non-white American like me.

At one time, I thought that policy and legal responses such as gun control could protect us. Furrow and Smith and others before them used guns to express their inner demons. Guns are among the deadliest of instruments. So are bombs. Sure, regulate them to the hilt, but there are so many guns in private hands—more than two hundred million—and bombs are so easy to make with instructions off the Internet that reining in these deadly weapons is not a practical solution to ridding white supremacists of their hatreds.

At some other point, I thought "education" would do the trick. But what exactly does "education" mean to a Buford Furrow or a Benjamin Smith? They, and others like them, got "educated" in ways that are completely foreign to me.

Besides, reason and logic hold no sway among white supremacists. The United States has a growing "non-white" population. Some people naively trumpet our burgeoning "multiculturalism" as a strength. If that is so, why then do Furrow and Smith, among others, regard non-whites (and Jews and gays and lesbians) as "mud people" to be exterminated?

There's been a lot of rancid debate over "identity politics" related to America's increasing multiculturalism, but most people realize they are of multiple identities, whether related to race, ethnicity, gender, age, generation, geography, work, or any other category. Furrow and Smith are or were obsessed with a single identity—as white Christian extremists. That is more frightening, and more un-American, than anything I have heard from people who celebrate multiculturalism.

I Am a Gook

San Francisco Examiner, February 23, 2000

I hated the gooks. . . . I was referring to my prison guards.

—JOHN MCCAIN

Dear Sen. McCain:

I am a gook, even though I was not one of your North Vietnamese cap-
tors who tortured you and other American prisoners of war more than
thirty years ago.

I am a gook, even though I was not a Viet Cong sympathizer who helped
the North Vietnamese Army battle Americans and South Vietnamese soldiers.

I am a gook, even though I was not allied with the South Vietnamese
military who fought alongside American GI's in that unfortunate war in
which you and other U.S. Navy pilots were shot down.

I am a gook, even though I did not join the North Koreans and Chinese soldiers in fighting South Koreans and Americans half a century
ago.

I am a gook, even though I did not march with Mao Zedong or take
up arms with Chiang Kai-Shek during the Chinese civil war in the 1930s
and 1940s.

I am a gook, even though I was nowhere near the Japanese Imperial military that cut a violent swath through East and Southeast Asia and the
Pacific islands in the 1940s.

I am a gook, even though I did not do battle alongside Filipino soldiers
when the Japanese military invaded the island nation that had been an
American colony for the first half of the 20th century.

I am a gook, even though I was not around when European imperial
powers carved up a weakened China in the mid-19th century.

I am a gook, even though I was not among the desperate men fleeing
the Pearl River Delta region of southeastern China for the lure of gold in
California in the late 1840s and early 1850s.

I am a gook, even though I did not suffer from the virulent bigotry of
white Californians who beat and killed Chinese men for working the gold
fields, building the transcontinental railroads, toiling in the farm lands and

in low-level city jobs such as operating laundries or peddling vegetables or handling explosives during the last half of the 19th century.

I am a gook, even though I was not personally excluded from legal entry into the United States because of the Chinese Exclusion Act of 1882, which was passed by a hateful U.S. Congress, goaded on by hateful white union leaders, politicians, and editors.

I am a gook, even though I did not have to pay extra taxes on my business or bribe politicians and policemen for the right to earn a living from the mid-19th century to the mid-20th century.

I am a gook, even though I was not Vincent Chin, who was beaten to death in 1982 with a baseball bat by a couple of white Detroit autoworkers who mistook him for being Japanese at a time when the American auto industry scapegoated Japanese automakers.

I am a gook, even though I was not among the young school children killed or wounded by Patrick Edward Purdy in the 1989 Stockton schoolyard massacre.

I am a gook, even though I was not Jim (Ming Hai) Loo, who was killed in 1989 by two white North Carolina brothers who thought he and his friends were Vietnamese.

I am a gook, even though I never raised funds for the Democratic Party from rich Indonesians.

I am a gook, even though I have never worked for the Los Alamos National Laboratory and never spied for China.

I am a gook, even though I was born in Oakland, California, and lost my primary language (a Chinese dialect). I knew I needed English to survive in this often intolerant society. I was thus unable to fully communicate with my immigrant parents before they died after devoting their adult lives to rearing seven children to be productive citizens of the United States.

7 Class

Yin and Yang

Picking on the Most Vulnerable

Nieman Reports, Summer 1999

During the Congressional debate over welfare reform in 1996, a new villainous image emerged to supplement that of the old welfare queen. This image was of an elderly Chinese immigrant undeservedly getting Supplemental Security Income (SSI). The foreign-looking senior instead should be supported by his or her middle-class children, not by the U.S. Treasury, the image implied.

Thus was born a new kind of welfare cheat, and that image helped propel the most significant change in social legislation in decades. It was no surprise, then, that welfare reform disproportionately hurt one of the most vulnerable and least powerful groups in our society—needy legal immigrants, including many from Asia.

The mainstream press helped perpetuate this fresh symbol of welfare fraud because, according to journalistic convention, it reports what politicians say. And some politicians were either fed up with real and perceived welfare cheats or spotted a winning issue with virtually no downside—the noncitizen ripping off our system. For the most part, U.S. news organizations played along.

That some Asian Americans abused the old welfare system is a given. Everybody did. But did they earn the ignominy of bearing an unfair brunt of Congressional wrath? Hardly.

When a political and media frenzy reaches fever pitch over something like anti-immigrant sentiments, it is too much for rational voices to

126

overcome. The press either was too impotent or it did very little to put into proper perspective the matter of whether elderly Chinese immigrants are stealing from U.S. taxpayers.

In fact, there are many needy old Asian immigrants who depend on the meager SSI monthly payments to survive, but the combination of conservative political voices and compliant press reports muted the reality. As a result, many Asian newcomers were frightened and confused—and a few even killed themselves—over whether they could depend on a U.S. government safety net to pay for shelter and food.

Ironically, the demonization of old Chinese immigrants was a new twist on press coverage of Asian Americans. Historically, people of Asian descent either have been ignored or have been targets of hostility. The press whipped up political passions against Chinese laborers in the mid- to late 1800s, fueling the acrid political atmosphere that led to the Chinese Exclusion Act of 1882. For the most part, the press did not speak out against the unconstitutional incarceration of 120,000 Japanese Americans during World War II, most of whom were U.S. citizens.

In the postwar era, press coverage of Asian Americans has improved, in part because more Asian Americans are mainstream journalists. But a goodly number of stories about Asian Americans still fall into two major categories—a "model minority" who excels in academics and business or bad guys like gangsters, influence-peddling political contributors, and spies for China. The old SSI-dependent Chinese immigrant joins the latter group of disreputable caricatures.

Immigrant advocates fought back after passage of the 1996 welfare reform act. Massaging the press and the politicians themselves, they were able to counter the cheating-immigrant portrayals with ones of genuinely desperate old people fearing for their lives and a few committing suicide because they had nowhere else to turn. This counter-image swayed enough lawmakers to restore some public-assistance benefits to legal immigrants in 1997. But the fear and confusion spawned by the 1996 battle to "end welfare as we know it" (in the immortal words of President Clinton) remains, according to immigrant advocates.

Let us stipulate that reforming the network of federal public-assistance programs is an extraordinarily complex undertaking and that disseminating clear, factual, and accurate information about this fundamental transformation in social policy is a Herculean task for both government bureaucrats and journalists. Besides, reporting on welfare reform swims against the awesome tide of a culture change in journalism. Many news-rooms in recent years have been feeling marketplace pressures to chase sexy, sensational stories. After all, the competition for readers and view-ers has grown intensely fierce. Thus many news organizations tend to ignore or downplay dull but important sagas like the impact of welfare reform on people who aren't likely to be prime targets of media adver-tisers and who aren't among a newspaper's most fervent readers or a TV station's most loyal viewers.

Compounding the problem is the question of language. The great immi-gration wave of the last third of a century has largely been from Latin America and Asia. Spanish, Chinese, Korean, Vietnamese, Khmer, Taga-log, and other Asian languages and dialects—to say nothing of a little Farsi, Russian, and other European and Middle Eastern languages—are the first languages of millions who have come to America to settle for economic and political reasons. This multiplicity of languages, and the underlying cultures, confounds, frustrates, irritates, and enrages some English-speaking Americans.

When some among this veritable United Nations of American new-comers become dependent on welfare, food stamps, and Medicaid, the challenge to government bureaucrats—and, by extension, the mainstream English-language press—to inform them of whether they remain eligible or whether they should seek work or whether they should cadge off rela-tives and not Uncle Sam becomes as daunting as climbing Mount Ever-est would be for an asthmatic.

For some immigrant advocates, it is simpler to deal with the news media of new immigrant communities than it is with the mainstream English-language press.

In getting the word out about welfare reform to their constituents, Vic-tor Hwang, a staff attorney with the Asian Law Caucus in San Francisco, said he and his colleagues don't use the English-language mainstream news media. His group instead turns to the ethnic media, but even they are lim-ited to middle-class immigrants, Hwang contends. Instead, the Asian Law Caucus has held numerous face-to-face community meetings to educate low-income Asian immigrants about welfare reform.

Karin Wang, a staff attorney and director of the Immigrant Welfare Proj-ect of the Asian Pacific American Legal Center in Los Angeles, said her organization has also concentrated on using the ethnic media because potential clients don't read mainstream newspapers like the *Los Angeles Times*. She noted, however, that some Asian immigrants, such as Cambodians and other Southeast Asians, are harder to reach through even the ethnic press because publications that serve them are not as well developed as Chinese-language newspapers and TV stations.

Despite their wariness of the mainstream English-language news media, immigrant advocates I have talked with say they would like to see more and better coverage of the impact of welfare reform on mostly ethnic minority immigrants. The big untold story, they tell me, is how English-deficient needy immigrants will fare under the new welfare-to-work rules. Welfare recipients now have two years to move from dependency to self-sufficiency. But many Asian immigrants are not proficient enough in English to take advantage of job training programs that are conducted only in English. They also are disadvantaged in seeking then securing jobs that require a high degree of English proficiency.

Overall, the plight of non-English-speaking Asian immigrants who are dependent on public assistance may not be a story of highest priority to a celebrity-hungry news media. But given the heavy hit that legal immigrants took from welfare reform, it would only be fitting to chronicle in depth the continuing obstacles they face in the land of the free and the home of the brave.

New Global Capitalists

Asian Week, November 28, 1997

The fourteen-month political fundraising scandal involving some Asian Americans has largely been framed in racial terms with mainstream journalists and Congressmen conjuring up a new Yellow Peril and Asian American activists screaming racism. While race has been a compelling point of discussion in the controversy, socioeconomic differences among Asians and Asian Americans have taken a back seat. A few Asian American analysts like Professor Ling-chi Wang of the University of California at Berkeley and long-time San Francisco civil rights advocate Henry Der have made clear class distinctions while taking into account the racist effect of mainstream critics.

A national conference organized by Professor Wang about the fundraising scandal put a spotlight on intriguing questions of class divisions in Asian America. These questions expose dirty little secrets about us in ways that a racial-ethnic framework does not.

Discussing class considerations in the Asian American political fundraising story does not mean racial concerns are irrelevant. Indeed, examining class differences within Asian America is necessary to fully understand our community's response to the scandal and, longer term, our political and economic development in the context of today's heightened global relationships.

When one reviews the questionable activities of John Huang, Johnny Chung, Yah Lin "Charlie" Trie, Pauline Kanchanalak, Gene and Nora Lum, and Maria Hsia, it is possible to conclude that here were wealthy and ambitious Asians and Asian Americans who inserted themselves aggressively in the high-stakes world of big-money national and international politics. Your ordinary waiter or garment worker doesn't have the means to buy access to the White House or to purchase a table at a glittery fundraising banquet.

Some Asian Americans implicated thus far were out-and-out hustlers whose only goal, it seems, was to get close to President Clinton for greedy purposes. They could use photos of themselves with Bill and Hillary to impress business partners—and as grease to cut big business deals for themselves and their friends. They are among the new global capitalists.

Did any of them represent the ordinary, hard-working Asian American worker earning a few bucks an hour sewing designer clothes or serving cheap Chinese grub? I know people who defend John Huang's integrity, and these are people I respect. They say Huang was promoting the Asian American community's political empowerment when he raised millions from Asian Americans (and apparently Asian nationals) on behalf of Clinton and the Democratic National Committee.

It depends on how you define "community." Does "community" mean all Asian Americans, rich, middle class, and poor? Does "community" mean self-anointed "leaders" who purport to speak for all Asian Americans?

Some journalists and Congressmen view Huang wholly differently. To them, he was a bagman for filthy rich Indonesian Chinese like Mochtar and James Riady. More shockingly, a few have all but accused him of being a Chinese spy. Without a full adjudication of the allegations against Huang, one cannot be certain what his motives were—to help the Asian American downtrodden move up the economic ladder or his wealthy associates gain business advantages.

Johnny Chung's motives appear clearer. Described as a "hustler" by a Clinton administration official, Chung apparently was eager to get close to the Clintons for photo ops. He reportedly pressed a $50,000 check into the wary hands of an aide to Hillary Rodham Clinton, with the exhortation, "You take! You take!"

At the same time, there were many middle-class Asian Americans who gave modestly to the Clinton campaign because, presumably, they believed he and the Democratic Party would best represent their political interests and those of the voiceless poor and working-class Asian Americans and Asian legal immigrants. It is this group that should be most aggrieved—and that has been silenced because criticism of their rich race-mates could be adversely used by outside journalistic and Congressional critics.

Somewhere in the middle was the handful of Asian American Democratic Party activists who have gotten enmeshed in the scandal. This group, like other semi-exiled Democrats, was ecstatic at Clinton's 1992 victory. These activists, at that time, were hopeful that Clinton would appoint them and their associates to administration jobs, a standard entree into national political power. Many, if not most, of the activists had strong links to or affinity for grassroots Asian Americans. They didn't necessarily represent Asian transnational capitalists. But they got caught in a classic vise—the big money game of global amoralists and the cries for empowerment of the lower classes.

As we know now, Clinton was motivated by fear and sheer ambition to escalate fundraising activities for his reelection campaign in 1996. The Republican Revolution in 1994, taking control of Congress, scared him silly. So he turned up the heat on his campaign staff (John Huang, among them) to raise more money, no matter what.

Perhaps the Asian American Democratic activists sensed that this was one clear route to political legitimacy for them and the "community" they purportedly represented, because everyone knew that Asian American votes were negligible nationally. They knew one doesn't quickly raise millions of dollars from small donors. A hundred bucks? Feggedaboutit. Come up with a hundred thou and you can share a cup of joe with the prez.

It was the moneyed Asians and Asian Americans who got wooed and who got to smile sweetly next to Bill and Hillary as flashbulbs popped—the folks who, if anything, could be oppressors of working- and lower-class Asian immigrants and Asian Americans. It was on behalf of grassroots Asian Americans that the party activists wanted to help by bringing their issues to the attention of the president. But the activists had to usher in the amoral rich Asians and Asian Americans because they have the kind of money that really impresses presidents who desperately want to win reelection.

An Obnoxious Status Quest

Asian Week, September 10, 1998

It is generally thought that American public schools aren't very good. They're not educating our kids well. Test scores are lousy. Kids are graduating without really knowing how to write or read well or much about math or science. Those are cruel generalizations, to be sure, but they hold sway in our political culture. Otherwise, we wouldn't have as many politicians making promises to "fix our schools." Otherwise, there wouldn't be so much talk of allowing public funds to be spent in private schools. In short, public schools have become a favorite whipping boy of the elite political class.

Schools are no trifling matter to Asian Americans. The model minority stereotype that adheres to Asian Americans like Elmer's glue is rooted in the drive of many Asian American parents securing the best educational opportunities for their children. Asian Americans are not the only Americans who revere education as a vehicle of future success for their children, but somehow our public persona, such as it is, is enveloped by educational ambitions.

Some Asian Americans say they detest the model minority stereotype, as I myself have too, but it does seem strange for us to collectively deny what otherwise should be a positive human attribute—the striving for knowledge. Or maybe I am missing the point. Perhaps many of us, Asian Americans or not, aren't really striving for knowledge. What we strive for is status and position and wealth and power that high educational achievements can bring. Again, Asian Americans aren't alone in this status quest, but we seem to stand out in this upwardly mobile climb.

While I see nothing wrong—and a lot that is right—about seeking out the best for our children educationally, I am turned off by the preening obnoxiousness one sometimes sees among upper-crust Asian Americans who boast of all the Ivy League schools their children attend. I realize such a boast plays out an Asian cultural trait of how an individual can bring honor to his or her family. When my son does something well and wins public validation, I feel great pride. Maybe I am deluding myself into thinking that my particular brand of reflected glory is significantly different and less obnoxious than the brand I see in wealthy, status-conscious suburban Asian Americans.

Well-to-do Americans, whether of Asian descent or not, will generally fare well educationally. The sad truth is that socioeconomic status is one of the major determining factors of whether a young person gets a good education or not. The other major factor is race. Class and race together account for the quality, or lack of quality, in our public schools.

Take California's recent experience in setting educational policy through the initiative process. The battle over bilingual education was reported to be between brown and yellow immigrant communities versus white-bread Americans. That was too simplistic a picture. Looking beyond the obvious, the Proposition 227 war was one between the haves and have-nots. Race and ethnicity weren't absent. It's just that class wasn't considered enough.

The class dimension of the bilingual-education debate got lost in the political rhetoric over 227. Kenji Hakuta, a Stanford education professor and expert on bilingual education, pointed out at a 227 forum before the election that 80 percent of the limited-English proficient (LEP) students in California were poor. Of the Asian LEP students, about 50 percent were poor. So maybe it wasn't just inadequate bilingual programs that held back LEP students from moving fluidly into English-instruction classrooms.

Over the past year, I have had occasion to visit some school districts in both northern and southern California. The class-race characteristics were obvious, not subtle. In Compton and Inglewood, two low-income cities adjacent to Los Angeles, the ten schools I saw were in pretty bad shape physically. But I couldn't help noticing the racial and ethnic makeup of the student population—predominantly brown and black. In visits to schools in Los Gatos, Saratoga, and Portola Valley—upscale towns near filthy rich Silicon Valley in northern California—the contrast was remarkable: predominantly white with some Asians.

In fact, Asian Americans are on both sides—the haves and the have-nots. I wouldn't say my old high school in Oakland is in the same socio-economic class as Compton or Inglewood, but it is nowhere near the haughty status of Los Gatos or Saratoga High Schools. What one sees at today's Oakland High School is a student population that is about 60 percent Asian, many of them limited-English proficient immigrants. But Oakland High also has American-born Asian Americans whose English language skills are somewhat deficient, being children of Chinese-speaking immigrants.

On the other side of the equation, Asian American "haves" populate schools in high-income communities like San Marino, Hillsborough, Los Gatos, Saratoga, Cupertino, Orinda, Moraga, and Piedmont.

Public schools have become a political whipping boy in the late 1990s. There are no quick fixes, folks, whether it be abolition of bilingual or affirmative action programs, or whatever. If Americans are intent on improving public education, we will have to find sensible and acceptable ways of truly equalizing opportunities so struggling families will have a chance at what well-to-do families take for granted: an educational system that serves their needs and, presumably, the needs of our society.

The Rich Can Be Nice Too

San Francisco Examiner, December 27, 1996

Here's the flip side to the current impression that wealthy Asian Americans made questionable political contributions out of greedy motives:

Charles B. Wang, head of a Long Island, New York, computer software company called Computer Associates International, made big news when he donated $25 million to the State University of New York at Stony Brook for a high-tech Asian American Culture Center.

Wang's story is quintessentially the American Dream: an 8-year-old immigrant fleeing with his parents in 1952 from a war-ravaged Shanghai;

settling in Queens, New York, with not a whit of English; a precocious immersion experience in which he quickly learned English; hard work and hard studying through Queens College; a risk-taking adventure in 1976 into the high-tech entrepreneurial world; and voila! twenty years later, a company with nine thousand employees in forty countries with $3.5 billion in revenue.

Wang told NBC Nightly News anchor Tom Brokaw he never thought about becoming "a very rich man in America." "I just wanted to survive in this country," Wang said. Level-headed about what he has accomplished thus far in life, Wang said he felt his achievements were "markers in the road. . . . I enjoy the journey more than getting somewhere. I tell my people over and over again, enjoy the journey because when you get there, big deal. . . . Push back the goal posts because you don't really want to say, I'm here now, and that's it. That's when we die."

For a man who's made a fortune in high technology, Wang is surprisingly skeptical about the long-term value of technology. He advises us not to make technology an end in itself. It is merely a tool, he suggests, to address real-world problems. Wang sees his proposed Asian American Culture Center as a multicultural vehicle to explore "ideas about East-West approaches to medicine, science, business, engineering and many other fields," including many forms of cultural arts. Its ultimate goal, he indicated, was to break down cultural barriers that divide us. "A central lesson I have learned from my parents is that mankind is well served when everyone does what he or she can to make the world a little bit better," Wang said.

Charles B. Wang hasn't been the only wealthy Asian or Asian American who has contributed to his community. Last year, Gordon Wu, a Hong Kong-based billionaire businessman, announced a $100 million gift and challenge grant to Princeton University's School of Engineering. Wu is a graduate of that school.

In the San Francisco Bay Area, Edward W. Chin, who grew up in Oakland's Chinatown, gave $250,000 earlier this year to help the Oakland Asian Cultural Center finish off its auditorium. "I've been fortunate to make money," Chin said. "I knew they needed money to finish the auditorium so they could become self-sufficient. So I said, 'OK, how much?'"

Exploiting Our Own

Asian Week, June 21, 1996

You need some new clothes, and you don't want to pay full retail. So you haul off to a suburban discount mall and troll Wal-Mart, The Gap, Eddie Bauer outlet stores, among others. Hey, great prices, great bargains! Look, here's a line of Kathie Lee Gifford's clothing. Same with Michael Jordan and Jaclyn Smith. Let's stock up!

Hunting for bargain-priced clothing with name labels is an American pastime. Does anyone think about who makes the clothes and how much, or little, they are paid? Other than a few human-rights and labor activists, no one—until the great Kathie Lee Gifford sweatshop scandal broke.

Gifford, the famous daytime TV talk-show personality married to the famous ex-football great who is now a famous TV sportscaster, was shocked to learn clothes bearing her famous name were being made by underpaid workers in Honduras and New York City, some of them children. Now she is on a crusade to wipe out sweatshops. Human-rights and labor activists and Labor Secretary Robert Reich are using Gifford's guilt and celebrity to promote the cause of garment-workers' rights.

This is an old story with new legs, thanks to Gifford's born-again social and moral conscience. It is a story familiar to Asians and Asian Americans.

Like many other businesses, the worldwide clothing business is hierarchical. At the top are the retailers (Macy's, Nordstrom, Wal-Mart, J.C. Penney, etc.) and the celebrities who sell their names on clothing lines, people like Kathie Lee Gifford and supermodel Kathy Ireland. At the bottom are the workers, many of whom make very little money under terrible working conditions. In the vast middle are contractors and subcontractors and others who manage to make their share supplying the retailers while, in some cases, exploiting their workers.

Asians and Asian Americans have long played key roles in this loosely knit fabric of relationships. In the U.S. clothing industry, Asians and Asian Americans are rarely found at the top levels. They are mostly players in the middle and lower levels.

In the Kathie Lee case, a 15-year-old Honduran immigrant girl, during a well-covered Capitol Hill press conference, pointed accusatory fingers at her South Korean employers, owners of a New York City sweatshop that turned out clothes for Wal-Mart carrying the Kathie Lee label. Wendy Diaz said her Korean supervisors insulted workers and yelled at them to work faster. She also accused them of sexual harassment. If Diaz is to be believed, an Asian middleman appears to be an exploiter.

In another well-publicized case, a San Francisco Chinese middleman supplied clothes for the famous designer Jessica McClintock. The contractor, however, owed his workers back pay and an Oakland-based group, Asian Immigrant Women Advocates, carried on an ultimately successful high-profile three-year campaign to get McClintock to make good. Here, it was a matter of Asians helping exploit other Asians and other Asians speaking out for the exploited Asians.

Women and children on the bottom rungs of the clothing business, the people who actually sew and stitch the apparel that are sold in fancy and discount retailers with famous names on the labels, are immigrants. More often than not, they are Asian and Latino.

For Asian Americans, sweatshops are a difficult and complex issue. You have immigrants who become contractors and subcontractors, small business owners who want to gain an economic toehold in Gold Mountain. Then you have other immigrants who are exploited workers, toiling away for long hours in lousy, filthy, unhealthy warrens, many at less than minimum wages. They too have an American Dream.

Labor, human- and civil rights activists among Asian Americans side with the workers. Middle-class moderates and conservatives lean toward the contractors and subcontractors.

How can you not feel the most sympathy for the most exploited, yet who among us, including Kathie Lee Gifford, can claim the moral high ground in a culture that revels in cheap materialism?

8 Affirmative Action

The Myth of Meritocracy

Between a Rock and a Hard Place

Asian Week, October 9, 1992

Are Asian Americans part of affirmative action programs? Should Asian Americans be part of affirmative action programs?

Those questions, and more, were indirectly raised by an agreement between the University of California at Berkeley's Boalt Hall law school and the federal government over the school's controversial admissions policies from 1988 to 1990. The U.S. Education Department's Office of Civil Rights (OCR) felt that Boalt violated federal civil rights laws and the 1978 Supreme Court Bakke decision that banned specific quotas in college admissions. Boalt officials denied "inconsistencies" in its admissions policies but signed the agreement with OCR anyway because the school believes it can administratively change its policies to satisfy the OCR, rather than to contest the government's findings in court. Within this bureaucratic and legalistic settlement are political and philosophic questions that affect Asian Americans.

Affirmative action has become a hotly debated issue in our society. Affirmative action programs were created to implement the civil rights laws of the 1960s. They were intended to correct past discrimination in employment and to equalize workplace opportunities for all people, not just those privileged by elite educations and class status.

What started righteously got caught in contentious politics, white-male backlash, and a shrinking economy, which triggers intergroup jealousies, conflicts, and fears. Some affirmative action programs also make some

138

program beneficiaries feel inferior, as though they were not worthy other than their special racial-minority status. At first, affirmative action programs were targeted to help African Americans but have helped other disempowered groups, especially white women.

The white-male backlash was personified by Allan Bakke, a white man who sued the University of California at Davis medical school, accusing it of reverse discrimination. The medical school at the University of California at Davis had set aside sixteen admission slots for certain racial minorities (not Asian Americans) whose qualifications were judged separately from the white and Asian-American applicants.

Denied admission, Bakke alleged his grade-point-average and medical-school qualifying test scores were higher than some of those affirmative action admissions. The Supreme Court ruled in his favor, saying the specific set-aside slots were illegal but also saying race can be a factor in admissions and hiring decisions. Since then, public- and private-sector institutions have continued some form of affirmative action but have abolished quotas.

The white-male backlash hasn't gone away. The battles rage on in the courts and workplaces over attempts by top officials to further integrate previously all-white-male police and fire departments and university faculties.

Ethnic politics were inevitable. The moral goal of equal opportunity clashed with natural instincts of those in power to preserve their privileges. In an expanding economy, affirmative action programs are generally tolerated. In a constricting economy, ethnic line-drawing and power plays take over because affirmative action programs, if they are enforced, can reduce potential jobs and admissions for white men.

In a law or medical school, the balancing act between promoting diversity and not discriminating against anyone is extremely difficult. At Boalt, one of the nation's finest law schools, officials have tried over the past several decades to increase the number of racial-minority and women students without resorting to strict quotas. Boalt got into trouble with the OCR over its separate waiting lists for African Americans, Latinos, Asian Americans (except for Japanese Americans), and Native Americans.

Most university admissions policies are a combination of so-called objective criteria (test scores and grade point averages) and other factors, such as racial-ethnic diversity, age, geography, special talents (artists, athletes), and heritage (your dad and grand-dad were alumni). The same is true for Boalt. Every year, Boalt gets 5,000 to 6,000 applications for the school's 270 slots. Some applications are administratively accepted because of exceptional test scores. Others are dismissed for opposite reasons. A middle group of possible admissions is referred to committees made up of one student and one faculty member.

At this stage, all racial and ethnic groups are treated the same. The problem the federal government had was the separate waiting lists for the four ethnic groups. All schools admit more students than they have room for. That's because some students admitted don't enroll. The waiting lists come into play when the school must fill slots turned down by those initially admitted but who don't enroll. Students ranked in the waiting lists were judged against only other students on the same list. Boalt officials said that they would sometimes choose a lower-ranked student on one list over a higher-ranked student on another list to fulfill the school's overall diversity goals. That was a no-no to OCR officials.

As part of the agreement with the OCR, Boalt officials said they are considering procedural changes including the abolition of separate committees to examine one minority group's applications. A probable change would be committees that looked over an integrated application pool at random. The school said it had already done away with separate waiting lists.

The OCR felt that Boalt relied too much on a racial criterion—Boalt denies it did—but school officials indicate they're looking at giving more weight to other factors, such as socioeconomic status, quality of undergraduate education, age, gender, and geography as part of the admissions formula.

The OCR's letter of findings was carefully worded and legalistic. It did not accuse the law school of using quotas. But Michael L. Williams, the education department's assistant secretary for civil rights, asserted in numerous press interviews he felt the school had illegally used quotas. Quota has become a buzzword for Bush Administration officials. President Bush criticized the 1991 Civil Rights Act as being a quota bill, when the act specifically outlaws quotas. The assumption of affirmative action critics is that those given college admissions or jobs because of these special considerations somehow aren't "qualified."

The dichotomy between "affirmative action" and "qualifications" is false and disingenuous. Mistakes have been made when unqualified people have gotten jobs under an affirmative action imperative over better-qualified people. But, in general, racial minorities and women who get special consideration in affirmative action programs are qualified to hold those jobs or be admitted to a college. That is clearly the case with Boalt's minority and women students. The OCR finding never alleged that minority and women students enrolled at Boalt under the school's affirmative action program weren't qualified.

Conservative Republicans have waged a holy war over the past decade against affirmative action programs. Cynically and hypocritically, conservative whites have used conservative blacks, Latinos, and Asian Americans—themselves beneficiaries of Republican affirmative action programs (Clarence Thomas comes to mind)—to criticize and belittle liberal and progressive positions.

One perpetrator is a conservative Republican Representative from Huntington Beach in southern California, Dana Rohrabacher, who prodded the OCR to investigate Boalt's admissions policies. No student claimed any harm from Boalt's admissions policies. Rohrabacher complained in part on behalf of Asian Americans, who have gotten caught in the crossfire of the volatile affirmative action wars.

Rohrabacher's office churns out press releases reflecting the Congressman's valiant defense of Asian Americans who, he says, feel discriminated against by affirmative action programs that principally help African Americans, Latinos, and perhaps Native Americans. To some Asian Americans, Rohrabacher is a hero, a stolid defender of purported injustices against Asian Americans. But I suspect Rohrabacher's real target is black and Latino Americans whom he considers to be less qualified than white and Asian Americans.

It is noteworthy that the OCR finding in the Boalt case doesn't accuse the school of discriminating against Asian Americans, a favorite theme of Rohrabacher's. His statement after the Boalt finding praised the OCR for finding Boalt had used quotas, when the OCR letter never mentioned quotas.

Some affirmative action programs exclude Asian Americans altogether. Reasons vary. In some cases, Asian Americans are statistically "over-represented" in the particular field. Or Asian Americans are invisible, or have no political clout to demand equal justice. Or Asian Americans aren't thought to have been victimized by discrimination. At Boalt, all Asian

Americans except for Japanese Americans were part of the 23–27 percent minority admissions goal.

Henry Der, executive director of San Francisco's Chinese for Affirmative Action, feels that Asian Americans have benefited from Boalt's program. He said he doesn't believe Asian Americans would do as well in an open admissions competition because the LSAT (law school aptitude test) doesn't have a mathematics component. It emphasizes English analytical and comprehension skills. The SAT (scholastic aptitude test) for undergraduate admissions gives equal weight to math and English comprehension. In general, Asian Americans usually do proportionately better in math than in English, Der said.

Large philosophical questions emerge for Asian Americans, many of whom believe in the merit system—that is, if I do well on a test, or score high grades, I should be rewarded with admission to a prestigious university. I believe in the merit system too, until one discovers that not everyone plays by these same rules, that privilege, class, and heritage count for more than test scores. Many Asian American students and scholars delude themselves into believing in the merit system.

I am not arguing against achieving high scores or doing well in school. We should think about our society and whether high test scores are the only criterion upon which we should be judged. Are there competing values of equal merit, such as equal justice and equality of opportunity?

We should be alert to snakes in the grass who claim meritorious achievement is the only way to get admitted to college or to get a plum job. In many workplaces still, it's politics and who you know and what school you went to—connections, juice, influence, alumni status, social standing—that still count more than merit. Asian Americans ought to be concerned about being used for the nefarious purposes of maintaining white-male privilege.

Furthermore, Henry Der makes a cogent point. Since the law school at the University of California at Berkeley is publicly subsidized, why shouldn't its students reflect the range of California taxpayers, who come in all colors and socioeconomic classes? And why should a taxpayer-subsidized law school create lawyers only for the corporate ruling class?

Calling for Magician Administrators

Oakland Tribune, July 25, 1995

In the near future, University of California administrators will have to become magicians to comply with new policies set by the regents of the world-famous public university system. These new policies, passed after a tumultuous twelve-hour meeting, state the university should reflect California's "diversity." To reach that goal, administrators cannot use race, ethnicity, or gender.

Hmm. Let's review that imperative. Diversify the university's student, staff, and faculty population and business contracting practices but don't use racial, ethnic, or gender criteria.

Candidates for the University of California president's job, which will become vacant soon with incumbent Jack Peltason's retirement, will have to have considerable magical skills.

The regents created their Alice-in-Wonderland world in defiance of reality. California and the United States aren't yet free of racial, ethnic, and gender considerations. One wishes we could be, perhaps, but we aren't there yet.

The powerful, unelected governing board of the widely admired university system kowtowed to Governor Pete Wilson's presidential ambitions. As dissident regents and others pointed out, there was no educational urgency to do away with affirmative action practices that take into account race, ethnicity, and gender.

From Wilson's perspective, there is political urgency. He needs to keep alive his candidacy for the Republican presidential nomination and one of his planks is to abolish affirmative action programs, a popular stance among Republicans.

To further his goals, he made a rare appearance at a regents meeting to support his close friend Ward Connerly's proposals to do away with racial, ethnic, and gender considerations from university decisions in admitting students, hiring faculty and staff, and awarding business contracts.

The governor won, but that was predictable, considering the fact eighteen of the twenty-six regents were either appointed or reappointed by him or former Republican Governor George Deukmejian.

"This is a sad day in the history of the University of California," said Delaine Eastin, a regent by virtue of her position as state superintendent of public instruction. "This rush to judgment is a terrible mistake."

The regents heard six hours of public testimony, including that of the Reverend Jesse Jackson, a possible Democratic candidate for president. But the majority of regents were not swayed by pro–affirmative action voices.

State Senator Diane Watson, an African American, noting that the University of California is taxpayer supported, said if the university "reverted to an all white and Asian institution, why should taxpayers support it?"

Colleen Sabatini, a white student at the University of California at San Diego, asked the regents, "Why are you attacking a solution and not the problem?" She said her campus has few African Americans, Latinos, and Native Americans. "I am being denied learning and living in a multi-cultural [environment]."

Regent Tom Sayles, who voted against Connerly's proposals, said, "We have not progressed to the point of declaring victory over racism." He cited his own experience as an African American man from South Central Los Angeles, a Harvard graduate, and a corporate attorney. "My modest success hasn't insulated even me from racial insults and prejudices."

State Senator Tom Hayden made a cogent point. "We need to reframe this debate to focus on the loss of educational opportunity instead of a Darwinian rationing of seats." He lamented the "disastrous downsizing of higher education in our state."

Eastin, the state schools superintendent, complemented Hayden's message when she challenged Governor Wilson "to put his money where his mouth is," regarding improving the kindergarten-to-twelfth-grade system to better prepare African American and Latinos to compete on their own at the University of California. Angrily, she said, "The governor hasn't done anything to implement K–12 funding." Instead, Eastin said, his recent budgets emphasize building prisons. "The best crime prevention is an education," she said.

For University of California administrators, the immediate task is to suddenly become color- and gender-blind in a state teeming with racial and gender issues. Outgoing University of California President Peltason said achieving greater diversity without considering race and gender is going to be "more difficult." Regent Ralph Carmona was more direct. "It's impossible not to take in ethnic factors" when attempting to diversify the university. "There is no way you can get around it."

Meanwhile, one wonders whether the California Constitution needs to be amended to accommodate the regents' new color-blind policies. Article 9, Section 9, paragraph (d) states: "Regents shall be able persons broadly reflective of the economic, cultural and social diversity of the State, including ethnic minorities and women."

The Selfish Versus the Altruists

Oakland Tribune, July 26, 1995

A fascinating aspect of the University of California (UC) affirmative action debate is the role of Asian Americans. In fact, Asian Americans are on both sides of the debate. That was more than evident at the UC regents' meeting where affirmative action policies were abolished.

Two of the regents voting to eliminate race, ethnic, and gender considerations in UC's admissions, hiring, and business contracting practices are of Asian descent, David S. Lee and S. Stephen Nakashima, both Republican appointees. A former regent who is of Asian descent, Yori Wada, pleaded with his erstwhile colleagues not to significantly change the university's affirmative action policies.

For the most part, Asian Americans have not benefited from UC's affirmative action admissions policies, which are aimed at increasing the numbers of African American, Latino, and Native American students.

Most of the Asian Americans admitted to UC's eight undergraduate campuses have gotten in through high grades and test scores. In the last school year, Asians made up 39 percent of UC-Berkeley's undergraduates. At all eight campuses, they were 35 percent of the undergraduates. Those two figures more than double the percentage of Asian Americans in California's high schools. On that basis alone, Asian Americans shouldn't have any complaints about getting into UC.

But some have a gripe. Chinese Americans and other Asian Americans who have been denied admittance to UC-Berkeley or UCLA despite high grades and test scores have not been happy. Some feel they have been discriminated against and blame affirmative action policies.

The Berkeley and Los Angeles campuses, UC's most popular, are the toughest to get into. Berkeley doesn't have enough freshman slots to accommodate all the straight-A students who are eligible, regardless of race or ethnicity.

All UC undergraduate schools have used a combination of high grades and test scores along with "supplementary criteria" to admit students. Those supplementary criteria have included race, ethnicity, and gender, as well as socioeconomic status. Thus, UC admissions policies and practices have not been based solely on "merit" or on "racial preferences." The goal has been to reflect the state's incredible diversity from the eligible pool of the top 12.5 percent of California high school graduates.

That is another key point. Those African American, Latino, and Native Americans admitted with some consideration to race and ethnicity are eligible for UC by virtue of being in the top 12.5 percent of their high school classes. The rub comes when, on average, the grade-point averages and test scores of African American and Latino students admitted are lower than those of white or Asian students.

Those who don't like affirmative action say "individual merit" should be the guiding criterion for UC admittance. Those who like affirmative action say it's important for a public institution supported by all taxpayers to serve all the people of California, not just an elite few.

Those polar perspectives emerged at the regents' meeting. Nakashima, a San Jose attorney, recalled being a victim of racial discrimination when he and other Japanese Americans were locked away in camps during World War II. That is why he doesn't like UC's affirmative action policies, because they discriminate against some people, he said.

Lee, a Chinese immigrant who is now a Milpitas high-tech businessman, said he doesn't like to be looked on as a "member of a race." He said, "I like people to judge me as an individual."

Wada, the former regent, also invoked past racial discrimination against himself and other Japanese Americans but said as a past beneficiary of affirmative action, he supported its principle of "inclusion." He added that UC's affirmative action policies were a "living symbol" of the university and the people of California.

Henry Der, executive director of Chinese for Affirmative Action and a longtime analyst of California higher education trends, cited UC figures that said a higher percentage of white and Asian applicants get admitted than African American and Latino applicants. He also said a majority of Asian American applicants admitted to UC-Berkeley don't actually enroll there.

"Where is the perceived harm to Asians in gaining access and admissions to the university?" he asked rhetorically, in urging the regents to retain affirmative action. "If Asian American students were to attend certain UC campuses that are exclusively Asian and white, such segregated education would not prepare Asian American students to assume leadership positions in a multiracial California society."

This debate can be characterized as the "meritocrats" versus the "social engineers." But it can also be called a battle between the selfish and the altruists.

When Values Collide

San Francisco Examiner, March 3, 1999

When two laudable values collide, does anyone really come out ahead? I am frankly hard put to answer definitively in the aftermath of the settlement of the San Francisco schools desegregation case, also known as the "Lowell case."

This case has been exquisitely painful for Chinese Americans who support a traditional civil rights agenda that seeks to desegregate American society and to provide equal opportunities for Americans who have been discriminated against because of segregation. In the context of the times, that meant mostly African Americans.

That is one admirable goal placed under scrutiny in the Lowell case. The other is equal treatment under the law. The two goals have been at odds in the years since San Francisco schools were ordered by a federal judge in 1983 to desegregate. The judge was responding to a suit brought by the National Association for the Advancement of Colored People on behalf of poor black children in San Francisco.

In the intervening years, the number of Chinese American schoolchildren has increased, giving rise to allegations of unequal treatment of Chinese American students under the desegregation plan as devised by the

San Francisco Unified School District to remedy the discriminatory treat-
ment against poor black children. The so-called discrimination against
Chinese Americans was most telling at the city's prestigious Lowell High
School, according to critics of the desegregation plan.

Some Chinese American parents sued the school district, and the parties recently settled the case. Beyond the specifics of the settlement and
the effect on individuals, the Lowell case conjures up issues that are gut-
wrenching to address without resorting to tired clichés of both liberal and
conservative persuasions.

For one, the case pits Chinese American liberal advocates of poor black,
Latino, and Asian American children against Chinese American conservative defenders of middle-class Chinese American children.

Were Chinese American liberals abandoning their own ethnic group
in favor of black and Latino interests? Were Chinese American conservatives acting only in their own interests without regard for the well-being
of all San Francisco schoolchildren?

Is the kind of plan the San Francisco school district came up with to
integrate the schools—busing and imposition of quotas by racial and ethnic category—workable in a city of such breathtaking racial and ethnic
diversity and whose racial and ethnic demographics change from year to
year?

What better way is there to close the gap between middle-class privilege and opportunities and lower-class despair and isolation?

Is integration as a societal value still worthy of our attention?

Should entry to elite institutions like Lowell High be based mostly or
solely on "merit," as defined by grade-point averages and test scores? And
if a "meritocracy" means a student body that is predominantly white and
Asian American, does that bother a society that is otherwise more diverse?

Is it fair to ask Chinese Americans, who themselves have been victims
of racial discrimination by American institutions, to sacrifice their opportunities in order to support plans designed to help disadvantaged African
Americans?

Chinese Americans and other Asian Americans are "over-represented"
in certain educational institutions (such as Lowell and the University of
California at Berkeley), but has that led to equality of opportunities for
them to attain leadership positions in society at large?

Who should take responsibility for improving the educational readiness of poor and working-class black, Latino, and Asian American children—parents, community, or the schools?

No clear-cut answer has emerged to satisfy all the tangled interests involved. All I know is that self-interests are forever battling with self-sacrifice. It may be superhuman to ask each of us to give something up for the good of all of us.

9 Gender

He Said, She Said

The "Hottest" Dating Trend

Asian Week, December 14, 1990

Here is the status of racial-sexual politics as it relates to Asian Americans and white Americans, according to one theorist:

- Some white men covet Asian women because they (the men) can't deal with strong, independent white women.
- Some Asian women prefer white men because they (the women) can't stand the more sexist Asian men.
- Some white women feel rejected by white men who covet Asian women.
- Some Asian men also feel rejected because they see Asian women preferring white men and they (Asian men) can't seem to get the time of day from white women.
- It is seemingly impossible for white women and Asian men to become romantically linked because strong, independent white women— the epitome of feminism—can't possibly stand Asian men, who are apparently the most sexist of sexists.

This is the blueprint of the "hottest" interracial dating "trend," as reported by Joan Walsh in the December 2 issue of *Image* magazine of the Sunday *San Francisco Examiner*. This confusing and narrow scenario leaves out a whole world of other cross-cultural relationships that are as real and certainly more profound than the kinds of sexual-racial couplings in Walsh's article.

150

Did Walsh and *Image* magazine sensationalize and trivialize the phenomenon of Asian women–white men couplings, and did they perpetuate stereotypes, or does the vehement and emotional response to the story, especially among Asian Americans of both sexes and some white women, reflect denial of dark truths about relations between the sexes and races? Probably a little bit of both.

Walsh's story struck a deep emotional chord among San Francisco Bay Area Asian Americans and other Bay Area residents. The topic of interracial romance sets off sparks because it is inherently provocative. It is enmeshed in age-old stereotypes and differences among men and women and various racial and cultural groups.

The emotional negative response reflects in part the frustration among some people of color over how the white-controlled media define and portray minority communities. Walsh and *Image* are the latest lightning rods for this frustration.

Some have criticized the quality of journalism, but the journalism question is a relative quibble. My most serious concerns are with the shockingly superficial attitudes of people Walsh quotes. The problem is more with the message, not the messenger.

Whether the Asian women–white men phenomenon is the "hottest" interracial trend is a debatable point. Walsh, in two conversations with me, expressed confidence that she's identified such a trend. The statistics she cites—mostly from Sonoma State University professor Larry Shinagawa—indicate that the so-called outmarriage rate of Asian women to white men far exceeds that of Asian men to white women.

Besides, Walsh emphatically asserted, many people she interviewed said to her privately that they see a lot of white men dating Asian women. She's on solid ground here, but it's not new ground. Walsh concedes that this trend is old, but with a new visibility, because of the growth of the Asian American population. The new twist, according to her, is that with more Asian-white romances in an era of interracial uncertainty, the most notable aspect of that trend (Asian women–white men) generates heat and tension.

In the diverse Asian American communities, especially those with third- and fourth-generation members, interracial dating and marriages are a reality. The quality of those interracial relationships ranges widely, from troubled to copacetic.

But these relationships should be discussed in much more profound terms than Walsh's sources appear to be capable of doing. They are pre-occupied with superficial factors, especially the white men, so much so that I still can't fathom how any of these people can carry on long-term, multifaceted relationships with anyone. Whatever happened to commitment, respect, compatibility, flexibility, a sense of humor, rather than the flimsiest of reasons to get together: racial-sexual stereotypes and physical appearances?

The truth about interracial romances is elusive. Walsh said her intent was to focus on white men seeking out Asian women and vice versa. Within this limited universe, the messages of the people she quotes—white men who prefer Asian women, Asian women who prefer white men, a white women threatened by Asian women, several Asian women who prefer Asian men, and several Asian men who lament their lowly social status—appear to be honest expressions, but they are most disturbing.

The subliminal messages of these people reflect (1) white-male fantasies, (2) subtle and not so subtle Asian bashing, and (3) the utter superficiality of values with which they engage in relationships.

What's missing is a discussion of Asian men having long-term relationships with white women. I say this not only because I happen to be in this situation—and I know others who are—but because the impression left by Walsh's sources is that (1) white women feminists have driven white men into the arms of compliant and more submissive Asian women, and (2) Asian men have little, if any, physical attraction to anyone and certainly little of cultural value because they're so sexist.

Walsh said she was writing about the Asian women–white men trend, not about any other kind. But is this particular "trend" truly so significant, or is it part of a larger picture of even more interesting interracial relationships?

Here's why I believe the subliminal messages suggest white-male fantasies and anti-Asian sentiments: Walsh quotes at length three white men who either have dated Asian women or specifically prefer Asian women:

- "Eric" admits to having "a thing" for Asian women's looks: "They have bodies that modern clothes fit really well." According to Eric, Lydia (a Taiwan immigrant, not her real name) was "lured in part by rumors about the sexual endowment of white men—white men are reputedly to Asian men what black men are supposed to be to whites," Walsh wrote. She added, parenthetically, "I heard this piece of folklore from four white men and no Asian women, and I was unable to confirm it personally."

- "Mike Arnold" told Walsh: "I get some breaks from Asian women. Their standards are lower. . . . I have an inferiority complex with white women. . . . I eventually realized that being white, I could make it with an Asian woman who's more physically attractive than I am, just because she's got a cultural inferiority complex."

- "Tom Knight" told Walsh: "I see something of a feminist backlash in [dating Asian women]. . . . I know I feel less threatened by Asian women. . . . I'm more comfortable with Asian culture, where interpersonal relations are more ritualized, and women are graceful, polite and considerate." Speaking of his first Japanese American girlfriend, "Tom Knight" said, "I liked looking at her. She didn't look threatening, mean or sad. She was pretty, but not beautiful—beautiful is threatening too. I thought, I could live with this person. . . . She did a lot for me: She had tea ready when I came home, she scrubbed me in the bathtub. I liked it." This relationship ended. "We couldn't communicate," he told Walsh. "We weren't mental equals. Her whole world was her relationship with me."

Even though Walsh cites stereotyping-busting traits of some Asian women she talked with, such as analytical, articulate, bright, attractive, assertive, overall the Asian women come across as being somewhat pathological. They criticize Asian men for being sexist, for not allowing women to be independent or equal.

The few white women and Asian men represented in Walsh's story come across pathetically. One white woman says she's "threatened" by Asian women, whom she believes embody what men want in an "ideal woman"—small, thin, fragile, almost doll-like, chic, exotic. Another white woman feels sorry for Asian men: "It's Asian men who really get the short end of the stick" because they can't get dates with white women.

Even the one Asian women who for political reasons dates only Asians had very little positive to say about why she's dating Asian men. Instead, according to Walsh, she "reluctantly agrees" that Asian men are more sexist than white men. And the Asian men quoted—three or four students at the University of California at Berkeley—whined about not being able to get dates and criticized Asian women who date white men for having self-contempt. Couldn't Walsh have found some Asian men who have healthy relations with women of whatever racial-ethnic background?

Walsh says that this Asian women–white men trend reflects "cultural anxieties" brought about by the growing racial-ethnic diversity of the country. She maintains that rather than ignore these anxieties and other confusing feelings, we as a society should talk about them openly. Agreed, but there must be a less titillating, more comprehensive approach to examining the diversity of interracial romances.

Special Assets

Oakland Tribune, December 7, 1990

After reading the cover story in a recent Sunday *San Francisco Examiner Image Magazine*, I grew faint. The story was about the "hottest" interracial trend—white men dating Asian women. As an Asian man, a species described in the story as having no appeal to the opposite sex, I envisioned the following conversation:

"Yo, dude, what's wrong?"

The Asian man, his form-fitting black tank top hiding none of his muscular, if lean physique, approached his Asian male buddy, whose thick glasses and "nerd pack" of pens marked him as a left-brain logician.

"Can't get a date," Thick Glasses said. "All the Asian women I know are dating white guys. And white women won't give me the time of day. I thought it was just me, but after that *Image Magazine* piece—boy, am I depressed!"

A third man, also Asian, looking preppy and prosperous, became aroused. "That was a bunch of crap. I've never had problems getting dates."

"That's because you drive a Beemer, man," Black Tank Top said. "Women just like rich guys. I'm not rich, but I've what it takes, you know what I mean?" Black Tank Top flexed his muscles. At a glance, you'd swear the late Bruce Lee, he of the flying feet and quick kung-fu moves, had risen from the dead.

"What do you mean?" Thick Glasses asked.

"Hey, if I have to spell it out—You know, my thing."

"What 'thing'?"

"Jeez, you know, my thing."

Preppy and Prosperous could barely suppress a laugh. "He means, uh, you know, his thing."

Thick Glasses shook his head, then it hit him. He recalled a reference in the *Image* story to how men believe there is a male anatomical pecking order (so to speak), with Asian men supposedly holding white men in high esteem in the same manner that white men hold black men.

"Ah, I get it," Thick Glasses blurted out. "You mean, women really like your, uh, thing!"

"That's right," Black Tank Top smirked.

"I don't believe you," Preppy and Prosperous challenged. "That's all male-fantasy stuff. Women tell me they don't give our *things* much thought. It's men who are fixated with length and sizes of *things*."

Thick Glasses looked puzzled. "You mean Asian women date white guys because guys have longer *things* than we Asian guys?"

"That's what some white guys seem to think," Preppy and Prosperous said.

"I also hear some Asian women like dating white dudes because Asian men are more sexist than white men," Black Tank Top said. "That's baloney too. These white guys are scared off by aggressive white women— you know, feminists. They think Asian women are submissive. They drool at the 'exotic' Asian look."

"These Asian women who date only white guys do so out of self-hatred," Preppy and Prosperous said. "This culture degrades men of color, so Asian women can't stand Asian men, whom they view as weak. Asian men just don't have any value in American culture."

"Yeah," Thick Glasses said. "Look at all those Asian women TV stars— Connie Chung wannabes. Do you see any Asian male TV stars?"

Thick Glasses slumped forward, weariness draped over his shoulders. He lamented, "I just want a date!"

"I've got it," Black Tank Top said. "You're this math-whiz computer genius, right? Why don't you make women an offer they can't refuse? In exchange for a date, you'll teach them how to upgrade their computers or hook up their VCRs. There must some women with a computer-genius fetish out there. It may not be sexy, but, hey, sell your assets, I say."

Thick Glasses thought to himself. "I may not be Tom Cruise or Kevin Costner, but Black Tank Top is right. I've got some value that women will recognize."

He began composing a personals ad for one of those San Francisco alternative weeklies. "Supercharged Asian male with significant asset seeking woman who wants an avant-garde, high-tech experience."

Hiding Behind a Cultural Defense

Asian Week, November 19, 1993

Writing about domestic violence from a male perspective can be an exercise in ignorance and insensitivity. Most, but not all, reported instances of domestic violence are committed by men against women. The issue gets complicated when Asian and Asian American men are involved. Some Asian-born men hide behind a so-called cultural defense when they batter their female partners or spouses.

At the same time, Asian and Asian American men often are made to feel less than equal and without as much value as Asian and Asian American women. Some may subsequently hold grudges and act out their anger on women.

I became much better informed about domestic violence in the Asian American community after I read a study of domestic violence in San Francisco and heard a presentation made by Beckie Masaki, executive director of the Asian Women's Shelter in San Francisco, at a forum sponsored by an Asian American philanthropy coalition.

The study released by the Family Violence Prevention Fund found that 59 percent of all women killed in San Francisco in 1991 and 1992 were victims of family violence. The San Francisco Commission on the Status of Women conducted the study along with the fund, with the collaboration of the San Francisco Police Department. "More women are killed in San Francisco by a husband, boyfriend, or family member than women killed in drug, carjacking, robberies and arguments combined," the study said. "A family violence homicide does not begin with the act of murder. It often begins with years of prior physical and mental abuse of the woman that is illegal and preventable."

The 59 percent figure in the San Francisco study was greater than an FBI statistic that one in three women are killed nationwide because of domestic violence. Jacqueline Agtuca, one of several Asian American women involved in the study, said, "The most dangerous place for a woman in San Francisco is her own home."

Masaki of the Asian Women's Shelter and a board member of the Family Violence Prevention Fund said domestic violence crosses all racial, ethnic, religious, cultural, and socioeconomic lines. Nonetheless, she added, "the solutions toward ending domestic violence must take culture into account to effectively impact the role of violence in the family and to increase community awareness and responsibility."

Masaki said, "We believe the cause of domestic violence is embedded in how societies define and value power and control: the way we are raised. So boys are taught that being powerful means having power over someone else, and being in control means controlling others. Girls are taught that responsibility means putting everyone else's needs before yours, that nurturing and caring means sacrificing yourself for your families, and to give power, not take it. The unequal position of women and men in our societies, the deep patterns and values we were raised with, and the promotion of violence as a solution on every level of our society all create the seeds from which grows domestic violence."

While Asian and Asian American women face the same barriers as all battered women, Masaki said, some factors are magnified and others are unique. Some Asian women who are battered in the United States are isolated because they may not speak English well, if at all, and they may not have friends and family here. Many Asian battered women are "dependent on their batterers for sponsorship in the U.S., and the batterers will use this as another means of control," Masaki explained. American society reinforces the powerlessness felt by many Asian battered women, she added, through racism and cultural and language chasms.

Masaki noted that many Asian cultures value family or community over the individual. This can work both for and against a battered woman. An extended family can be supportive of an abused woman. At the same time, close family ties can inhibit an affected individual from escaping a bad situation.

"Culture is not static," Masaki said, "but for Asians and other groups who face the racism and marginalization of life in the U.S., we cling to 'tradition' and our perceptions of our home cultures. The result can be a 'cultural freeze' in which we . . . perpetuate beliefs that may in fact be outdated or changed in our home countries. . . . This cultural freeze can be destructive. Some Asian Americans attribute equality for women and the laws against domestic violence as western beliefs, and not Asian beliefs." She said the status of women and attitudes about domestic violence are changing in Asian countries. The feminist movement has had worldwide influence.

A New York case a couple of years ago involving an ethnic Chinese couple made national headlines. Using a "cultural defense," the husband got a light sentence for murdering his wife. He said his "culture" considered her alleged adultery to be wrong and therefore he had a right to kill her.

Masaki told me that the so-called cultural defense is often invoked by Asian and Asian American men. She feels it is racist for American society to accept such a cultural defense. She also feels the Asian American community "reinforces domestic violence by minimizing the problem. The Asian community may not want the larger society to use this as yet another negative attribute, and the Asian community may also believe that domestic violence is acceptable because it is 'traditional.'"

Which brings it back to men. Some Asian American men can be torn between two cultures. One is a more traditional unequal male-female relationship. The man is the master, the woman the slave. The other is equality between men and women. It would be incorrect to stereotype Asian immigrant men as holding only to traditional beliefs and Asian American men as "progressive." Both attitudes are likely held to varying degrees by both immigrant and American-born Asian men.

Making matters murkier is the often-perceived lowly status of Asian and Asian American men in American society. Some of us feel devalued and put down by Asian and Asian American women who occupy a higher status than we do in a culture dominated by white men. On the other hand, some Asian and Asian American women feel they have a right to reject us because some of us are control freaks.

Some Asian American men are caught in a double bind. This is certainly no excuse for battering your female partner, but this psychological vise could at least explain why some Asian and Asian American men take out their frustrations and anger at women.

As some Asian and Asian American battered women seek out a shelter like Masaki's, more Asian and Asian American men need to examine the impulses of power and control and the still-unequal relationships some of us have with women in our lives.

This kind of behavior modification is not easy to accomplish. It requires consciousness-raising and courage. It means defying machismo tendencies. It means resisting mass-media, peer-group, and cultural influences that continue to objectify women and glorify manhood.

We must somehow find psychological sustenance to strengthen our own egos, while at the same time not ride roughshod over women who are important to us. This may seem an unfair burden, but we've got to deal with conflicting pressures brought about by forces beyond our control.

It is possible, I feel, to be both "sensitive" and "manly."

The Hero of Asian Men

Asian Week, December 18, 1992

As a self-respecting male of the Asian persuasion, cognizant of tiresome media stereotypes of us as wimps, as having little or no sexuality (except for the ferocious Bruce Lee), I just had to see *The Lover*, a movie, according to its own hype, that features an Asian guy as a live sex object. Not only that, the woman objectifying him is a French teenager. Oh! Forbidden love, across racial, cultural, and generational lines.

Better yet, the story takes place in French colonial Saigon, long before French political and military failures, long before America got involved only to return home, tail between legs (I tell you, these sex films get my prose all aroused), leaving a culture despoiled, women raped, children parentless, and men embittered at the cultural and political imperialism.

But I'm being much too grave. *The Lover* is only a movie, a sweaty, erotic affair, to be sure, which must be its strongest selling point. Nonetheless, from an ethnic, gender, and class perspective, this movie, directed by Jean-Jacques Annaud, bears discussion, for it roils deeply held feelings among Asian American men and women, because a racist and sexist history has divided us and makes us insecure in each other's company.

On one level, *The Lover* is a sensuous trifle, an episode in a long life, a modest memoir. Based on an autobiographical novel by Marguerite Duras, the movie evokes the desperate cultural chasms between French colonialists and the Asians of Saigon. The principal Asian in this case isn't Vietnamese but a dapper dandy of a bored, experienced Chinese man whose refined manner bespeaks a cosmopolitan lifestyle, one that takes him to Paris on a whim. His white-linen suits look, well, cool.

The young Duras character is something else. She's stuck in a rural village in Saigon, living with her teacher mother and two brothers, one an opium addict good-for-nothing who steals to support his dastardly habit, the other a quiet, artistic sort. They define the word *dysfunctional*. And they are relatively poor.

So, here we have a rich Chinese man smitten with this young woman's pubescent beauty, who, without much explanation other than perhaps an attraction to his wealth, covets his body, as he covets hers. In this sense, the movie turns on its head what we might otherwise expect. The French, after all, are the colonialists, the invaders, of Asia. The twist here obviously is that the Asian character is a rich Chinese, a minority in Vietnam. Alas, this inside-out class theme isn't explored in *The Lover*. To do so would have made a completely different kind of a story, not the erotic mood piece that it is. Would there be a story at all, had the man been a schlump, a pauper, someone without money, status, a chauffeured car? I doubt it.

The sex scenes hide little (I guess they aren't fully "pornographic" in that they do not show, you know, *everything*, but they show plenty). They spend every afternoon together in his apartment hideaway in Cholon, Saigon's Chinese district. This is where he has his amorous assignations, for he has no work and no hobbies other than to bed down beauties. The man and his inamorata don't talk much. They just, well, you know. We're talking serious sexual obsession here.

Predictably, their relationship can't last. She eventually ships off to Paris, after the rich Chinese man has helped her groveling family settle some debts and after he gives her his mother's precious diamond ring. Theirs can't be anything more than a hot tropical fling, an awakening experience for a 15-year-old girl (in the movie, perhaps to make it more palatable to general sensibilities, she is eighteen), a deeply impressive experience for a man caught in a cultural and class vise.

Racism on both sides dooms their affair. He knows his culture and class standing make impossible a long-term relationship, or even marriage. During his affair with her, he is about to be married to a woman he's never met. Your classic Chinese arranged marriage. For her part, she says she doesn't like Chinese. Neither does her family. Except he's rich, and thus maybe he can be used. Several times, she asks him if he's ever slept with white women before.

The most unsettling scene for me was the dinner the Chinese man hosted for the girl's family at a fancy French restaurant. He tried to make idle conversation. The girl and her family ignored him. They ate as if they were ravenous animals. The mother poured down good French wine. The girl never looked at her lover. Looking exquisitely bored, she nibbled at her food.

The after-dinner activity was body-to-body dancing, the girl with one of her brothers, while the other brother smooched conspicuously with an Asian taxi-dancer. The Chinese man sat stoically, but you feel his rage. After leaving her family, he takes her back to their love nest, and playing out his rage, he slaps her down, pulls off her panties and rapes her. She gets something out of this. She asks, "How much would it cost in a brothel to do what you just did to me?" He pulls out his gold-tipped leather wallet and angrily removes a wad of bills and tosses it onto a table.

Their affair has been reduced to commerce. They you-know-what, he gives her money. They you-know-what, he gives her his mother's heirloom diamond ring. They you-know-what, he pays off her brother's opium-den debts and pays for his ocean passage back to France, to boot. But their affair isn't only so crass, the film's voice-over tells us. In the final scene, we see an elderly woman, her back to us, at her desk. The voice-over says after her more conventional life (multiple marriages, children), her Chinese lover calls her out of the blue and says he still loves her, after many years of a conventional Chinese marriage. And she indicates she hasn't forgotten him either.

We who have not experienced such intense sexual obsessions may have little sympathy for or understanding of how these characters feel. Can "love" be sustained by a wholly physical relationship? Or is this some kind of male-chauvinist fantasy dressed up in a liberated Frenchwoman's story-telling?

For us mere mortals, the film stirs emotions that reflect, at least in spirit, some of its racial, gender, and class themes. At a superficial level, we see a Chinese stud, an image that's almost never portrayed in mainstream commercial films. You don't see a studly Asian male in any of Hollywood's regular repertoire of action adventure melodramas. You don't see Mr. Asian Sex Appeal on any of commercial television's regular programming, whereas you are more likely to see an exotic Asian woman—still mostly in the background—the object of a white man's lust.

And since so much racist and sexist history (in both the West and the East) has muddied the relations of contemporary Asian American men and women, giving rise to the exotic Asian female ready to serve her man and, conversely, the docile, meek, mild Asian male simpering somewhere in the background, *The Lover* is bound to rattle our inner cages of stereotypes, insecurities, and anxieties.

Asian American men might envy the Chinese man's predicament in the movie. He's rich. He's handsome. All he has to do is make love to a nymphet. And, since so many Asian American women seem to favor white men over Asian American men, this Chinese man's journey on the far side of restrictive conventional wisdom is indeed heroic. Male fantasy, writ large.

Another part of this prototypical Asian American male, though, might wince at the Chinese man's situation. How wasteful. How politically incorrect. How debased.

Asian American women are likely to have very different reactions, and I cannot pretend to accurately articulate those reactions. Whether *The Lover* will help Asian American men and women drop some of the discursive barriers that separate us, or whether it will stimulate meaningful conversations among some of us, I really don't know.

Given my settlement into comfortable middle-agedness, I am, as they say, out of the loop on what clicks or doesn't click between Asian American twenty- and thirtysomethings when it comes to the relationship thing. Having been married for more than twenty-four years to the same woman (not of Asian descent) puts me further from the psychic power centers of the yellow gender wars.

If truth be told—and I must constantly tell it to myself, more than any-one else—these stereotypes I and others complain about, regarding wimpy Asian men and exotic Asian women, aren't as restrictive and awful as we sometimes make them out to be. They aren't good, I'll grant you that. But none of us should take them too seriously or believe that all non-Asians swallow them whole. A lot of non-Asians do, of course, as do, I suspect, a fair number of Asians who can't or won't think for themselves.

In real life, we must know people who break the stereotypes in living, breathing ways. So what if Hollywood and French film directors perpetu-ate some awful stereotypes of us or create new ones?

I'm not backing off from objecting to one-dimensional outrageous stereotypes of Asian men or women. I just feel that life is more than movies or TV. Decry these limiting media as we must, we should also realize that the range of the human condition is indeed virtually limitless and that we enter relationships or break them for many reasons, some having to do with sex, race, class, religion, culture, mixed together deliciously, some having only to do with one more than the others, perhaps.

If we let ourselves, we can become trapped in both stereotypes of our making and those of fanciful filmmakers. *The Lover* gives us food for thought, even while the two principal characters aren't much interested in thinking as much as you-know-whating.

10 Race Relations

Why Can't We All Get Along?

Just Who Is the Victim Here?

Asian Week, September 21, 1990

From the glitz of Park Avenue, on the east side of Manhattan, to the low-rise earthiness of Church Avenue in the Flatbush section of Brooklyn, two different worlds are joined by a thirty-five-minute subway ride. That's how long it took me on a Saturday morning in late August.

In a prosaic way, I was on a pilgrimage—in search of the best-known battleground in a frustrating and protracted dispute between two racial groups, African Americans and Koreans: The Family Red Apple store on Church Avenue near St. Paul's Place in the Flatbush section of Brooklyn. It and another Korean-owned grocery store across the street have been targets of a boycott by an African American group known as the December 12th Movement.

What started out as an altercation between a Haitian woman customer at the Red Apple and a Korean grocery clerk in January has escalated to a great morality play that embodies a host of insecurities and inequities of two groups that are themselves victims. While not blaming the media for the origins of the dispute, some observers believe the boycott has been nurtured by media hysteria in the media capital of the United States. Why has this dispute gotten sensational national news attention? Because New York City has seen some startlingly raw racial conflicts in recent times. Remember Bensonhurst, Central Park, Howard Beach, Bernhard Goetz?

Whether we like it or not, the Flatbush case has become a symbol of American racial and economic conflict at a time when America's racial-ethnic and socioeconomic profiles are evolving. Flatbush has forced Asian Americans, African Americans, and, indeed, Americans of other racial-ethnic backgrounds to either choose sides or become confused about this nightmarish dilemma.

In turn, each side has victimized the other in Flatbush. Racial animosities have been exchanged. Anger, hurt, and bitterness are there in abundance. Numerous efforts involving veterans of the civil rights movement—African American, Asian American, white, and others—have attempted to mediate the dispute. No one yet has succeeded.

The Flatbush incident isn't the first time that black customers and Korean grocery store owners have clashed. Throughout the 1980s, in places like Washington, D.C., Harlem in New York City, Philadelphia, and Los Angeles, black customers have alleged racist treatment on the part of Korean grocers, who in turn have alleged petty criminal activity by some black customers.

The Flatbush case, though, has meaning far beyond the grittiness of Church Avenue and St. Paul's Place, the nearest corner of the Family Red Apple store owned by Bong Jae Jang, the principal target of the boycott. In a larger context, the dispute involves the aspirations of an immigrant group (Koreans) and the abject disappointment of a long-suffering American minority group (African Americans). One doesn't follow the other, but through no grand design, they collide. Yet another culture clash.

By and large, Korean immigrants come to America seeking a better life, a goal shared by newcomers from all over the world. Because of language and cultural barriers, they find opportunities limited—and end up establishing grocery stores in tough inner-city neighborhoods. That is the territory of many black Americans, whose economic dreams are snuffed out by racism and lack of opportunity.

It is now fashionable among neo-conservatives to blame poor black Americans for their own circumstances. Black poverty and hopelessness aren't society's fault, this trendy and insidious argument goes. Other downtrodden people have "made it" against adversity, why can't black Americans? the neo-conservative line continues.

Many black Americans have. But others have not. Ever since civil rights laws opened opportunities for many black Americans (and other disenfranchised people), many have done relatively well economically.

But it takes longer than a generation to overcome the inequalities of the slave system.

Thus far, the so-called permanent underclass of American cities— a code term for poor black Americans—has had little hope of achieving the relative economic success of other Americans. So, when they see Korean immigrants—or any other newcomer group, for that matter— come into their neighborhoods and start small businesses, one can understand their frustration and suspicion.

The two sides literally do not speak the same language. Their customs and body languages are different and can lead to miscommunication and hurt feelings. Spike Lee's seminal film, *Do the Right Thing,* gave us a sense of the grim realities of multicultural misunderstandings.

I wanted to hear first-hand the perspective of the boycott leaders. Twice, I tried to talk with boycott leader Sonny Carson or other representatives of the December 12th Movement. In one phone call, an unidentified male told me Carson wasn't available. He suggested I call back a couple of days later. When I told him what I wanted to talk about—the boycott and the black-Korean dispute—he said, "This is about one incident at one store. Don't make it out to be black people hating Koreans."

The second time I called, a woman who refused to identify herself didn't want to be interviewed. She said that her group has gotten negative publicity from almost all news organizations. "This Korean thing has put problems on the shoulders of black people. . . . You're an individual. You are incidental to all this. The black nation of people are the one who's continuing to be victimized."

On my sojourn to Flatbush, I missed the Family Red Apple store when I passed it. Its name on the awning had been obliterated. I circled back and found it. It shouldn't have been so difficult. Most of the outdoor bins that would usually hold fresh fruit were empty. One had sad-looking plantains. Another had shriveled oranges and sickly looking apples. Inside, most bins were empty. The shelves still had bottled and canned goods, but the musty and pungent smell of cured pork tails and snouts in open vats attacked the senses. The store smelled rotten.

Bong Jae Jang, grim faced, is near the rear. Several men are nearby. A clerk sits head lowered near the cash register. There are no customers. The store had been doing about $2,000 a day in sales. Now, it gets maybe $20 a day. Jang has little to say. It's not as though he's unfriendly. He seems distracted, staring outside at police barricades against the sidewalk. No boycott demonstrators are in sight. Jang chats animatedly in Korean with one of his colleagues, who's on the phone.

Another talks with me. He says that Jang is determined to stay open, no matter what. Jang and the other grocer have been getting financial assistance from other Korean grocers and the Korean American community. "If he [Sonny Carson] shuts this shop, he'll target others," the man says.

Both Jang and his companion express disgust with the administration of Mayor David Dinkins. "What have they done? It's the same situation. It's eight months now," the man says. "I can't trust the city," Jang says. "I trust Koreans."

A lone boycotter—a black youth wearing a green T-shirt—shouts into the store, "Boycott! Boycott!" It's early yet, I am told. Wait till 2 P.M., the Korean grocers say. They'll be here.

Two young people, perhaps Hispanics, walk into the store. They browse the mostly empty bins and dusty shelves. They leave. No sale. Outside, a police officer leans against the empty outside bins. He looks bored. Across the street, four police vehicles are parked in an alley. More police officers lean against the wall of the other boycotted store, Church Fruits & Vegetables, not far away.

I cross the street to see what, if anything, is happening in that store. Nothing. Its bins too are empty. Dusty canned and bottled merchandise lines the shelves. A man sits on a crate near the cash register. I approach him. He excuses himself to fetch the owner. Kyung Ho Park emerges from the back, sleepy-eyed, in a T-shirt and jeans. I start asking questions. He's more talkative than Jang. Park is the brother of the store's owner, Man Ho Park.

"Why do we stay open? This is my store. They can't stop my business," Kyung Ho Park says. No one else is in his store but him, me, and another man. The store used to take in about $18,000 a week in sales. Now it's lucky to do $160 a week. Park asks rhetorically why his brother's store is being boycotted. He said after the protesters started boycotting the Family Red Apple, his brother's store did great business for about half a day. Then boycotters started picketing Church Fruits for no apparent reason, he says.

He denies mistreating customers, most of whom have been African American or Haitian immigrants. "I treat all customers the same. If I treat customers bad, I lose customers," he says in broken English.

Upon questioning, Kyung Ho Park tells me a little about his life. He came to America seven years ago from South Korea as a 21-year-old. He had graduated from high school but didn't go to college. Upon arrival in Flatbush, he worked at a fruit stand owned by his sister.

His image of America was pristine. "I heard about America. America was beautiful, good education, people so nice. I think America is nice." He says he didn't understand English when he came. When someone said something to him in the store, he had to ask his sister what was said. He learned sometimes that what was said wasn't friendly, or nice. "I learn they were saying bad language. I don't say anything to anybody. Why they treat me like this?"

Not long after his arrival in America, Park says he learned American swear words. "I just can't believe this country," he says in an agitated tone. Some customers have called him "Chinaman" or "Chink," but, he says, "I never call them names."

As he talks, a black woman enters the store. She asks about olive oil. Park's helper points to a shelf with olive oil bottles. She selects one, a sixteen-ounce bottle that costs $5.29. She pulls money out of her purse, pays for it and leaves with her purchase.

I ask him how he feels about the boycott and about his life. "My feeling? Very angry. I want to kill everyone."

Playing Together

Oakland Tribune, July 30, 1990

Meet Kenny Walton and Art Sato, high school basketball junkies. Their story may or may not be typical of everyday interactions between people of different racial and ethnic backgrounds, but in light of a rancid atmosphere of racial hostilities emanating especially from New York City, we might be able to learn a lesson or two from these two men.

Walton grew up in Harlem. He is African American. Sato grew up in Sacramento. He is Japanese American. Somehow, they were destined to collaborate on what they both love: youth basketball.

Through a mutual friend, the two met five years ago and quickly discovered their addiction to basketball. Sato's son, Ilyich (known to his friends a "E"), was playing in a Buddhist church league made up mostly of

Japanese American teenagers. Sato was asked to coach a team. He asked Walton, who had coached youth basketball in New York City, to coach with him. Both men had initial trepidations—Walton would be the only African American in an all-Asian setting—but Walton has fit in easily without problems.

This summer, looking for further competition, they came upon the Oakland Neighborhood Basketball League, founded eighteen years ago by junior high school teacher Jesse Guidry. The league is a de facto all-black league that provides organized competition for teenagers (eighteen and under), most of whom don't have high school playing experience. When Guidry heard an Asian American team wanted to play in his league, he was delighted. Guidry coaches some Asian American youth but hasn't been able to persuade them to compete in the senior division (15 to 18 years old) in his league.

As it turned out, Walton and Sato aren't fielding their regular team. Instead, they have recruited several Asian American players from the Buddhist league and several African American youth. They call themselves "Prime Time Performers," wear gray shirts, and have become the talk of the Oakland Neighborhood Basketball League.

The Prime Time Performers won the league championship by winning all five games. In all five games, their opponents were much taller. That didn't faze the Prime Time Performers, however. They won because they played disciplined, heady basketball. Their defense, speed, quickness, and tenacity overcame any height disadvantage.

The black and Asian players contributed equally. Marlon Hendrix, who will be a junior at McClymonds High, provided speed and athleticism. Two San Francisco high school teammates, Antoine Lewis, who is black, and Jeff Cariaso, a Filipino American, gave the team overall rebounding and scoring strength. Sean Wada, a Japanese American who is only five feet seven inches tall, played a gutsy game as point guard. This black-Asian team has earned respect among the all-black teams. One former Oakland high school star told Walton that the Asians on his team were the best non-black athletes he's ever seen.

Basketball isn't a sport that is associated with Asian Americans, who are thought to be too short for the sport. Basketball has become known as a black sport, especially in cities. This summer, at an Oakland high school gymnasium, a different picture of the sport developed. As the prime movers behind this stereotype-shattering experience, Walton and Sato unobtrusively provided a game plan worthy of emulation.

As different as they are, they have much in common. Walton, who is 32 years old and an attorney, left Harlem for a prep school in Connecticut, then Williams College in Massachusetts. He came to California ten years ago to attend Boalt law school at the University of California at Berkeley. Sato, who is 46 and works in a San Francisco preschool, was born in a Japanese American internment camp in Colorado. He developed a love for sports and jazz, which drew him to San Francisco.

Both men live multicultural lives. Now, without fanfare or even much discussion about racial differences, they are showing black and Asian youngsters the value of playing together.

Plenty of Blame to Go Around

Oakland Tribune, November 5, 1990

The Oakland Chinatown restaurant is busy, but not full. It is well past the regular dinner hour, about 10 P.M. Two black men enter. The older of the two—slender, with glazed eyes—weaves his way to a table. The younger one—hefty and stout—follows.

A couple of minutes pass. A waiter (Chinese, of course) stops by their table. I do not hear what he says. What the younger black man says is, "We want to eat." The waiter departs to go to the kitchen for other orders.

The younger man begins to show impatience. The older man sits impassively slumped in his chair. In a raised voice, the younger man asks the woman cashier for menus. She appears to ignore him. He repeats his request in a stern tone. She responds by passing two menus over the shoulder of the older man and releases them so they fall on top of the man's folded hands. The man turns his head and glares at her.

Next, the younger man demands tea, again in a raised voice. He gets no response. About five minutes have passed since they came into the restaurant.

The younger man gets out of his chair and starts shouting profanities. He complains that he and his friend can't get served, haven't gotten tea, and got menus thrown at them. He starts walking around the restaurant, which is now thick with tension and anticipation.

The restaurant manager emerges. He asks the younger man what is wrong. The man continues his stream of profanities. He says he's eaten at this restaurant before and has never had any problems.

The manager tells the two men to leave. The younger customer continues his agitated pacing and shouting. Finally, he says to his friend, who had remained seated all this time, "Come on, let's leave this (bleeping) place."

Suddenly, the older man lifts the table and spills the plates and tray of condiments onto the floor. The crashing sound jolts the room. The older man weaves his way out quickly. The younger man stays. He alternates between being apologetic—"He shouldn't have done that"—and belligerent.

The manager ducks into an alcove. A few minutes later, a group of about six young Chinese men appear at the front door. They confront the younger black man, who is still inside the restaurant. They block the doorway and a few of them exchange harsh words with him.

The younger black man eventually works his way outside. From my table, I do not hear any sounds of fighting. I see a small crowd milling about outside. Then I see the reflections of a flashing police-car light. The two black men have apparently left the scene. Inside, the manager directs a Latino busboy to clean up the mess.

Other than this being a raw slice of life in the big city, what are we to make of this scene? I do not take it as "typical" of relations between African Americans and Chinese or other people of Asian descent. But I would be naive to think that hateful confrontations haven't occurred or won't occur again with racially charged currents surging to the surface.

My thoughts immediately flashed to the well-publicized tensions in New York between some black people and Korean immigrant grocers sparked by a dispute between a black woman customer and a Korean store clerk.

If anyone has an easy answer, please offer it up. Were the Chinese in this case racist? Probably. Were the two black men threatening because of their drunken-like demeanor and belligerent attitude? Probably.

I know some Chinese and other Asians are racist toward black people. I also know some Chinese waiters are rude to everyone they serve. I know some poor black people, burdened by drug and alcohol problems, can threaten businesses of all kinds.

Complicated and seemingly irreconcilable value differences and stereotypes hang over us. Pieties about a harmonious multicultural future mean nothing to the downtrodden or parochial business owners.

Middleman Myopia

Asian Week, March 10, 1995

The O. J. Simpson case is a metaphor for American race relations, including Asian Americans. The cast of characters is clear: O. J. Simpson, African American, is the defendant, accused of murdering his former wife, Nicole Brown Simpson, and her friend, Ronald Lyle Goldman, both European Americans.

Defending Simpson are Johnnie L. Cochran (black), Robert Shapiro, F. Lee Bailey (both white), and Carl Douglas (black). Prosecuting him are Marcia Clark (white), Christopher Darden (black), and William Hodgman (white). The jurors are eight African Americans, two whites, one Latino, and one mixed white–Native American. (The racial composition of the jury can change at any minute, as it has a couple of times already.)

The judge is Lance Ito, Japanese American. He's right in the middle of the media and legal madness, a fitting metaphor for the place many Asian Americans find themselves in a society drenched with racial contradictions and conundrums.

Nothing is simple in American race relations, even the classic black-white model. In the Simpson case, some old animosities are playing themselves out along historic black-white lines. Polls indicate that more than two-thirds of African Americans surveyed believe Simpson is innocent, while 60 percent of whites surveyed think he's guilty. Through the trial's first month of testimony, the percentage of black people polled who believe Simpson to be guilty has fallen below 10 percent from 15 percent in November.

Lance Ito isn't Every Asian American. None of us is. Right now, however, he's the best-known Asian American. Judge Ito's role has been both crucial and enigmatic. He won't make the final judgment of Simpson's guilt or innocence. But he's the essential rudder of this legal proceeding, steering it ever so carefully in an impossibly public and zany atmosphere.

As with the other main characters, Ito's behavior, character, and essence have been scrutinized by everyone. Early in the trial, he was said to be reverential to Cochran, a celebrity Los Angeles defense attorney. It has been said Ito is treating Cochran with kid gloves, allowing him to talk on and on without interruption. When Ito intervenes, it is in a sweet and deferential tone. When lead prosecutor Marcia Clark speaks, however, Ito has been thought to be rude and curt, cutting her off and addressing her in a stern manner.

This has led to speculation that Ito was being sexist, or that he was bending over backwards because he himself was a prosecutor so he wants the world to know he is not partisan to his past colleagues. And let's not forget Ito is married to a white woman who happens to be a ranking Los Angeles police officer, so his solicitous attitude toward Cochran, once again, may reinforce a desire to be fair to the defense and not be viewed as a dupe for the prosecution and police, his more natural allies.

Ito's middleman role is emblematic of how Asian Americans survive the racial politics of America. Many Asian Americans believe we are "middlemen" in American society. Respectable Asian American intellectuals and political leaders extol such a role. It is suggested, for instance, we possess the psychological and cultural goods to "bridge the gap between black and white."

This is nonsense because such a view assumes Asian Americans are omniscient, that we stand above the racial fray, like a judge (Ito?) on a raised docket looking down on battling blacks and whites. This view also assumes Asian Americans are free of prejudice and aren't victims of prejudice. Nothing could be further from the truth.

Honesty requires us to acknowledge the usual range of human flaws, not unlike white and black and brown people and all shades in between. At one time or another, Asian Americans are both prejudiced and victims of prejudice, even simultaneously.

Think about how many Asian Americans survive in an America torn between black and white. Depending upon where we grow up, either the white kids or the black kids are "cooler," so we emulate one or the other, or both. The mass media are filled with white and black culture. There's little or nothing about Asian or Asian American culture.

This is not to dismiss the seminal influence of parents, but sometimes our parents are too uptight, and the pressures are great in America to conform, to be accepted by your peers, to be part of American culture.

If an Asian American kid isn't in an Asian cultural setting, like a Chinatown or a Little Saigon, then he or she tends to be racially isolated. Sure, the family remains important and depending upon personalities and character, the Asian kid in an American suburb could certainly survive, Asian identity intact. But one hears too many stories about self-hatred and self-loathing, about the desire to be white (or black), anything but yellow. Chinatown and Little Saigon denizens tend to have a stronger Asian identity, but they aren't immune from the general culture that is so heavily white Christian or Jewish and black.

Another way to view this conundrum is from the perspective of the white American majority. White folks can be both sincerely nice and condescending, or in the extreme, cruelly racist. In recent times, Asian Americans have won an acceptance from white people, who see us as (you choose) the "model minority," the hardworking inheritors of thousands of years of civilization, exotic, able, smart, obedient, trustworthy. In their eyes, we may not really be as good as they are, but we're certainly "better" than black people.

At the very same time, we can be so foreign to some white people that they don't know what to make of us, the inscrutable Oriental. Undoubtedly, some white people probably loathe Asians, while others love us.

Then, again, we can be completely invisible to some white people even though we are around them, within sight, if they would only see us. Maybe our opaqueness is a function of our "quiet, reserved ways." Or they may see us but they dismiss us as inconsequential since there may be questions about what exactly have we done in America, other than the laundry and cook up some pretty good, cheap grub?

Do we entertain America the way black superstars in show business and sports do? Do we make movies that cause critics and moviegoers to go gaga? Do we make deals on Wall Street that will stop the shouting on trading floors? Do we make a difference, positive or negative, in the halls of Congress, the state capitol, city hall, the school-board meeting, and in the neighborhood?

Many Asian Americans have uneasy relationships with black people too. In many urban schools, for instance, some black kids pick on and beat up Asian American kids (some of whom are fighting back). In some cities, black criminals target Asians because they sense Asians won't fight back and won't report the crime to authorities. (Asian American criminals know the same thing about docile Asian victims.) Some black people can be cruelly prejudiced or hateful toward Asian people. (The reverse is equally true.)

At another level, some Asian Americans feel closer to black Americans than to white Americans. There's a shared "victimization," of being targets of specific or generalized racist behavior by whites who hold more positions of formal and informal power in America.

Where we get outflanked by African Americans is in cases where white people in power play us against each other. Some white employers have unofficial "minority quota slots" over which white women and black, Latino, Asian, and Native American men and women compete with one another to fill that token slot.

On another tangent, consider the matter of racial hierarchies in America as though it were ranked on a spectrum from "good" at one end to "bad" at the other. African Americans occupy the extremes, both "good" and "bad." They are "good" because of white guilt over the slavery experience. They are "bad" because of the poor, welfare-dependent, and criminal stereotypes.

Asian Americans, on the other hand, occupy the center portions of the spectrum. We're much more acceptable than black people are to many white people. But we're not nearly as feared or listened to as black people are when black people point out white racist behavior. When that happens, liberal white people usually respond with compassion and understanding without trying to be too condescending. (Yet they and other white people deeply fear black people, especially young black men, who scare a lot of people, Asian Americans included.) But when Asian Americans gripe about white racist behavior toward us, our complaints fall on deaf ears.

So here we are, in the middle, even though I don't think we offer any special gifts to "bridge" the gap between warring black and white people. We have our own wars to fight, on both fronts.

The point is, we are not really in a position to broker any kind of racial-ethnic-religious-class-gender peace in America. We are but one of many groups seeking more power, more action, more recognition, more validation. Yes, some of us have made impressive marks in academics, the sciences and the arts. But we are still political wimps. And we have not earned the respect of others who have long battled for equality and justice in America.

Instead of concentrating on "building bridges" across the cultural divide, I think we need to concentrate on empowering ourselves, fighting for our rights, fighting for other people's rights, not allowing ourselves to be taken advantage of, not kowtowing to the white elite, who have an altogether different agenda than we might have. Once we win our rightful place in

American society, a place of respect and equal opportunity where we need not worry about quotas against us or stereotypes about us or hate violence aimed at us, then we can turn our attention to the business of "building bridges." Maybe.

Lance Ito has a tough job. Some court observers believe he's not been tough enough on either side, that he's let the case wander all over the place. Others see him as being scrupulously fair and careful. Indeed, when he has been forced to, he's held his ground against some powerful egos.

His lofty role has risks. Because emotions are so high in this case, he and other principals surely will continue to be criticized, depending upon the jury's final judgment. Despite his symbolic middleman role, he can't be expected to solve any of the entrenched racial complications, other than to deal with them in as even-handed a manner as he can. That alone will be quite an accomplishment.

Yellow Pride Versus Multiculturalism

Asian Week, July 3, 1992

As some of us remembered Vincent Chin, we couldn't get Los Angeles out of our minds. The tenth anniversary of the death of Vincent Chin, the Detroit Chinese American beaten to death by two autoworkers and reigning icon of contemporary anti-Asian violence, yielded a number of public forums in the San Francisco Bay Area and elsewhere, including Detroit. I attended two and what I heard was both encouraging and troubling.

Part of Asian America's soul remains wounded and unattended. Regardless of our larger numbers and increasing presence in all walks of life, we still feel invisible. For the most part, opinion leaders and power brokers don't include us in any discussions of race and class in America. Our absence is preposterous, especially when Asian ethnics are specifically picked on (or, on occasions, precipitate racial friction). In significant discussions in national publications of America's race relations after the Los Angeles riots, the question is posed in black and white terms only.

That Asians aren't considered a player in national race relations is appalling, given the defensive posture Asian Americans have been forced into in recent years. Korean American merchants and other Asian

American stores are targeted for looting and burning. Japanese Americans and other Asian Americans get blamed for Japan's economic hegemony.

Remembering Vincent Chin gives us a chance to spill our guts and vent our rage. The ten years since his brutal beating haven't been a blank slate. Many other anti-Asian assaults and some killings have taken place. Los Angeles happened. So any remembrance had to embrace the new sobering realities for Asian Americans, not just one "isolated" incident, but a disturbing random pattern of them.

It is important for Asian Americans to learn more about ourselves. We must define our own problems, voice them in our own terms, and try to control the agendas. Doing only that, however, is limiting and ultimately myopic in polyglot America, a place that barely knows us to begin with except as gooks, Chinks, Japs, and slant-eyes.

Given the complexity of race and class relations today in America, we Asian Americans can't simply stick together and let it go at that. We have to start with ourselves, learning of one another's histories, cultures, sensibilities. We may not always agree, but we shouldn't disagree if we don't at first have knowledge of each other.

Sticking together is still a fantasy in Asian America. It's become more difficult to do so since the tremendous growth in our communities over the past twenty-five years. That we don't stick together now isn't anyone's fault. We're much too diverse, and too few of us have appreciation for the other person's heart, mind, and soul. The cries for "unity" and "solidarity" sound fine, but realities make genuine unity and solidarity virtually impossible. Not only do we Asian Americans have differences in culture, language, history, and American experiences, we have distinct political differences.

Not all Asian Americans, for instance, are sympathetic toward African Americans. Not all Asian Americans hate the "model minority" stereotype. Not all Asian American activists believe that greater political power ought to be exercised on behalf of a pluralistic society, rather than simply for one narrow ethnic group's interests. Some of us talk about seeking more political power but do little to achieve it. Some of us disdain working with or knowing more about other Asian ethnic people.

One forum was a decidedly multicultural affair, organized by Asians and African Americans, held at a black-led church near Japantown, and attended by a rainbow of people, mostly Asians and African Americans.

It was called "Sharing Histories—Building Bridges: A Town Meeting on Hate Violence and Intercommunity Relations." This forum emanated from a liberal-progressive perspective. Some speakers, predictably, denounced racism and the white power structure. Others called for "unity" and "solidarity" among people of color. As one African American man put it, "We've got to learn to cover each other's back. . . . We've got to make it our business to share each other's cultures." Alluding to world population proportions, which have more people of color than white people, he asked, "What do the majority of the planet think?"

The most hopeful aspect of this forum was the candor of individual Asian Americans and African Americans. Russell Lowe, a long-time San Francisco Chinese American activist and an aide to retiring U.S. Senator Alan Cranston, challenged Asian Americans to examine our own racism. Who among us is free of prejudice against blacks, whites, and others? Does our racism precipitate problems? In the case of Korean Americans, did their racism create, exacerbate, or have nothing to do with some of them being targeted for looting and arson in South Central Los Angeles?

Then a black speaker said, "I hate to say this, but I hear a lot of biased statements in the black community against Asians—they're coming in here to take over, blah, blah, blah." He suggested we all practice "common courtesies" and not call each other names other than what or who we are. Simple as it is, this is a good idea.

Maurice Lim Miller, another veteran Asian American activist in the Bay Area, took us on a personal journey into his racial interior. "In my heart, I'm Mexican," he said of his mixed Mexican-Chinese heritage. He said he remembers when he was first called a "Chink." "I always thought I was Mexican," he said. "I didn't want to be Chinese. My mother would tell people we're all from India" because, for some reason, she thought being from India was better than being either Chinese or Mexican. Miller noted that, in America, one becomes "compartmentalized," and he didn't want to "fall into the Asian stereotype. I thought it was much worse than being Mexican."

Then he went to Vietnam as a U.S. soldier. There, he quickly discovered, American troops were killing Asians, and he learned that American soldiers who were white, black, or Latino dehumanized the Asian enemy. He was seen by his fellow GI's as an "Asian," and there was a unity among the other American soldiers against Asians. Once back in the United

States, however, he rediscovered the fact that black people are at the bottom of America's racial pecking order.

At another San Francisco forum, this one sponsored by AT&T, the communications company, similar sentiments were expressed, but the main difference was the participants were all of Asian descent. AT&T invited about 100 Asian Americans in five cities (San Francisco, Los Angeles, Houston, Chicago, and New York) to talk with one another via the company's videoconferencing technology.

Selected speakers from each city summarized anti-Asian activities in their areas. Then, in a round-robin format, other people commented or asked questions. The most provocative question came from Henry Der, executive director of Chinese for Affirmative Action, a San Francisco civil rights group. He asked whether Asian American leaders weren't "letting down" Asian American victims in Los Angeles by not pressing harder for hate-crime prosecutions against looters.

Stewart Kwoh and Bong Hwan Kim, two Los Angeles activists, answered him politely without really getting to the heart of what Der was asking. After the videoconference was over, the fireworks over Der's question got started. Several in the San Francisco crowd felt it was impolitic of Der to raise this question because the assumption was that, if hate-crime prosecutions are pressed against people who targeted Asian American merchants in Los Angeles, African Americans would bear the brunt of any legal case, and it was unwise to go after a community we Asian Americans should want to work more with.

Der said he wasn't blaming African Americans or Latinos for the looting of Asian American stores, but he was concerned about the "consistency" of the Asian American civil rights leadership, which doesn't hesitate pressing hate-crime charges against white people who target Asian Americans.

The feeling I got from Der's critics was that because people of color need to be unified in their approach to redressing social wrongs, going after some African American looters and arsonists would be divisive and set back efforts to build bridges with African Americans. Besides, they said, how could one truly determine whether the action of looters and arsonists was racist in nature, when it could have just as much been class envy?

As this off-camera—and much livelier—debate ensued, I thought about the dilemma that faces Asian American liberals and progressives who believe in the merits of multiculturalism, that racial and social injustices elsewhere affect us too. But we also believe in asserting our ethnic pride, speaking out for our rights, and demanding a fair share of society's spoils. Los Angeles put us uncomfortably in the middle. We decried injustices to black people, but at the same time, we denounced the racist attacks on Korean Americans and other Asian Americans, even if those attacks came from black people.

Der's question lingers like the smell of a skunk. How does Asian America get justice from Los Angeles and other cases of anti-Asian violence if we don't press legal authorities to bring whatever charges need to be brought? The trouble is, doing so endangers coalition building with other communities of color, if people from those communities perpetrated these racist crimes.

There is no easy answer. Asking the question, however, forces us to think through our values and priorities. Asking the question forces us to confront who we are and what we believe. That is both healthy and constructive.

Beyond Black and White

Asian Week, July 25, 1997

It is an unavoidable human trait to care first about yourself and your immediate circumstances. That banal truism was brought into focus by President Bill Clinton's "national conversation on race." As a Chinese American and Asian American, I am naturally most interested in what happens to me and other Chinese Americans and Asian Americans. But the "national conversation on race" mostly ignores yellow folk. We rant and rave in our own fashion, but almost none of what we say is ever heard or heeded. Frankly, it has become tiresome to whine about being left out of the national conversation on race, which is usually between white Americans and black Americans.

Alas, a letter I received in early June silenced me (at least temporarily) on the matter of being left out. The unsolicited letter was from Kweisi Mfume and Myrlie Evers-Williams. Mfume, a former Maryland Congressman, and Evers-Williams, the martyred widow of slain civil rights leader Medgar Evers, are president and chairwoman, respectively, of the National Association for the Advancement of Colored People, or NAACP, one of the foremost civil rights organizations. They were inviting me to help the NAACP think through some of the challenging race-relations issues America faces.

Rather than occupy my usual outsider role, I took Mfume and Evers-Williams up on their invitation. The group was small, about twenty-five people in all. In addition to African Americans, there were three other Asian Americans—Karen Narasaki, executive director of the National Asian Pacific American Legal Consortium; and David and Frances Namkoong, of the Cleveland branch of the Organization of Chinese Americans. There was a Cuban American, at least two Jewish Americans, and several other white Americans. The lack of more Latinos, such as from Texas or California, was noticeable.

The fact that Mfume and Evers-Williams convened this multiracial consultation indicates they aren't necessarily locked into a black-white model of U.S. race relations. That in itself is a bold statement by the current leadership of a proud but tarnished organization founded to fight for the civil rights of African Americans. Christopher Edley, a Harvard law professor, was part of the consultation too. Edley, a bright, insightful man, is advising Clinton on race matters.

We had honest and frank discussions in the day-and-a-half meeting. Narasaki, the Namkoongs, and I reiterated the need for a national racial dialogue to go beyond the historic black-white narrative. Evers-Williams, who seemed sincere and open-minded, told us that she and the NAACP were looking for a "new approach" to a discussion of race—"something that grabs the imagination of this country." She asked us to "help the NAACP be a leader" in future racial discussions, much as it has been a leader in past ones.

As flattering as it was to be included in a discussion about race with some of America's leading African American officials, I sensed that a multiracial agenda wasn't one that could be fully embraced by the NAACP. Mfume so much as said that when he indicated the need of his organization to deal first with black-white issues before addressing multiracial ones. At the same time, he recognized that America was "headed for a much different scenario in the next twenty years. . . . We hear you loud and clear [on multiracialism]."

In a speech to the NAACP, Clinton emphasized the need for our society to come to grips with our multiracial relations, a point he raised when he introduced his race initiative in San Diego. The panel he appointed to advise him is multiracial. Interestingly, the chair of that panel, a distinguished African American, John Hope Franklin, has said the black-white issue is preeminent.

This newest incarnation of a national conversation on race seems to be boiling down to whether we examine the past or the future. On purely selfish grounds, I favor a multiracial, multicultural approach. Otherwise, I and other non-white, non-black Americans will feel left out (again). That doesn't mean we should disrespect the complicated and legitimate black-white model. There is no reason why the conversations over the next year can't accommodate both.

11 Politics

A Seat at the Table

Right Man, Wrong Time

Asian Week, November 20, 1992

Michael Woo strides confidently, with a smile, into the second-floor dining room of the Silver Dragon restaurant in Oakland's Chinatown. Gathered around in clusters, some sitting, some standing, are about eighty men and women, most of them ethnic Chinese, most of them middle-aged or older. Woo, a slender, energetic 40-year-old, seems out of place. But he isn't.

He is on a mission and the men and women waiting to have dinner with him are, in a sense, his missionaries. More accurately, they are his financiers. Woo is a Los Angeles city council member, the first Asian American to hold that high elected office in America's second largest city. Now he is reaching higher the mayor's office. His quest comes in the wake of the worst urban riots in the country's history, riots that, among other things, harmed and deeply affected Asian Americans, Korean Americans in particular.

His ambitious journey makes him one of the most interesting Asian American politicians at this time. And his candidacy symbolizes the slow, but sure, ascendancy of Asian American political empowerment. It raises enduring questions about the value of ethnic politics for an ethnic group that has so little political power but yearns for more. Woo appears to be an ideal vehicle for an expanded desire of Asian Americans for a bigger piece of the political pie.

Woo is in Oakland to raise money for his mayoral campaign. He's already raised about $500,000, but he figures he'll need from $2 million to $2.5 million to wage a competitive battle, which climaxes on April 20. If no one wins a majority of the votes—and it's unlikely anyone will, given the already crowded field of eight and probably more—there will be a runoff election six weeks later.

His visit to Oakland on a Sunday, and to the San Francisco peninsula the day before, was worth his while. He raised more than $20,000 over the weekend. An array of Oakland Chinese and Asian American groups sponsored the $100-a-plate dinner. The key sponsors were the Oakland lodge of the Chinese American Citizens Alliance, or CACA, and the Gee How Oak Tin Association. Woo's banker father, Wilbur, was once national grand president of CACA and is a member of the Gee How Oak Tin Association.

These old-time family-association connections are an important component of Woo's fundraising strategy. They provide him funds, and the link is clearly ethnic, not ideological. If the elderly Chinese men at the banquet tables have any American political affiliation—which is improbable—they would likely be Republican. Several middle-aged men in the crowd, more acculturated to the American mainstream than the elders, are Republicans. They are business people and believe the Republican Party protects the interest of business. Two told me they voted for George Bush.

Michael Woo is a liberal Democrat whose strength is building coalitions between various ethnic groups. His ideological stances, if known to these older men, might be offputting. But that wasn't the point of their attendance and financial support. Tong and family-association members attend dutifully, perhaps only vaguely aware of who or what Michael Woo is. It is important to them that he is the son of a Gee How Oak Tin Association member.

This part of Woo's appeal exemplifies the multiplicity of roles an Asian American candidate plays. He or she must connect to his or her ethnic base, regardless of political ideology. Another part of Woo's strategy is to reach out beyond his own ethnic group, as he (and most other Asian American candidates) must. To be sure, fundraising dinners and events for Woo aren't all elderly Chinese men belonging to tongs and family associations. Younger Asian Americans, more his generation, attend also, but they don't have the resources to help Woo reach $2.5 million. And, of course, Woo solicits funds from non-Asians as well.

Woo's message to the Oakland banquet audience was clearly ethnic. He explained why he was running for Los Angeles mayor. He recounted how divided and troubled Los Angeles is, attributable to a sliding economy and the middle class moving to the suburbs. He noted how ethnic groups have become pitted against one another. "It tears me apart to see our city go down the road of Newark, Detroit, and even New York," Woo said.

As an urban planner, Woo said he has a vision for what cities can be, and he's using the political arena to try to realize that vision. He lost his first run at public office, but, "I never gave up." He ran for the city council in 1985 and won, making history. His reelection in 1989 was with 71 percent of the vote in a district that is only 5 percent Asian. "I want to make history again by becoming the first Asian American mayor of the second largest city," he said. His election would "change how others look at us. It will shatter stereotypes and [signal] that we're ready to come to positions of power."

He made a promise. "I want to come back, not only to raise money, but to help you by being a role model. I want the younger generation to know it's honorable to go into politics, to provide leadership." He added, "I may be running for mayor of Los Angeles, but I represent a broader constituency of Asian Americans who know they ought to exercise leadership, to get into the mainstream of American political life."

Woo did not invent an ethnic appeal in politics. The Irish and Italians in East Coast cities perfected the strategy. At its worst, ethnic politics can divide and self-segregate. At its best, it can lift under-represented groups to positions of political parity. Beyond his ethnic appeal, he offers a thoughtful three-pronged, interrelated message for Los Angeles voters—build interracial coalitions, grow the city's economy and reduce crime.

Many of these are image-building acts of ambitious politicians, regardless of ethnicity. Woo has a natural political temperament—an ebullience and enthusiasm working a roomful of people, an articulate chattiness needed to endure fundraising crowds. He's a good example of a "crossover" politician, one based in an ethnic community but who can easily work in different ethnic settings.

Woo knows the job of Los Angeles mayor will be tough because of the racial-ethnic gaps so explosively exposed in April. He said he would try to boost Los Angeles's sagging economic fortunes by consolidating local-government efforts to develop businesses. "There's a close connection between race and economics," he said. "If we fail on economic growth, then the violence will happen again."

He said he would use dollars as a unifying force, not a divisive one. An example is getting Asian American and African American bankers to join forces to create a community-development bank to lend money to minority businesses that have a difficult time getting financing from white-owned banks.

If elected, he would create an urban Peace Corps to "cross over the invisible boundaries" of Los Angeles. Instead of Americans going overseas to serve in the Peace Corps, he would recruit Los Angeles residents of all backgrounds to work in communities different from their own. "Los Angeles is actually a mentally segregated city. Unless leadership can point the way to a more integrated city, then there's no hope for us."

Does he have a chance to win? Yes, but it won't be easy. Early polls put him in the lead or second place. Already, there are eight announced candidates, including Woo. Say this about Michael Woo. He's a gambler, a man willing to take, in his words, "bold steps" to risk a political future in a wide-open contest. He must give up his council seat to run. If he loses, I wouldn't count him out of future political considerations.

[Woo made the runoffs but lost to millionaire Republican businessman Richard Riordan by eight points. Woo became a fellow at the Kennedy School of Government at Harvard University, then West Coast regional director of the Corporation for National Service, followed by director of Los Angeles programs for the Local Initiative Support Corporation.]

Race and Ideology: Bumping into Each Other
Asian Week, October 21, 1994

Ted Dang surprised a lot of people last spring when he declared his candidacy for Oakland mayor in the primary election that already had seven challengers to the incumbent, Elihu Harris. He surprised even more people when he got into a run-off against Harris by pulling almost 30 percent of the June vote against Harris's 37 percent.

From the start, Dang, a soon-to-be 43-year-old, has run an aggressive campaign, defying stereotypes that Asian and Chinese people don't dare speak up. He's attacked Harris as a "career politician" who has failed to stem Oakland's economic and social slide.

Beyond the specifics of Dang's campaign against Harris, his candidacy is an object lesson in how Asian American candidates compete for political office in complex times. The Oakland mayoral race also illustrates the frequently confusing intersections of ethnic and ideological considerations.

Some Chinese American voters make a simple choice at the polls. If a candidate is Chinese, I'm for him regardless of party affiliation, political experience, or ideological leanings because it's about time a Chinese person runs for mayor. That's not a terribly sophisticated position, but it reflects a pent-up frustration with not having power in a society that has historically discriminated against people of Chinese and Asian descent.

The Asian pride argument is not realistic in these times, at least in most cities and especially at state and national levels. For one thing, what is "Asian pride"? There is pan-Asian sentiment among some Asian Americans. Many Americans of Asian background, though, don't embrace the vague "Asian American" sobriquet. The identity label of choice ranges from plain old "American" to a particular Asian ethnicity.

Equally significant is the lack of a critical Asian mass. It's extremely rare that Asian American candidates run in areas of high concentrations of Asian people. Oakland's Asian American population doubled in the 1980s and is now a little more than 15 percent of the city of 385,000. African Americans make up about 40 percent. Latinos are also about 15 percent, leaving non-Hispanic whites and others about 30 percent. Asian American and Latino voters do not match their population proportions.

Individual Asian Americans in Oakland have enjoyed past political success—a Chinese American and a Japanese American were elected to the city council in the 1960s, when the city's Asian American population was much smaller. Only recently have Oakland Asian Americans consolidated some of that power by successfully campaigning for an Asian plurality district, but the Asian American candidate put up to run for the city council seat representing the new district lost badly to a more experienced white candidate. Oakland Asian Americans split between the two candidates, illustrating starkly the divide between an ethnic bias versus an ideological one.

Ted Dang's mayoral candidacy has some of the same elements, with Oakland Asian Americans supporting both him and his rival, Mayor Elihu

Harris, who happens to be African American. Riding a nationwide anti-incumbent wave, Dang, an Oakland native and a successful real estate developer, is running as an antipolitician candidate, a "businessman with a conscience." That doesn't necessarily mean he'll win, but his "outsider" status has helped him among Oaklanders fed up with politics as usual.

Various observers think the race is close and, depending on voter turnout, he could pull off an upset. The conventional wisdom is that if mostly black, poor, and working-class people turn out in significant numbers, Harris will win. If flatland voters stay home, Dang has a real shot because he is stronger among wealthier and more conservative voters in the hills, mostly whites and Asians. In short, the contest has lots of racial implications.

Although party affiliation is officially irrelevant in the Oakland mayoral election, both men are Democrats, but of different stripes. Harris, who served in the state assembly representing Oakland for twelve years before he was elected mayor four years ago, is a liberal with solid party connections in the state, while Dang calls himself a "Kennedy Democrat" when in fact he sounds much more like a conservative Democrat.

On the stump, Dang has had to be both "Chinese" and "American." At a Chinatown fund raiser, he read his remarks when he could have spoken extemporaneously. Moreover, he didn't use his quite passable Cantonese. On another occasion, he used Cantonese in a way that was both comforting and discombobulating. At a mayoral forum, an elderly ethnic Chinese woman asked a question in Cantonese. Dang answered in Cantonese, even though the majority of audience was white or black, all English speaking. As he was speaking Cantonese, someone in the crowd muttered in a loud whisper, "Aw, come on, speak English." Another white woman, who spoke a French-accented English, criticized Dang's call for more bilingual police officers to help people like the elderly Chinese woman who had a complaint about police service. This critic said she didn't see the need for bilingual officers because this is America and you should speak English.

This electric moment over bilingualism has many potential effects. Dang seemed to enjoy more support from the crowd than Harris did. Yet, one wonders whether his use of Cantonese, to make the Chinese-speaking woman feel more comfortable, might not have turned off some otherwise supportive voters. Was their friendliness to him muted by his use of a foreign tongue, which can be an alienating device?

That's but one of the dilemmas for Dang and probably other Asian American candidates. At some point, they want to be identified as "Asian." At others, such a label could be disadvantageous. Sometimes, Asian Americans candidates simply want to be treated like any other candidate. At others, they undoubtedly like the "special" feeling that attaches to their ethnicity.

A challenger like Dang pushing an outsider's antipolitician, reduce-government message will attract zealots who hate taxes and career politicians. Some conservatives have embraced Dang because of his rhetoric about overhauling City Hall and the "bloated bureaucracy." Whether the angry passion of his core supporters will lure undecided Oaklanders or turn them off is also a key to whether Dang will win or lose.

[Dang lost to Harris by thirty points, as black voters in the Oakland flatlands turned out in sizable numbers, while Dang lost some of his core support in the wealthier hills.]

An Asian American "Mr. Fixit"
Asian Week, October 25, 1996

In full campaign throttle, Gary Locke tells the poignant tale of a "one-hundred-year journey from houseboy to the governor's mansion," a story as American as Horatio Alger, Bill Clinton, and Bob Dole. Locke's grandfather emigrated from China some 100 years ago and became a houseboy in Olympia, the state capital of Washington.

On November 5, Locke, a 46-year-old former state legislator and current top county administrator, is heavily favored to become governor of Washington and thus preside over the state government about a mile from where his grandfather began the Locke family's American saga. More than that, Locke would assume symbolic leadership of the burgeoning Asian American political movement by becoming the first Asian American governor of a mainland state and first Chinese American governor of any state. (Hawaii has had three non-Chinese Asian American governors.)

The symbolism isn't lost on Locke. "Being the first mainland Asian American governor, I could help elevate, articulate and amplify Asian American issues," he said in an interview. These issues include affirmative action, "glass ceiling" barriers, immigration policies, and the impact of welfare reform on legal immigrants.

Nor is the symbolism lost on Asian American political observers outside of Washington State. Locke's prospective victory would be "a breakthrough to a level of leadership we have never seen before on the mainland," said Don Nakanishi, director of the UCLA Asian American Studies Center in Los Angeles. "There is potential for some positive consequences that could come from Gary being elected. He is sensitive to and knowledgeable about Asian American policy concerns." When Locke meets with other governors and issues of significance to Asian Americans are raised, his would be a new and credible voice at the table, joining the Hawaii governor's.

The burden would be heavy, but Locke seems up to the task. A Democrat, he emerged first with 24 percent of the vote among a crowded bipartisan primary field in September. Ellen Craswell, a former state senator, was the top Republican vote-getter with 15 percent. Recent polls have shown Locke ahead, but his aides say he is running as though he were the underdog. Locke appears to have wider appeal than Craswell, a conservative with strong support from the Christian Coalition who favors privatizing schools and other government services. Craswell's far-right positions have prompted moderate Republican leaders to support Locke.

Locke calls Craswell a "formidable opponent." But at a fund raiser held for him by wealthy Asian Americans in California, Locke said he was "confident" of victory. He notes how Craswell's campaign has launched negative ads against him, accusing him of being an "extreme liberal," which he is not. He said her charges ignore the fact that he has worked to streamline government and has considerable law-enforcement support.

His supporters are confident he will win. Paul Berendt, the state Democratic chairman, has said Locke will win because of his experience and dynamism and because Craswell's views are out of step with most Washingtonian's. Locke's campaign hopes to raise $1 million for the November 5 run-off election. It spent $800,000 during the primary. About 20 percent of the latter amount was raised outside of Washington, much of it in Asian American communities in California, New York, and other states.

Because of recent national publicity over Democratic Party solicitations of donations from Indonesian and other Asian sources, Locke can't escape questions about possible illegal contributions from Asia. He objected to the characterizations of these contributions as "Asian." They are "foreign" contributions in the same way that German, Canadian, or Israeli sources give money to American political campaigns, he said.

Whatever the momentary controversy, no one can question Locke's qualifications. He served for eleven years as a state legislator, including five years as chairman of the powerful budget-writing committee. For the past three years, he has been King County Executive, heading up the second largest governmental unit and the largest county in the state. Before his fourteen years as an elected official, Locke was a deputy prosecutor in King County, which includes Seattle.

Locke doesn't attach a political label to himself. Others, however, call him either a "new" or a "moderate Democrat," in the mold of President Clinton. One Seattle Asian American activist, who asked to remain anonymous, called Locke "a closet Republican." His campaign platform melds Democratic and Republican stances—strengthening public education, stimulating economic development, increasing public safety, protecting the environment, and streamlining state government.

According to his supporters and his record, he didn't come upon his moderate-centrist agenda overnight. Locke earned his reputation as a first-rate legislator through hard work and a keen intelligence. He distinguished himself when he chaired the House Appropriations Committee for five years, according to several sources.

Art Wang, who served in the state legislature with Locke for much of the 1980s, said, "Everyone respects him as being one of the best, brightest, most knowledgeable legislators. He has an incredible mind for details." Martha Choe, a Seattle City Council member, said Locke "has a remarkable ability to reflect the priorities of the community while taking into account budget realities. There is no better budget guru than Gary. He really knows the [budget] details. This knowledge made him a stand-out legislator."

Terry Mark, a legislative assistant to Locke for two years, describes her former boss as "a computer brain who can spout out numbers. . . . He looked critically at every public dollar." Mark said Locke was so well prepared during annual state budget hearings that state agency officials and others seeking a piece of the budget had to endure rigorous questioning from him. "Everyone had to justify every dollar they requested. If they weren't prepared to do that, they realized they might not get funded. Gary did his homework. He was cordial and kind, but he asked very direct questions that needed direct answers." Joan Yoshitomi, a former Locke aide and now director of community relations for King County, said Locke has always "worked both sides of the aisle [Democrat and Republican]" in the legislature. "He was able to craft dollars for programs he cared about that would normally fall through the cracks," she said.

Locke developed his political skills not through the conventional backrooms-and-bars venues but with his technical knowledge and an open, collaborative style to try to resolve public issues, his supporters said. As he moved up the legislative ladder, Locke didn't shy away from issues important to Asian Americans. Over the years, he sponsored or supported bills that established a minority and women's business enterprise office, authorized the practice of acupuncture, provided low-income housing for refugees, gave redress for Japanese American municipal employees, expanded nursing home beds for ethnic minorities, and created an "English Plus" state policy that tolerates other languages.

When Locke won the King County Executive seat in 1993, he faced different challenges. The Kingdome, where the Seattle Seahawks football team and Seattle Mariners baseball team play, was in embarrassing disrepair. Ceiling tiles fell during games. Locke oversaw the upgrading of that facility. Then the Seahawks owner, Ken Behring, wanted to pull his team out of Seattle. Locke stood up to him and has fashioned a tentative deal for Microsoft billionaire Paul Allen to purchase the team and keep it in Seattle. Locke successfully promoted public assistance to keep the Mariners afloat, then helped promote a plan to build a new baseball stadium to be financed through a public-private partnership.

Throughout his political career, Locke has won widespread support from Seattle's diverse Asian American communities. In the primary, however, some Asian Americans backed his opponent, Seattle Mayor Norman Rice. "We hate him and we love him," Joan Yoshitomi, one of his supporters, said. "Some groups feel he doesn't do enough for Asian Americans. Others think he is wonderful." Yoshitomi said some Asian Americans have criticized Locke for not having enough diversity on his staff or for not appointing enough Asian Americans to boards and commissions. Locke supporters point out many Asian American appointments.

His work to keep the Mariners collided with some Asian Americans. They didn't like the fact that Locke, as the top county administrator, didn't name any Asian Americans to the seven-member governing body of the Public Facilities District (PFD), the quasi-governmental unit created to own and operate the proposed Mariners baseball stadium, which will be going up right next to the district where many Asian Americans live and work. These activists remain troubled that the environmental impact report on the stadium siting didn't include provisions that would address some of the negative effects that a stadium would have on the mostly Asian American neighborhood, such as heavy traffic and heightened public safety concerns. Locke named four Asian Americans to a sixteen-member citizens advisory committee to the PFD and his supporters say Locke tried to persuade at least two Asian Americans to take a PFD appointment but was turned down for different reasons.

Even while Locke has not been able to please all Asian Americans all the time, there is no doubt about his Chinese background. His pioneering grandfather worked in Washington canneries and logging camps and cooked in various guises. His father, also China born, served in the U.S. Army and was part of the allied Normandy invasion during World War II. Locke's parents operated a restaurant in Seattle's famous Pike Place Market and a grocery business too. Even today, Locke's father cooks for his campaign staff.

"My Chinese/Asian heritage are an integral part of me," Locke said. "I can't separate that from who I am. It has helped shape my values—the importance of family and education." He said that given an Asian American history of contributing to this society, "It's only fair that Asian Americans be at the table making laws that affect us all." Locke said he didn't speak English until he went to kindergarten. As a child, he grew up in a public housing project. Later on, his smarts got him into Yale, then to Boston University for his law degree.

His wife of two years, Mona, a former TV news personality who is pregnant, has called Locke a "straight arrow." Supporters describe him as an "Eagle Scout." In fact, Locke was an Eagle Scout and his life embodies a squeaky clean image. He doesn't drink alcoholic beverages or smoke. He doesn't even use swear words in private or demonstratively express anger.

Contrary to his public image as a workaholic policy wonk, Locke is "well rounded," his friends say. For instance, he has a good voice and has been known to sing solos at wedding banquets. He enjoys hiking and camping in the natural wonders of Washington State. He is an amateur photographer and botanical buff. And he is good at making ice cream from scratch. Perhaps his favorite nonwork activity is as a "Mr. Fixit," an accomplished handyman who has elaborately remodeled his home. Indeed, some friends say, Locke's idea of fun at a party is to fix someone's leaking faucet.

Governors today have to be public Mr. Fixits. Locke said if he's elected he won't abandon needy people in his state, including legal immigrants who might lose social-service benefits. Given his record and values, Gary Locke is more than ready to assume the top public job in a state with only a 5 percent Asian American population. His ascension would symbolize another realization of the American Dream.

[Locke won, and in November 2000, he won reelection.]

Riding a Yellow Wave

Salon.com, October 27, 1998

Just ten days ago, California seemed on the verge of electing its first Chinese American senator, Republican State Treasurer Matt Fong. But as one of the most-watched races in the country enters its final week, the momentum has swung back to incumbent Democrat Barbara Boxer, at least for now.

After several polls gave Fong a slight lead over the incumbent, the most recent surveys indicate Boxer leads Fong by five points, in part because of hard-hitting TV ads charging that Fong would weaken abortion rights and block tough HMO reform—ads that have gone largely unanswered by Fong. The Republican challenger has also been hurt by the revelation that he contributed $50,000 in leftover funds from his 1994 state treasurer campaign to Rev. Louis Sheldon's Traditional Values Coalition, a Christian-right lobbying group, which could threaten Fong's moderate image with voters. And the Congressional impeachment mess, which was expected to help Republicans, might actually be hurting them with voters.

The campaign is expected to be tight in its closing days, though, as Fong begins to combat Boxer's media barrage with one of his own. The tight race has put a spotlight on one group of voters who have the power to make or break Matt Fong: California's Asian Americans. Although they're 12

percent of the state's population, they are 6 percent of the California elec-
torate, and they've been neglected politically because they tend not to go
to the polls. In San Francisco, for instance, where Asian Americans are
34 percent of the population, they are only 16 percent of the city's registered voters.

But Fong's candidacy has energized California Asian Americans, particularly Chinese Americans. Their sentiments have gone undetected in
the major statewide polls. Unbelievably, the last *Los Angeles Times* poll
measured white, Latino, and African American voters' preference, but
not Asians', calling them "statistically insignificant" and citing language
difficulties in accurately polling Asian voters. They're significant enough,
however, to be getting attention from both candidates in the race. And
Fong could get help from an unlikely source—Asian American Democrats,
who are torn between their support for many of Boxer's political stands
and their desire to see their community taken more seriously by both political parties.

Many Asian American Democrats still resent their party for abandoning Asian American fund raisers accused of soliciting illegal foreign contributions in the 1996 presidential campaign. The party then intensified
the insult by investigating the citizenship status of Asian-surnamed donors,
the vast majority of whom were U.S. citizens. The Boxer campaign's finan-
cial-solicitation materials, several Asian American Democrats noted bit-
terly, spell out that she is accepting donations only from American citizens, leaving out legal permanent residents, who are eligible to contribute.

One longtime party activist, who asked not to be identified, said the
fundraising scandal showed "how vulnerable we were. Our entire community felt chastised by the party. . . . Some traditional Chinese American Democrats are now saying, 'It's time for one of us Chinese Americans
to get a high national political office, and if we have to sacrifice ideology
and issues, so be it.'"

That's the position of San Francisco attorney Bruce Quan Jr., a long-
time Democrat who is supporting Fong. "Matt Fong is from my community," Quan says. "Barbara Boxer has not been there for us. Boxer can't
point to any leadership on issues like immigration or anti-Asian violence.
She hasn't nominated Chinese Americans for federal appointments."
Quan sees today's Democratic Party as "the party of black and white, not
of brown and yellow."

Rose Tsai is another Chinese American Democrat supporting Fong. Tsai, who says she is a "lifelong Democrat," is a candidate for San Francisco supervisor this November. "Matt Fong holds many of the values of the Chinese American community—fiscally conservative, concerned with education. His candidacy is historic, an inspiration to the younger generation. We see Matt Fong as one of our own. When we call him, he returns our calls. What has Barbara Boxer done for us? We are sick and tired of being ignored. We will be loyal to the [Democratic] Party when it is loyal to us."

Quan and Tsai may have a lot of company, according to June-primary exit polls. An exit poll conducted by political consultant Tom Hsieh Jr. in liberal San Francisco found that 74 percent of Chinese American voters supported Republican Fong in the state's open primary, while 81 percent of them chose a Democrat in the race for governor. In Los Angeles, an exit poll conducted by Vision 21, a nonpartisan Chinese American political group, found that 84 percent of Chinese Americans voted for Fong—including two-thirds of Chinese American Democrats.

"Matt Fong will probably get some crossover votes from Asian American Democrats," concedes Rose Kapolczynski, Boxer's campaign manager. "But Barbara will get some support from Republican women" who disagree with Fong's support for more restrictions on abortion. She said the campaign has formed an "Asian Americans for Boxer" group. "We're working hard to reach Asian Americans," Kapolczynski says, touting Boxer's record of Asian American federal judicial appointments and support of other issues of interest to Asian Americans such as Japanese American reparations, Filipino American veterans' benefits, and family reunification provisions of immigration laws.

Alicia Wang, vice chair of the California Democratic Party, says, "Matt Fong is the first major Chinese American candidate for the U.S. Senate from California, so it is perfectly understandable that the Chinese American community will feel pride in his candidacy. But that doesn't mean we should not apply the same standards we apply to other candidates. What is his track record on issues that matter to me, like affirmative action, immigration, education? Barbara Boxer has been there for us on those issues." Wang notes that Fong supported Propositions 209 and 227, the California initiatives that abolished affirmative action and bilingual education programs, respectively.

Asian Americans make up almost 4 percent of the nation's population and about 40 percent of the nation's ten million residents of Asian descent live in California. Their voter turnout is the lowest of any major racial group in the nation.

California's Asian American voters are a hard group to characterize politically. Like Fong, they supported Proposition 227, which abolished bilingual education, and which most Democrats opposed. But they opposed Republican-backed Proposition 209, which did away with affirmative action. According to the Field Poll, the state's leading public-opinion survey firm, California Asian Americans are 45 percent Democrat, 35 percent Republican, and 20 percent independent or "other."

According to the Chinese American Voter Education Committee, San Francisco's Asian American voters are 43 percent Democrat, 20 percent Republican, and 37 percent independent, other, or "decline to state." In Monterey Park east of Los Angeles, Chinese American voters are virtually evenly split among Democrats, Republicans, and independents, according to Don Nakanishi, director of the University of California–Los Angeles Asian American Studies Center.

Some analysts expect the Asian American vote to get more conservative. As the number of Koreans and Vietnamese rises—two groups that tend to vote Republican—the proportion of traditionally Democratic Japanese and Filipino Americans is going down. The Fong-Boxer race is expected to break down the same way, with Korean Americans and Vietnamese Americans going for Fong, Japanese Americans and Filipino Americans going for Boxer, and Chinese Americans supporting Fong. On balance, California's Asian American voters tend to line up right in between whites and Latinos politically and are usually much closer to white Californians than to black Californians, according to Mark DiCamillo, director of the Field Poll.

Until recently, the affable Fong has made it easy for moderates of every ethnicity to support him. The son of California's longtime Democratic secretary of state, March Fong Eu, he comes across as a bland but likable middle-of-the-roader, not the right-wing conservative that Boxer has said he is. During the campaign, Fong has presented himself as a moderate on issues such as the environment and abortion rights. He has cultivated ties to the business community and avoided right-wing appeals on abortion, crime, and gay rights.

He benefits from the contrast with Boxer, who stands solidly on the liberal wing of the Democratic Party and alienates many moderates with a strident image. "Matt Fong is a moderate, not a flaming right winger," stresses Democrat Quan. "We do not have extreme philosophical differences."

That's why Fong's $50,000 contribution to the right-wing Traditional Values Coalition could damage him with Asian American Democrats and others considering a crossover vote. It might not sway Asian Americans who are emotionally invested in his candidacy for ethnic-pride reasons—just as Republican women crossed over to Boxer in 1992 despite ideological reservations. It will likely hurt him most with moderate female supporters who believe in abortion rights.

Fong may also suffer from an unexpected impeachment backlash. In a September *Los Angeles Times* poll, 14 percent of registered voters said the Clinton-Lewinsky scandal made them more likely to vote, and two-thirds of those voters were going for Fong. But in the *Times* poll released last week, 26 percent of voters said they were driven by the scandal, and half of them went for Boxer, 44 percent for Fong.

Whatever the result, Fong's candidacy is inspiring activism among Asian Americans, especially Chinese Americans. "Both parties give our community a lot of lip service," observed political consultant Hsieh. "In reality, neither party has done a very good job of courting our vote. Our voting community has a way to go for full maturity. We are beginning to show the first signs of adolescence. We are starting to come out to vote."

[Fong lost to Boxer, who got 1,805,788 votes to his 1,569,390.]

A Common Human Affliction

San Francisco Examiner, July 25, 1996

The Lotus Fund fiasco in San Francisco is a painful lesson not just for Asian American Democrats but for all Asian Americans seeking a higher American political profile. The 4-year-old political action committee has had a horrible ten days. After bursting out in the public spotlight two weeks ago with the glittery announcement President Clinton would be the group's keynote speaker this week, the fund got hit with a triple whammy of bad news.

First, one of its officers turned out to have an illegal guns possession conviction. Then, Democratic National Committee sources told me Clinton wouldn't show up at the fund's awards dinner. Finally, Chong Lo, the group's ambitious leader, was arrested by federal authorities on a fourteen-count indictment including fraud in some Bay Area real estate transactions. Even though the charges aren't apparently connected to her political fundraising, the timing of her arrest couldn't have come at a worst time for the Lotus Fund. The fund's dinner, scheduled for Tuesday night at the same San Francisco hotel as a Democratic National Committee fundraiser featuring Clinton, was abruptly canceled.

Local Asian American Democrats who aren't involved with the fund are worried about the fallout, and well they should be. Democratic Party staff members with whom Lo dealt must be feeling sheepish and embarrassed too. It is a measure of the insecurities of Asian American political activists that some are expressing dismay at how the fund's problems will reflect badly on all of them. The fact is, the Lotus Fund isn't the entire Democratic movement in the unpredictable Asian American political scene, either locally or nationally.

The fund began four years ago as an alternative to a political action committee formed earlier by local activists called the Coalition of Asian Pacific Americans, or CAPA. CAPA's founding members are generally American-born liberal and progressive Asians who have been raising money to support candidates and issues consistent with CAPA's viewpoints. The Lotus Fund's founders were from both major political parties but had more moderate political views. Internal differences, however, changed the group's leadership, and Chong Lo emerged.

Lo, a well-to-do immigrant with ties to Hong Kong and Shanghai, was able to raise a lot of money, especially for the Democratic Party. But she wasn't considered part of the Asian American Democratic regulars who concentrated on party and community issues. From the party's perspective, it apparently was sufficient that Lo raised money. She also reportedly temporarily housed a few Democratic National Committee staff members.

Lo and her colleagues at the Lotus Fund aren't the only political wannabes among Asian Americans, who feel relatively powerless in politics despite impressive economic gains in San Francisco and other American cities. Some feel the quickest access to the American political game is through giving money to candidates and their parties. Others, however, look at the longer haul and believe campaign and advocacy work is a more effective strategy to earn respect from the established powers.

President Clinton's visit to Chinatown Tuesday before the Democratic fund raiser was designed to offset the impression the party leadership was abandoning local Asian Americans in the wake of the Lotus Fund problems. Asian American activists shouldn't be overly concerned about the Lotus Fund embarrassment. After all, blind ambition is a common human affliction.

A Question of Loyalty
Asian Week, April 4, 1997

Not long ago, Asian American activists could say with assurance that our community's issues and overall profile were virtually invisible. That can no longer be said, not with all the attention the political fundraising scandal has gotten from the news media elite. We can no longer say the national news media don't know we exist. Having said that, I know many Asian Americans continue to rage over how we collectively seem to be portrayed by news media reports and by Democratic Party officials.

The essence of what makes many Asian American activists discomfited is that the possible wrongdoing of a handful of Asian and Asian Americans is somehow ascribed to an entire group—Asian Americans in general. What remains unclear is whether the news media have set out to "get" Asian Americans or whether Asian American activists are excessively paranoid in part because such national scrutiny at its feverish, competitive pitch is a wholly new experience.

Not excusing the biased performance of some mainstream and ideologically extreme journalists, it is hard to believe an anti-Asian conspiracy on the part of all news media is afoot here. What the cumulative effect of the reporting has shown is that most, if not all, mainstream journalists know very little about Asian America. They are beginning to learn because of the howls of protests from many Asian Americans.

For Asian American activists, this has been a painful lesson in being a target of a voracious, sometimes unthinking and insensitive press. Asian American political and community leaders have to toughen up to withstand inaccurate, biased, and slanted reporting. Moreover, they must acknowledge that some Asian Americans may have violated the law or were duped into questionable activities by a superambitious president.

After many months of media bombardment, one troublesome issue emerges as a distillation of how far we Asian Americans yet have to travel in order to be considered truly American. That issue is a question of loyalty.

Since the end of the Cold War, the loyalty dilemma has receded in the political culture. As a youth in the 1950s, I well remember abrasive debates over one's loyalty to the United States because the Red Menace (Russia mostly, but China too) loomed large. For some Chinese Americans, there was a stretch of recent history in which some of us assumed a psychological ostrich stance for fear of appearing too enamored of "Red China," when Mao's Marxist-Leninist doctrines could be interpreted as a resuscitation of nationalism after a century of humiliation under Western and Japanese colonialism. That is, some Chinese Americans may have leaned toward Maoism not out a Marxist ideological bent but because they felt an ethnic or cultural affinity for a reviving Middle Kingdom. Other Chinese Americans forced the issue with China-leaning Chinese Americans because the former favored the Nationalists who had escaped to Taiwan following the fractious Chinese civil war.

This China-versus-Taiwan dispute has animated internal Chinese American politics for decades, but it has not touched all Chinese Americans. Second-, third-, and fourth-generation Chinese Americans are much more remote from these maddeningly emotional "family" conflicts.

The broad brush of possible disloyalty among people of Chinese descent living in the United States is never far from the surface and can easily be revived by demagogues and ideologues at the drop of a news leak from U.S. intelligence sources hoping to manipulate public opinion in this muddled post–Cold War world in which China is the main candidate to be the next Evil Empire.

It remains a huge psychological burden for many of us if we who have nothing whatsoever to do with U.S.-China geopolitical manipulations can be thought to be venal spies for the land of our forbears despite having lived in the United States most, if not all, of our lives and having never shown an ounce of disloyalty to this society's values, principles and precepts.

Trolling for the Big Fish

Asian Week, July 23, 1998

A few familiar Asian names—pushed out of the limelight by true celebrities like Monica Lewinsky and Tina Brown—crept back into the Washington, D.C., news scene in recent weeks. I missed those old names—Johnny Chung, Maria Hsia, Pauline Kanchanalak. In late 1996 and early 1997, they (along with a few others like John Huang and Yah Lin "Charlie" Trie) were among the best-known Asian Americans, mentioned in the highest political and media circles. The good old Asian names that embarrassed a lot of Asian American Democratic political activists re-emerged, albeit on the inside pages and without much fanfare this time around.

Johnny Chung, everyone's favorite hustler, was in the news again last month because he reportedly told Justice Department investigators that high-ranking Democratic Party officials "knowingly solicited and accepted" improper contributions from him. *Sacre bleu!* Chung has already entered into a plea agreement with the Justice Department so federal investigators are milking him for whatever they can get out of him. Maria Hsia, also implicated for allegedly funneling illegal contributions to the Democratic Party, was in the news not because of political fundraising funny business but on an indictment for failing to file personal income tax returns in recent years. Pauline Kanchanalak was indicted earlier this month for allegedly steering $679,000 of illegal foreign contributions to Democrats.

What we are seeing is a continuum—Chung, Hsia, and Kanchanalak, among others, were identified as fund raisers in the Asian American community who collected hundreds of thousands of dollars, some from "illegal" sources, for the Democratic Party and the re-election of President Clinton and Vice President Gore. Now, as Justice Department and Congressional investigations drag on, the suspects are being charged with a crime. In a couple of cases—Nora and Gene Lum, Johnny Chung—the suspects have pled guilty to a variety of charges. What is still ahead is some kind of resolution on the John Huang and Yah Lin "Charlie" Trie cases, among others.

This story—stretched out over many months—nettled a lot of Asian American Democratic activists who were alternately horrified at broad hints of "guilt by association" with these characters and angry at the voracious Washington press for seemingly targeting Asian and Asian American individuals for practices that aren't all that uncommon among both Democrats and Republicans. There was a lot of hysteria and finger pointing at the height of the scandal, and a good deal of harrumphing about slurring all Asian Americans for the alleged foul-ups of a few.

Most Asian Americans and Americans generally, far from the foul odors emanating from the Potomac River, simply lost interest because they felt this was national political business as usual. Besides, what do we expect of a campaign financing system that encourages influence buying of the kind alleged of these few Asian Americans? Fair-minded people (yes, even Republicans) ought to refrain from finding these Asian American operatives guilty of any wrongdoing until their cases are properly adjudicated.

That brings us back to Johnny Chung. The portrayal of Mr. Chung in the mainstream media elicits feelings of pity, embarrassment, and condescension. It has been difficult to get beyond that portraiture. He seemed eager to please, too eager. He wanted desperately to gain access for his Chinese business friends and associates, who may or may not have wanted to impress President Clinton to cut deals for themselves and entities in China. But let's listen carefully to his latest alleged assertion—that top Democratic Party officials willingly accepted whatever Johnny had to offer and that they solicited him for the funds. In effect, Johnny is saying, "Hey, this political fundraising game isn't a one-way street. I give, someone receives. Someone wants money, I get them the money." Sounds reasonable to me.

After almost two years of off-and-on media and politician-bashing, leading many of us to dismiss them as oily sleazeballs, is it time to stand up for them, at least to the extent of saying, "Hey, yeah, maybe Johnny and Pauline and Charlie, et al., went over the top with collecting money from their friends and associates to give to the Democrats and the Clinton presidential campaign, but they didn't do that in a vacuum, did they? Someone wanted their money. Someone needed their money. Someone accepted their money."

I am not defending possible illegalities allegedly committed by a small handful of Asian and Asian American eager beavers. But do they stand alone as transgressors in a corrupt campaign financing system? Should they be the only ones to pay a high legal and personal price for whatever wrongdoing they either admit to or are eventually found guilty of? Who among the highest ranks of the Democratic Party should share the blame?

My questions are not knee-jerk racial paranoia. They are more a reflection of knowing how the world works. In other settings that have nothing to do with Asian Americans, the little guy often takes the fall, while the powerful big guy survives intact. Let's hope the Asians and Asian Americans already implicated in the fundraising scandal aren't the only ones targeted by the legal-political might of the state, if some higher-ups who aren't Asian American are as culpable, if not more so.

Scientific Scapegoat
San Francisco Examiner, March 17, 1999

A few years ago, I was invited to the Los Alamos National Laboratory in New Mexico as part of an Asian Pacific American Heritage Month observance. My speech and informal conversations with about two dozen lab employees, most of them ethnic Chinese, were about the history and growth of the Asian American community.

I don't know whether Wen Ho Lee was in the audience. I do know there was no discussion about whether Chinese American scientists at the lab could be spies for China. Now there is a chorus singing that tune out of Washington, D.C., and the music sends chills through Chinese Americans, especially those in sensitive technology-related jobs.

Lee, a computer scientist at Los Alamos, was very publicly dismissed last week, suspected of illegally giving data that has helped China advance its missile capabilities, although he has not been arrested or charged with a crime. His dismissal casts a long shadow over his loyalties—and perhaps those of other Chinese American scientists.

The Lee case is the latest act in an enduring international serial melodrama featuring the United States and China and whether the world's most powerful nation and the world's most populous nation are friends, allies, partners, or enemies, or some combination.

While the two countries have had more or less normal relations for more than twenty years now, some Americans are clearly irritated, if not downright hostile, about continuing dealings with the rising force of Asia. They complain about China's human rights record. They accuse China of trying to influence U.S. politics with illegal campaign contributions. Now they are screaming about China stealing U.S. technology.

But more sober analysts say China is still decades behind the United States in nuclear weapons development. It is also not at all clear whether China used stolen U.S. technology to make recent missile advances. Chinese scientists could have developed such technology on their own or gotten help from the Russians or simply acquired it through open international exchanges among scientists from many different nations.

When one is so publicly fired from a sensitive job, as Wen Ho Lee was, the tendency is to assume he is guilty. The fact that the FBI has not yet arrested and charged him with any crime after several years of investigation means we ought to withhold judgment on whether Lee, who was born on Taiwan, is a Chinese spy. Some of his colleagues contend he couldn't have done what he is suspected of doing. Nonetheless, prominent Republicans and the Washington media elite have all but convicted Lee.

In a rational world, one would not assume scientists of the same or similar background might also be disloyal. But Chinese Americans have good reasons to feel insecure when such explosive allegations roar out of Washington. Some remember the exclusion era, when ethnic Chinese found it virtually impossible to settle in the United States solely because of race. Others—more recent arrivals—feel the push-pull of dual identities and loyalties, a dilemma not helped by subtle institutional racism that blocks their progress despite excellent credentials, qualifications, and experience, to say nothing of demonstrated loyalty to the United States.

It could very well be that the Lee case will turn into a serious breach of national security. But it really has the smell of political and possibly racial hysteria, almost an annual rite of spring but not nearly as affirming as the blossoming of daffodils.

[The U.S. government indicted Wen Ho Lee in December 1999 on fifty-nine counts of mishandling data, including downloading classified materials on to unclassified computers, but did not charge him with espionage. After being denied bail and held for nine months of solitary confinement, Lee pled guilty to one count of mishandling classified data and was freed. The judge hearing the case sharply criticized the government's prosecution of Lee, saying it "embarrassed our entire nation . . . for the unfair manner in which [Lee was] held in custody by the executive branch." The resolution of the Lee case set off a national debate over national security lapses, racial profiling of Chinese American scientists, and sensationalistic journalistic and prosecutorial practices.]

12 Crime

Bang, Bang, You're Dead

"It Makes You Feel Special"

Oakland Tribune, May 15, 1994

On a recent morning, I was sitting next to Samantha Vong and Lap Neou on a stage at the Federal Building auditorium in downtown Oakland. As they spoke at an Asian youth conference, I felt as though we lived in two different worlds, despite the fact we are all East Bay residents.

Our worlds are far apart in terms of age, ethnicity, education, experiences, and world outlook. I was both awed and depressed by what I heard. It's not that I've not heard stories like these before. It was simply that I was beginning to tire of hearing them again, as though nothing has changed, as though nothing will change.

Samantha is 16-year-old Oakland high school student. She was born in Cambodia and came to the United States when she was four or five. She told the mostly Asian American youth audience why she chose "the streets."

"I was having family problems," said Samantha. Her parents didn't want her to go out. "I'm living in America and I wanna go out, have fun. So I hooked up with friends. We hung out on the streets till one or two in the morning. Why did I choose the streets? I wanted to be, like, somebody. I got into trouble [stealing cars]. I went to juvvie [Juvenile Hall] for a week. I came out and did it again. I didn't care what anybody said. I went to juvvie for a month. That made me think about my life. My dad, who's buff, strong, but old . . . he started crying. That really touched me. He was crying for me. He told me to do good. That made me think about my life. I can't stay a little thug all my life."

"Here's what politicians can do [for young people]: build more youth centers, offer more counseling, deal with family problems." Later, she reiterated, "We have solutions [to youth problems], but people don't want to listen to our solutions: jobs, training, education, places to have a good time."

Lap Neou, a 17-year-old who came from Cambodia when he was a year old, said he wanted to be like the "older guys, be like a gang . . . more powerful." He got into trouble stealing cars and car stereos, "anything you can get for money. I traded stolen goods for guns and other good stuff." Some in the audience chuckled.

He speaks in a clipped street argot. "[We] kids drink beer, smoke cigarettes, marijuana. We don't touch crack. We talk with each other, watch [each others'] backs." He said he's been "in and out of the [youth criminal justice] system." He was first caught "joyriding in a stolen car. Got caught in the front seat. . . . I'm not that bad." Again, some laughter. "My parents got mad at me, cussing me, 'You gonna end up a bum.'"

He got caught a second time driving a stolen car. "They found bullets in my pocket. I tried to lie: I said I was carrying bullets for friends." For that, he spent five months in the "hall." "I thought my life was over. . . . They treated me like a dog."

Matter-of-factly, he related some fights he's been in. In one, he was one of four against ten. "They couldn't beat us. Someone came at me with a knife. No one got hurt except for me." Another time, he got into a fight in a suburban mall. He was with a friend, smaller than him. They confronted "a couple of Mexicans. They were big and fat. I go one-on-one with one. I started it. I won. I beat him. Reason I'm telling you this is that I broke my hand hitting a door. Fightin's not good." More laughs.

His future? "I just wanna finish high school. Don't know about college. I want a good job, get paid, big house, fancy car."

Someone else asked why young people fight one another. Samantha said, "Kids want to be somebody, they want to have power." A third person asked Lap why Asian kids fight other Asian kids. "Some Asians think they're more powerful," he said. "Some don't like your race. It's Cambodians against Vietnamese against Chinese. . . . My brother's gang used to fight Vietnamese gangs. They didn't like each other."

Samantha offered, "We don't learn about each other's cultures at school. We need to learn more. Why do Chinese fight Cambodians and Laotians?

American people know about Chinese and Vietnamese. . . . Cambodians and Laotians aren't well known. We want to show power."

Why do they feel the need to join gangs? Samantha: "It makes you feel special. You wanna be a part of something. You want somebody to back you up, your own little crew. Some don't see a future for themselves. They don't want to be out of their gangs, their homeboys, homegirls. You want the power, fame. You want a pager. You're tight. You want a cell phone, ride in a Honda Civic, lookin' fresh. If you don't have anything else, then the group's gonna give you power."

Samantha and Lap typify some children of Cambodian refugees. These kids, according to Oakland school board member Jean Quan, are dropping out of school at very high rates now. With the exception of a few groups that are trying to help, these youngsters are on the loose, culturally severed from their parents, who themselves are adrift in a strange environment. These support services, sincere and conscientious as they are, are merely fingers in the dike.

Remember: These children are a legacy of the American misadventures in Southeast Asia a generation ago.

The Model Minority Criminal

Asian Week, January 29, 1993

With several sensational crimes involving so-called model-minority Asian Americans in recent months, one is tempted to ask whether these incidents debunk the myth that Asian American youngsters are goody two-shoes. We might even ask whether Asian Americans ought to be unduly alarmed about the emergence of sociopathic behavior among some of our very best.

Why individuals who are wealthy and well educated and who come from seemingly controlled family circumstances turn bad is a question perhaps unanswerable even when we know the specifics of an incident. It takes expert examination over time to determine possible roots of aberrant behavior. I am in no position to judge these cases.

Oddly, I am not displeased that these incidents have been made public, because they cause people who look on Asian Americans one-dimensionally, as a model minority, to rethink their stereotypes. Hardcore criminality is not exactly what one wants to advertise as being "representative" of Asian America either. But that's exactly the point: These accused criminals shouldn't be thought to be "representative" of the eight million people of Asian descent in America. Asian Americans are a diverse lot. It shouldn't surprise anyone that some of us will commit shocking crimes.

I once reacted to news of Asian American gangsters with some alarm. Other Asian Americans did too. It was as though we were ashamed to admit some of us could do wrong. Perhaps we subconsciously bought into the model-minority stereotype. Part of the problem with this earlier response had to do with how the mass and news media portrayed Asian Americans. In the absence of in-depth coverage of Asian Americans, occasional stories of criminality by Asian Americans distorted the reality of Asian America, and people who otherwise knew nothing about us could conclude that all young Asian American men were gangsters.

We can't make the same analysis today. Our depictions in the mass and news media aren't much improved over the bad old days, but at least the model-minority stereotype has emerged to offset the Asian American gangster stereotype.

Now, with incidents of shocking crimes allegedly committed by model-minority Asian Americans, we're faced with a dilemma that deserves examination. The most notorious case involves Wayne Lo, an 18-year-old accused of killing two people and wounding four at Simon's Rock College in western Massachusetts on December 14.

Lo was born in Taiwan to a career military officer and a music teacher. At seven, he moved with his family to the Washington, D.C., area where his father took a diplomatic post. According to the New York Times, young Wayne Lo played violin with the Montgomery County Youth Orchestra. The family returned to Taiwan in 1983 and came back to the United States four years later when the parents opened a restaurant in Billings, Montana. Lo reportedly did well in school, continuing his passion for violin and playing competitive basketball too, despite his five-feet-four-inch stature.

In September 1991, Lo entered Simon's Rock College, a small institution known for attracting bright teenagers as young as 14 years old. Something happened at Simon's Rock to turn Lo from a high-achieving, violin-playing youth to one who became attracted to so-called hardcore punk rock and fascist, racist views. The New York Times reported he hung out with fringe rockers and espoused hateful anti-Semitic, anti-black, and homophobic sentiments.

Whatever was troubling Lo came together on December 14, when, police say, he bought a Chinese-made SKS semiautomatic assault rifle and some ammunition. That night, according to police, he proceeded to shoot two people and wound four others at the college over a twenty-minute period. He gave himself up after the shooting spree. A photo in the *Times* shows Lo as a shaved-head young man wearing a sweatshirt with the words "Sick of It All" on the front. "Sick of It All" is the name of a punk-rock band.

A second equally sensational case involves six southern California teenagers, at least five of whom are Asian, according to their surnames. The two principal teenagers are of Chinese descent and both are excellent students, destined for an elite Ivy League university. What's mind-boggling is that the two are alleged to have been part of a conspiracy to rob an Anaheim, California, computer store. Something went wrong with their conspiracy and, according to police, five of them ganged up on the sixth and bludgeoned him to death with baseball bats and a sledgehammer on New Year's Eve.

The dead youth is Stuart Anthony Tay, a 17-year-old honor student from Orange in Orange County, south of Los Angeles. His chief assailant, according to police, is Robert Chien-Nan Chan, 18, of Fullerton. Tay was described in news reports as being part of a wealthy Singaporean immigrant family. Chan, a native of Taiwan, is the son of an engineer and a homemaker.

Police said Chan masterminded the killing of Tay because Tay used an alias while they and four other teenagers plotted the computer heist. When Chan and the others discovered Tay had used another name with them, they suspected he would snitch on them and thus, police said, they decided to kill him.

Two cases, however shocking and sensational, do not a trend make. Maybe not. Separately or together, they certainly get the attention of Asian America. Mental-health professionals I talked with were understandably reluctant to discuss these cases because they had no first-hand knowledge of the individuals involved. Nonetheless, three of them were willing to share general thoughts on the cultural context of these cases.

Dr. Stanley Sue, a professor of psychology and director of the National Research Center on Asian American Mental Health at UCLA, surmised that America is hearing about these cases now because there are more Asian Americans than there were twenty years ago, and today's Asian American population is more diverse than it was a generation or two ago. "With greater diversity, we have to anticipate lots of problems that are likely to come up" among Asian Americans, Dr. Sue said.

He speculated that some Asian immigrants, coming from more tightly controlled societies, lose control over their children who become Americanized, which can be both good and bad, he said. The children may do well in school, but "education doesn't guarantee you'll be mentally healthy."

As America becomes more multicultural, including larger numbers of diverse Asian Americans, this society is going through a "state of transition" and hasn't found appropriate institutional ways of handling these kinds of dysfunction, Dr. Sue indicated. Parents and community members are at a loss for what to do.

Indeed, in both the Lo and the Tay-Chan cases, parents and relatives expressed dismay their relatives became involved in such sociopathic behavior. Wayne Lo's mother, Lin-Lin Lo, told the *New York Times*: "These things that happened I still cannot figure out. . . . Wayne's a fine boy, a lovely boy. He cares about family, he cares about friends. I really don't understand what happened." Edward Djang, lawyer for the Tay family and a family friend, told the *Los Angeles Times*: "The family really doesn't understand what happened. It doesn't make sense. We're all sort of numb, just blown away by what has happened."

Dr. Evelyn Lee, who teaches psychiatry at the University of California at San Francisco Medical Center and is executive director of the Richmond Multi-Service Center in San Francisco, said many Asian American parents and children aren't used to communicating with one another. In a traditional, old-country setting, families of two or more generations worked and lived close together. Here, in America, the communications link is broken by differing adjustment problems to a new culture.

She said she sees many Asian American young people with two personalities, one at school, the other at home. Parents don't know much, if anything, about the school (or outside the family) personality. Dr. Lee surmises that many Asian American parents focus on their children's academic progress and will reward (or punish) them on their achievements. But they don't either know about or pay much attention to their children's development in other areas. "Some parents complain about their children's behavior, but they don't understand some of this is normal adolescent behavior."

She believes newcomer parents should be given parenting-skills lessons. In her practice, she said she tries to introduce to Chinese American parents the idea that they are not raising Chinese kids. "They are raising Chinese kids in the United States. That's a big difference. They have to learn about their kids' world. Love is not enough. They have to learn parenting skills" to fit their new cultural circumstances.

Dr. Benjamin Tong, a clinical therapist who teaches at both the University of California at Berkeley and San Francisco State University, said his work with Korean and Filipino American families tells him that some Asian American families are a "pressure cooker." "Their whole world is family, and if things don't work out, there's hell to pay," he said. "Across the board, Asian American families are coming apart."

His speculation echoes in some ways Dr. Lee's. In their root countries, Asian families were tightly knit, self-contained clans, in response to distrust of what passed for government. Asian families had many children as a way of increasing their numbers, much as an army needs more soldiers. Dr. Tong said he and writer Frank Chin have theorized about traditional Asian societies that are modeled on military organizations. "For all the modernization in Asia, feudal values still prevail," he said.

Using the army analogy for typical Asian family structure, Dr. Tong said, "In an army, you don't do as you feel. You act for the survival of the collective." This mentality explains in part why many parents push their children to be the best because the parents themselves can't seem to be selfish. "It's as though a parent says to a child, 'I raised you to make me and the family famous. Whatever you do enhances my status.'"

Coming to America, however, upsets those value systems, and the resultant discord in families may mean some children run away, or possibly turn bad. Dr. Stanley Sue cautions Asian Americans not to "overreact" to news of these model-minority Asian Americans gone bad. "If we do, then we buy into the notion that we are a model minority."

That's good advice. The tragedies of the two cases are human tragedies, exacerbated by cultural fissures we in Asian America are only beginning to understand.

Born to Kill

Oakland Tribune, January 22, 1995

The spread of criminal youth gangs across America is hardly news. Most of the attention has been on African American and, to a lesser degree, Latino gangs. There's been some local press on Asian American gangs, primarily those linked to Chinese and Hong Kong triads. Nothing in depth has been written about Vietnamese gangs.

T. J. English's *Born to Kill* fills some of that gap. A new book, published by William Morrow & Co., documents three years in the life of a violent Vietnamese gang with that all-American name based in New York that carried out crimes in faraway places like Georgia, Florida, and Texas.

Born to Kill is an entertaining, exciting, but ultimately chilling account of that gang's crime sprees until federal agents, with the help of a gang-member-turned-informant, arrested gang leaders, who were convicted a couple of years ago under federal anti-racketeering statutes.

Author English, in mostly matter-of-fact and detailed prose, tells of the gang's rise and fall, personalizing the tale in the form of gang leader David Thai and one of his minions, Tinh Ngo, a teenager who becomes the government informant after he became distressed when a fellow gangster shot a crime victim in the head.

The gang took its name from a slogan some members recall American soldiers wore on their helmets during the Vietnam War. After wrenching dislocations from their native country, these young Vietnamese men, many still in their teens, found solace in the gang life after finding no legitimate avenues here.

English writes that Ngo, for instance, valued the "brotherhood" his gang membership brought him more than loot garnered from robberies or illicit drugs he and other members ingested. Like some other Asian American gangs, the Born to Kill gang targeted Vietnamese and other Asian victims because, they surmised correctly most of the time, the victims wouldn't report the crimes and wouldn't cooperate with authorities.

English, who has written a book about Irish American gangs, said some Asian American gangsters know they can prey on Asian Americans because the victims "won't go to the cops and won't be taken seriously by mainstream society."

Mainstream America, he said in a phone interview, looks on Asian gangs as a "blur, faceless hordes of Asian youth gang violence." He maintains a book like his is "long overdue" because it sheds light on a situation that has been hidden behind myths and stereotypes about a "closed" Asian American society.

While the New York news media have done stories about Asian gangs, they have mostly been sensationalistic and haven't explored the social and cultural context of the gang phenomenon, English said.

Born to Kill is mostly a detailed look at the gang's structure and operations, but it puts into a larger context why some young Vietnamese Americans join gangs and commit crimes. The author rightly traces the roots to the Vietnam War and Vietnamese communist government policies of kicking out ethnic Chinese in the late 1970s and the refugee wave into the United States and the cultural and linguistic difficulties some of the newcomers encounter.

"The reason [some young Vietnamese refugees] got into gangs here isn't that they were criminals over there. They came here as children. It's because of their experiences here that they fell into a gang life. There's been absolutely no attempt to work them into the fabric of American life."

While focused on a New York–based gang that lived a violent nomadic life, his book is really a cautionary tale for other communities that have significant Asian American populations, especially refugees.

Born to Kill isn't a quaint, ethnic book. "There's something very American about [the Vietnamese gang story]," English said. It's a story that has precedence in how immigrant groups have acculturated themselves into American life. Many immigrants make the transition over time without severe problems. Others, however, slip into a life of preying on their own. It happened with Irish, Italian, Jewish, Chinese, and other immigrant groups. We shouldn't take this book as representative of Vietnamese American life, but it does provide a jarring reality check on one aspect of it.

Boyish Appeal
Asian Week, February 9, 1990

A dark side of the Southeast Asians' American experiences is beginning to come out—the sexual exploitation of Southeast Asian children. A conference in Oakland, California, opened my eyes to this apparently growing phenomenon. The conference was sponsored by the Oakland Police Department's Asian Advisory Committee on Crime and the Asian Community Mental Health Services.

Child sex abuse is now beginning to garner some public attention. We generally know that sexual exploitation of children mostly occurs between adults (almost always males) and children they know. We also know that the victims—and perpetrators—cut across all racial, ethnic, and socio-economic lines. Nonetheless, according to police and community-agency officials, and pedophiles themselves, Southeast Asian children have become a special target.

Perhaps there's no better authority on why Southeast Asian children are coveted targets for some pedophiles than a convicted pedophile, Theodore Benjamin Unterreiner. Unterreiner spoke at the Oakland conference, a rather odd circumstance, you might say, but his appearance was a galvanizing moment. The prospect of his appearance stirred up controversy in the Oakland Asian American community, especially among those he victimized and social-service agency workers who have been counseling the families of the victims. Some people were reportedly so upset at Unterreiner's scheduled appearance that there was talk of picketing the conference, but that never happened.

Unterreiner, who is 34 years old, faces charges of molesting five Southeast Asian children in Oakland, while he worked as a refugee resettlement worker. He has already been convicted three times of child molestation and was a registered sex offender when he got his job. Police officials asked Unterreiner to address the conference because he is intelligent and has expressed remorse for his crimes.

Adults who show an abnormal sexual interest in children are known as pedophiles. Unterreiner said he wanted to dispel myths about pedophiles and to offer help to police and psychiatric, social, and community workers. I found most everything he said fascinating, while at the same time,

I could never be sure whether to believe him. His intelligence was evident; he expressed remorse for what he did; his advice seems sensible. Especially interesting was his explanation for why Southeast Asian children are desirable to pedophiles.

These children, he said, are "diminutive, submissive, and easily impressionable." They come from families who have gone through a lot of emotional trauma, referring specifically to Cambodian and Laotians who survived genocide and war. This applies to some degree to Vietnamese also. He also said he found that the children he worked with didn't have many friends and that their families were "pulled apart" both by the sudden relocation to the United States and by generational differences. The latter refers to a situation in which parents acculturated in Southeast Asia can't handle their children who are rapidly being Americanized.

In short, these are needy and vulnerable children. "They will latch on to the first person who will befriend them," Unterreiner said. In some cases, Unterreiner was just that person, but as he acknowledged with candor, "Not everyone, including myself, is good for them." He found that the Southeast Asian children he worked with "were hungry for physical affection. These kids needed to be hugged and if you don't," he said to parents, "then somebody else will. That somebody else may not be the most appropriate person."

After his speech, I and a couple of other journalists questioned Unterreiner while he was changing his casual sportswear for county-issued prison garb and while police officers were removing a bullet-proof vest. Some of the children would come running to him with their arms up, ready to be hugged, he indicated. He surmised that Southeast Asian cultures—and perhaps all Asian cultures—were "no touch" societies. "It's curious why Southeast Asian families wouldn't cuddle their kids, but allow me, a social worker, to do that."

Unterreiner's modus operandi wasn't to snatch a kid off the street and molest him. Rather, he ingratiated himself to Southeast Asian families over a period of time. He helped their children with homework and other problems at school. He bought them gifts. He was accepted as almost a part of the family. He picked up some of the language. Over time, the children learned to trust him and turned to him for help. Their parents were grateful to him for his intervention in a culture that still baffled them.

To this day, some Southeast Asians in Oakland still can't believe the accusations about Unterreiner, according to Robert Sayaphupha, Oakland's only Laotian American police officer. "He's still a hero to some people," Sayaphupha told me. But to the families of the children he allegedly molested, Unterreiner has lost his hero status, according to Phiane Sayarad, a Laotian case worker with the Asian Community Mental Health Services in Oakland. These families are hurt and ashamed, he indicated.

Unterreiner's background provides a glimpse at his own malady. He was molested, he said, when he was 8 years old. A year later, a man he and his family knew had a sexual relationship with him for a few months. The relationship "was rather reciprocal," Unterreiner said matter-of-factly. When he was 12 or 13, he acknowledged his homosexuality and his attraction to children. He's been molesting children since his mid-teens, he said. He started working with Southeast Asians about ten years ago, an outgrowth of his work in the San Francisco Recreation and Parks Department.

He attributed his attraction to Southeast Asian children to "a personality factor and their accessibility. I used to tell the families that they made their kids too accessible. Like kids playing on the streets late at night. This lays the foundation for all sorts of things. They didn't seem to understand that you just don't do that [allow children to play on the streets late at night]. They seemed to feel that living here [in America] was the same as living there [in Southeast Asia]."

He also said that to some pedophiles, Southeast Asian children are "physically attractive," but he didn't elaborate. A couple of child-sex-abuse experts later told me that these physical features of Asian children include relatively hairless bodies, smaller stature, and later maturing bodies, which means that Asian boys, in particular, remained boyish longer than white or African American boys.

The chief myth he wanted to dispel was that of the stereotypical child molester—a 40-year-old white man wearing a trench coat and driving a Cadillac. In truth, Unterreiner said, most molesters are like the man down the block, or "even daddy, uncle, or grandfather."

He advised his audience to listen to children, for they don't lie about being abused. He also cautioned parents to be wary of anyone who shows unusual interest and attention to their children. He said parents should be suspicious of anyone who works closely with children.

As a parent, I find this latter advice to be chilling, for it forces us to think through how trusting we can be with teachers, recreation directors, ministers, and a host of other people who work closely with children every day.

The subject of sexual exploitation of Asian children is one that tests the Asian American communities' willingness to look inward and find truth. On the whole, Asian cultures don't encourage open discussions about sexuality, normal or aberrant. Incest and other forms of child sex abuse surely occur within the Asian and Asian American communities, but they are things almost never discussed.

Yet, with the Oakland conference shedding light on a subject that's long festered in the dark, the time is appropriate to confront these demons that haunt not only Asian Americans but all people. Dysfunctional adults don't just happen overnight. Their dysfunctions usually begin when they are children.

One point made by several experts at the Oakland conference was that today's child molesters were yesterday's molester's victims. This is not to say that all persons who were molested as children will turn into molesters themselves, but some will.

Teddy Unterreiner said he's sorry and ashamed for what he did, and if we are to believe him now, he points us in a direction that will help protect our children and give them a shot at healthier and safer lives.

13 Stars

I AM *Somebody*

Colorblind Casting
Asian Week, August 24, 1990

The controversy over the casting of the male lead of *Miss Saigon* is deliciously chewy. It embraces so many issues that intersect and polarize a society that's grappling with the realities of multiculturalism.

Asian Americans have been at the intense center of this raging theatrical debate. Its lessons, however, go far beyond Broadway. It has disgorged a multilayered debate—over the politicization of art, affirmative action versus artistic freedom, reverse discrimination versus perpetuation of historic discrimination, and harmful stereotypes of excluded groups.

Miss Saigon has been a hit musical in London since last September. It is produced by Cameron Mackintosh, who also produced *Cats, Phantom of the Opera,* and *Les Miserables.* He cast Welsh actor Jonathan Pryce in the *Miss Saigon* male lead role of Engineer, a pimp. He cast Lea Salonga, a Filipino teenager, as the female lead. Some thirty-four of the fifty roles are Asian characters. The storyline is a 20th-century update of the Madame Butterfly opera, set in Vietnam in 1975, as American troops were withdrawing in defeat.

Mackintosh wants to bring his hit to Broadway, New York. He wants Pryce to reprise the Engineer role, which may or may not be a Eurasian character. Some critics have found in the libretto lines that indicate the character ought to be Vietnamese. Mackintosh, by casting Pryce, has made it a half-French, half-Vietnamese character.

There's some dispute as to whether the producer gave Asian American males a fair opportunity to audition for the Engineer character. One version is that Mackintosh searched worldwide for all roles but couldn't find an Asian American of appropriate age and "international stature" and requisite acting and singing skills. Another story is that he had his mind made up from the get-go for Pryce to play the role and the worldwide search was for the female lead and the fifty supporting roles, including the thirty-four Asian ones.

Asian American members of Actors' Equity, the union representing actors, mounted a protest to Mackintosh's intent in importing Pryce for the Broadway production. The American union and its British counterpart have a reciprocal agreement that each can veto the casting of lead roles in productions mounted in the other's country. The reason is that each union wants to protect as many jobs for its members in their country as possible. The key mechanism to exercise that veto is whether the other country's actor is considered a star. If so, then that actor usually gets approved.

After receiving complaints from Asian Americans such as Tisa Chang, creative director of Pan Asian Repertory Theatre in New York; David Henry Hwang, Tony-award-winning playwright of M. Butterfly; and B. D. Wong, Tony-award-winning actor of M. Butterfly, Equity's governing body exercised a technicality that barred Pryce from playing Engineer in the upcoming Broadway production of Miss Saigon. Interestingly, Equity didn't state that Pryce wasn't a star. It merely said it couldn't condone the casting of a white actor to play a Eurasian role.

Producer Mackintosh responded by saying he was canceling the show, which would have cost $10 million to mount and which had already sold $25 million worth of tickets in advance, a record. His action hit Broadway like an earthquake: Millions would be lost, as would hundreds of jobs. Mackintosh could have gone to arbitration, and according to Equity's lawyers, probably would have won.

In other words, Equity's initial technical response was a protest in principle and it fully expected Mackintosh to follow the quasi-legal procedure that would have allowed the show to go on with the objectionable white actor in the lead. Instead, Mackintosh steered the dispute into a much more public arena and thus set off a nationwide debate over the myriad issues raised.

Last week, Equity reversed itself, saying it's now okay for Pryce to play the role. Mackintosh hasn't said he would mount the Broadway production. I suspect he will go ahead with it, since so much money and so many jobs are at stake. Whatever Mackintosh's response, he has benefited from publicity that money couldn't buy.

Many in the Asian American theater community cheered Equity's initial decision to bar Pryce. They saw it as a victory for affirmative action in the theater world. Their position is based on the history of exclusion of Asian American actors from playing significant race-neutral roles, even though the buzzword in recent years has been "nontraditional casting."

Nontraditional casting means different things to different people. To racial-minority actors, including Asian Americans, it means enhanced opportunities for roles they historically couldn't touch. These roles presumably don't have racial or ethnic characteristics—that is, they are race-neutral.

The history of American theater (and film and television) is that white actors have been able to play any role, even black, Latino, and Asian ones. Nontraditional casting to some in the theater means "colorblind casting"—that is, anyone can play any role. That's fine in the ideal, Asian American actors tell me, but in reality it doesn't work that way.

Dennis Dun, a San Francisco–based Asian American actor, has labored hard in the Asian American theater world and gotten supporting roles in movies such as *The Last Emperor*, *Big Trouble, Little China*, and *Year of the Dragon*. He's also a supporting actor in television's *Midnight Caller*. Since his Hollywood roles, he thought he would get more chances to play race-neutral parts. That hasn't happened. He says he's auditioned only twice in the past six years for non-Asian roles and when he did, he was in effect asked, "What are you doing here?" He says Asian American actors get called mostly for Asian roles. Most of these are minor or perpetuate stereotypes.

Others active in the Asian American theater community in San Francisco, New York, and Los Angeles have similar stories to tell and share the pain of seeing prominent Asian roles go to white actors who give Asian stereotypes a continuing life.

Kelvin Han Yee, a San Francisco actor who's played both Asian and non-Asian roles, believes nontraditional casting is a one-way street for racial-minority actors to make up for past discrimination. It's a way for the dramatic arts to correct historic inequities. It is not a way for white actors to continue to play racial-minority roles. Since racial-minority actors still have a tough time getting work, they should at least be able to play parts fashioned after their racial-ethnic types. Many white actors, and others, of course, see this as blatant "reverse discrimination."

Asian American actors who want to practice their craft must then either accept those menial jobs that may or may not perpetuate stereotypes, or try futilely for nonracial roles, tilting at theatrical windmills. America still doesn't seem ready for true colorblind casting.

Frank Chin throws icy water on the whole dispute. Chin is an uncompromising intellectual presence who is highly critical of some Asian American actors who, in his estimation, are chasing success at the expense of cultural integrity and truth. Chin broke stereotypes and pioneered Asian American productions in New York City and San Francisco. His 1972 play, *Chickencoop Chinaman*, won critical raves in New York. He founded the Asian American Theater Workshop (now Company) in San Francisco and later split over creative differences.

Calling *Miss Saigon* a racist musical not worth the fight, he believes Asian American actors are fighting to portray stereotypes. Further, he says, once a production—any production, even a racist one—is mounted, then a producer should be allowed to proceed as he likes. In other words, he supports the creative freedom of the producer.

In a larger context, this dispute is rooted the 1960s civil rights struggles. The idea was to provide more opportunities for people who belong to historically disadvantaged groups so they could eventually catch up. Twenty-five years later, an intense backlash to affirmative action has set in. Some white people feel they are being discriminated against to make room for women and minorities. The issue gets complicated when affirmative action, which is a job regulation, is applied to an artistic enterprise like a big-money musical where the producer, understandably, wants to do whatever he (or she) can to make it a big hit.

The *Miss Saigon* flap is likely to be settled in a Solomonic fashion. The show will go on with Jonathan Pryce in the lead. The producer will be under intense pressure to cast an Asian American as Pryce's replacement in the future and find Asian Americans for road companies of the show. In the end, even if *Miss Saigon* wasn't the perfect vehicle to raise the principle of unequal opportunity for Asian American actors, it is proba- bly beneficial to the theater world—and to America as a whole—that the gnarly debate exploded so openly and in such a dramatic fashion.

Miss Saigon did open on Broadway with Jonathan Pryce in the lead male role, followed by Asian American actors taking the role. The musical has also spawned a traveling company that has featured Asian American actors in the lead male role.

Forbidden in More Ways Than One
Asian Week, January 26, 1990

The documentary film *Forbidden City, U.S.A.*, by Arthur Dong, preserves a piece of American cultural history that otherwise might have been lost. In getting key players associated with the Forbidden City nightclub in San Francisco to talk candidly about their experiences, Dong has captured for the ages a piece of Americana that has roots in both the Asian Ameri- can experience and the bicultural dilemmas of an America two genera- tions ago.

An enterprising Chinese American stockbroker and dress designer from Nevada named Charlie Low opened Forbidden City in December of 1938. The time seemed ripe for his "novelty." America was beginning to recover from the Great Depression. They were apprehensive about growing storm clouds of war in Europe and Asia so they were ready for a good time. Low offered something different. Mostly white people patron- ized the club, which did boffo business in the 1940s, as soldiers on leave and other tourists flocked to experience the uniqueness of an "all Chi- nese revue."

The Asian Americans who made up this "all Chinese revue" were gal- lant and brave, each courageously plowing new ground against great odds. They were rebels, in the words of one trouper. *Forbidden City, U.S.A.* makes clear that these rebels who wanted to sing and dance had few oppor- tunities to pursue their dreams and the barriers that stood in their way were erected by both their own communities and the larger white society.

Frances Chun, a Forbidden City singer, said, "What we did in the thir- ties and forties was shocking to the Chinese community and confusing for

Caucasian people." What they did was sing and dance in the American cultural mode. Their role models were white American performers, such as Fred Astaire, Frank Sinatra, and Eleanor Powell.

Jadin Wong, a Forbidden City dancer, said, "We used to get letters from Chinese people telling us we ought to be ashamed of ourselves doing what we're doing for a living, dancing in a nightclub. We should get a decent job and be respectable. . . . In the thirties and forties, the Chinese people were close minded. They were sure that anyone in show business had to be absolutely insane, immoral and everything else that's bad."

Dancer Tony Wing recalled, "An Oriental boy going into show business, an Oriental girl going into show business . . . the community thought something was wrong with them. If my father hadn't passed away and I finished school and became a pharmacist, a pill roller . . . oh, God, I'd be bored stiff."

It wasn't just resistance within the Chinese American community that made life difficult for Chinese American singers and dancers. (With the exception of one Japanese American performer, the other Forbidden City entertainers in the documentary were all of Chinese ethnicity.) Show business in those days was segregated.

Several Forbidden City performers remembered those barriers. Wing said, "If a white boy came in, he'd get the job before me." Dancer Dorothy Toy added, "We had to be much better than the American dance team, the Caucasian, or we wouldn't get the bookings." Jadin Wong recalled how some white club owners would say, "'We'll use you on Chinese New Year.' I said, 'That's once a year! Do you use Italians on Italian New Year and Jewish people on Jewish New Year? Now, come on, I'd get awfully hungry.'" Mary Mammon, a dancer, said, "They [white club owners] just weren't educated to the fact that we had talents in other fields than, I suppose, cooks or laundry boys."

For the most part, Forbidden City performers didn't come out of an intense Chinese American experience like a Chinatown. Thus, they didn't carry mental baggage from an insulated minority group that had unequal status, which Chinatowns did in those days. They were relatively free of strong ethnic identities, free to think and act openly according to their dreams and abilities. In the political rhetoric of the 1960s, some of these Forbidden City veterans were "bananas"—yellow on the outside, white on the inside.

Noel Tay, perhaps the most scandalous of the club's entertainers because she was the "Chinese Sally Rand" bubble dancer who hid her nudity behind two huge "bubbles" (or balloons), recalled, "Fortunately, we lived in a small town and didn't have all these old-time Chinese on top of us. That was to our advantage. That's how come we were a little more liberated. . . . I was brought up purely Caucasian. It wasn't until I went to junior college and saw an Oriental and I said, 'Oh, my gosh, there's an Oriental!' I never thought of myself as one." Tay was born and grew up in Inverness, California, a small town in Marin County north of San Francisco, "the only Chinese family there."

Mary Mammon said that when the call came from Forbidden City for a chorus line, "Girls from out of town applied. Chinese families in San Francisco looked down on such things and girls there didn't apply so we were the only game in town." Mammon was born and grew up in Clifton, a small Arizona town. "We mingled with the rest of the population, mostly whites. Our traditions were American traditions. This is what we learned in schools. Chinese traditions were not really that strong."

For a little more than two decades—the late thirties to the early sixties—the Forbidden City club gave Asian American entertainers a shot at their dreams. Just as its birth was the product of its time, so was its demise. Nightclubs of a similar genre died off as American entertainment culture took another turn in the road.

While the mostly white audience was undoubtedly surprised and entertained by the "all Chinese revue," the Asian American performers weren't free of racist reactions. Dancer Mammon said that on several occasions, "we heard people ask, 'Do Chinese dance? They don't have any rhythm. And their legs, they're terrible. They've got terrible legs.'"

Larry Ching, a Hawaii-reared singer whose role model was Frank Sinatra, said, "Those white guys would come in and say, 'That Chink can't sing, that Chinaman, that slant-eyes.' Being in the business, we had to take some of that. We were supposed to take some of that. But we didn't."

Forbidden City entertainers filled a niche, limited as it was. At least they were able to perform, to live out a part of their dream. The club itself both exploited and exploded stereotypes. It exploited them by marketing itself as an "exotic" entertainment, but it exploded them by putting on shows that mimicked white entertainment using Asian American dancers and singers.

The challenges faced by contemporary Asian American entertainers and performing artists aren't far different in spirit from those that confronted the Forbidden City group. More Asian Americans are employed in show business, both on and off stage and camera. The questions of whether they are true to their ethnicities—somehow reflecting their root cultures—or whether they are "selling out" their cultural integrity simply for employment remain debatable within Asian American intellectual circles. Some Asian American actors or entertainers perform nonstereotypically, but there are few consistent and long-term opportunities for Asian American performers to spread their creative wings wherever they might go.

Both paths—Asian American artists working the Asian American cultural vineyards and non-ethnic roles—have merit. We still haven't reached the day in American cultural life where either route is particularly well traveled. But if today's Asian American performers get disheartened by the artistic and employment limitations, they should remember the courage and pioneering efforts of Charlie Low and his "all Chinese revue."

The Connie Chung Syndrome

East-West News, November 26, 1987

David Louie, the popular KGO-TV reporter, had just made a knee-slapper of a joke—and, of all people, Wendy Tokuda, the most prominent Asian American journalist in the San Francisco Bay Area, was his "straight person." The occasion was a fundraising banquet in Oakland. Louie was the master of ceremonies, and Tokuda was receiving an honor for her contributions to the Asian American community.

After the standard tribute to Tokuda from the organizers, Louie stepped up to the microphone to Tokuda's right, stood shoulder to shoulder with her and said, "Don't I look like an Asian Dave McElhatton?" The crowd of 300 roared at Louie's pointed reference to Tokuda's stout and balding news-anchoring partner on Channel 5.

After the laughter died down, Tokuda turned solemn as she began an off-the-cuff commentary on a subject she said has gone on too long to ignore—why Asian American men aren't anchors of television news shows, locally or nationally.

"The reason why David and other Asian American men aren't anchoring news shows," Tokuda said, with a now-serious Louie at her side, "is simply racism." The banquet room hushed.

It was a remarkable moment. Here we had the Bay Area's most visible Asian American television personality calling a spade a spade. Tokuda could have let Louie's joke go unanswered, or she could have replied with a witticism of her own. Instead, she chose to provide some serious food for thought to go along with the roast prime ribs of beef.

The Asian male news-anchor brouhaha isn't new, and it isn't receding into the background. At the first national convention of the Asian American Journalists Association in Los Angeles two months ago, the subject pervaded the hallway gossip among the broadcast journalists.

A Chinese American male television reporter related to me how he was told by his news director, whom he described as a friend and mentor, why he would never anchor a news show. "This guy said that when people see me on the screen, they see someone who does karate, or kung fu, someone aggressive and threatening," he said.

The day after the banquet, I talked with Tokuda. I wondered whether this was a new and bold step she was taking. No, she said, she has been harboring such sentiments for quite some time.

I asked her whether she thought sexism wasn't more of a factor. She said no, because she thought it was racist for television bosses to select Asian American women over men for the high-profile anchoring jobs

Tokuda was gutsy to state so directly her views on a live controversy in her industry. Her position in Bay Area television journalism is solid; she ranks high in viewer popularity. She handles both anchoring and serious reporting duties with professionalism.

You may wonder what the big deal is. After all, there are Asian American men on television news; one (Rick Quan) even serves as a backup sports anchor for the same station Tokuda works for, and David Louie, Vic Lee, and Lloyd LaCuesta, among others, demonstrate their professionalism as reporters.

The continuing imbalance of responsibilities for Asian men and women on television news, on deeper analysis, represents another form of insidiousness among the mostly white men who are the station managers and news directors.

All this might be a tempest in a teapot if it weren't for television's pervasive influence in contemporary life. In the Asian American community, which has so few public heroes, our television personalities serve as those heroes, and therefore, whoever holds the visible and prestigious positions—in this case, Asian American women—garner the most public accolades.

Television bosses have apparently decided that the least offensive combination of anchoring talent—at least in the incredibly diverse Bay Area—is a white man with a woman, white or Asian usually. It's a cozy, non-threatening combination. Asian women are seen as exotic, or as objects of libidinous desires. Asian men? I guess even the so-called tolerant Bay Area views them as threatening or, worse, as non-entities.

This imbalance has a deleterious effect on Asian Americans. It drives a wedge between Asian American men and women. The overall relationship between the sexes is fraught with complexities and psychological land mines. The continuing gap between what Asian American men do on television news and what their female counterparts do can't ease the tension between the two groups.

By the actions of the TV bosses, one might conclude that Asian American women have a higher value in our society than the Asian American males do. Being an Asian male, I'm biased on this issue, but at least one prominent Asian American female—Wendy Tokuda—apparently feels the same way. On this issue, her word counts for a lot more than mine.

[More than a decade later, several Asian American men have anchored local weekend news programs in the Bay Area, but Asian American women are an even greater presence as reporters and anchors.]

Kowtowing to the Queen

Asian Week, September 10, 1993

And, to think, *this* was the one Asian American Journalists Association (AAJA) Convention I chose not to attend, the one at which Connie Chung was (finally) embraced with open arms, the "prodigal daughter come home," in the words of one attendee.

When AAJA first formed in Los Angeles in the early 1980s, organizers tried to get Chung, the most visible Asian American journalist, involved in the group. No thanks, she said. When the group went national in the mid-1980s, some hoped to get the superstar Chung for speaking gigs. No luck.

AAJA's 1990 convention in New York was Chung's Waterloo. She had agreed to be the convention's star speaker at the Friday night banquet. Finally, the group's leaders sighed with relief, Queen Connie was going to bless us with her presence.

Alas, as fairy tales go, she canceled two weeks before her scheduled appearance. In a written statement, she said she was paring back her schedule so she and hubby Maury Povich (a TV star too) could try to conceive a baby. Their heartwarming tale made the cover of *People* magazine and other national news.

It left AAJA leaders livid, although they were too polite to say so publicly. Chung helped find a replacement (Mary Alice Williams, a lesser TV news star) and the show went on. Connie sent a videotaped apology, which played at the Friday night banquet. When her saccharine apology aired, people booed and hissed. The prodigal daughter clearly was in the group's doghouse.

Fast forward three years. A scheduled speaker at this year's AAJA convention in Los Angeles, K. W. Lee, a widely respected veteran newspaper reporter and a past honoree of AAJA, couldn't make the Saturday luncheon speech because of illness. Chung was asked to substitute, and she readily agreed, according to Jeanne Park, a senior editor at *Entertainment Weekly* who as the New York AAJA chapter president was the key mediator.

"I knew how terribly she felt [about canceling in 1990]," Park told me. Park said Chung had planned on attending this year's convention anyway. At the same time, the AAJA board wanted to formally congratulate her on her ascension to the pioneering role of co-anchoring a network evening news show. "AAJA should be proud of her," Park said.

The initial reaction of convention goers to the news that Chung would, at long last, come to an AAJA gathering was decidedly underwhelming, according to several people I talked to. But you couldn't tell that from looking at a videotape of Chung's Saturday luncheon speech, which is how I was to witness the historic occasion. It looked like a lovefest. No hint of strain or anger at the woman who is now a syndrome—you know, the cultural norm that local newscasts must have one Asian American woman anchor.

AAJA leaders fawned at the Great One's appearance. They even passed a resolution that practically outdid the luncheon's dessert in sugar content. "Most prominent Asian American journalist . . . inspired many . . . generous supporter . . . first Asian American to anchor a prime-time newscast . . . AAJA congratulates her on her landmark achievement, wishes her the best of success and looks forward to a close association in the years ahead."

Never mind that lesser constellation AAJA members have for years done for journalism and the AAJA much more than Queen Connie (other than co-anchor a nightly network newscast and host a primetime TV magazine). The AAJA board (not without some dissent) chose to salivate all over Chung, oblivious to her past snubbing of the group and her community.

This says more about AAJA than it does about Connie Chung. This says AAJA, for whatever reason, hungers for association with the Supernova of Asian American women TV anchors. This concedes that Chung is bigger than AAJA and that AAJA apparently feels it must have Chung in its fold to gain legitimacy.

"She's very valuable to us," Park said. "She means so much to so many of our members. . . . She was completely mobbed [after her speech]. This has never happened before at an AAJA convention. Everyone wanted her autograph or wanted a picture taken with her. It was amazing."

What does Chung bring to the group? There were several references to Chung's "generous" support of the New York chapter. Park said Chung had quietly worked behind the scenes to help Asian Americans and other minorities get hired at CBS. Park told me Chung plans to make a "significant contribution" to a national scholarship program.

In the hyped fashion of TV, Chung at the convention offered to mentor one AAJA mid-career broadcast member, a generous gesture in the eyes of Chung's supporters, who are numerous among AAJA's younger female broadcast members. Yet, other AAJA members, busy people also, have mentored aspiring young journalists, both print and broadcast, without getting a national board resolution passed in their honor.

Chung's most significant contribution is star power, plain and simple. There are few Asian Americans with greater national recognition. Not politicians like Congressmen Norman Mineta or Bob Matsui, or, arguably, even Senator Daniel Inouye of Hawaii, even though a recent *Los Angeles Times* survey said that Inouye was seen by 7 percent of those surveyed as well known nationally, compared with 6 percent for Chung. Star power is what AAJA seems to want more than anything now. In that limited context, Chung's coming in from the cold should benefit AAJA. But is that what AAJA ought to be coveting and marketing?

In her rambling and disjointed speech, Chung never once uttered an interest in or a cogent analysis of coverage of Asian America, or other minority communities. Better coverage is the reason non-white journalists have been making a fuss about newsroom integration over the past twenty-five years, not star power.

She first talked about her immigrant family and her growing up in Washington, D.C., and how she broke into journalism. Then she recited third-party observations on the role of Asian Americans and women in journalism. Chung was essentially a reporter, not a passioned advocate for anything. She credited her own rise to the women's movement, not to the Asian American movement.

Here, I play a bit part, for she quoted from a past column of mine. Dragging me in was the latest chapter in the Connie and Bill subplot. In 1989, for the AAJA convention in San Francisco, I wrote a column criticizing her for staying away from her ethnic community and for not doing more to get Asian American stories told on shows she was associated with. (I have also defended her when a Washington, D.C., disk jockey slurred her on the air.) My point of view isn't unique. Other Asian Americans feel similarly underwhelmed by Chung's star status.

Her speech showed what little she has to offer other than star power. After listening to her (twice), I found myself saying, "Where's the beef?" Continuing the food metaphor, her speech was more like cotton candy. Sweet, but ultimately not nutritious.

After her personal story, she talked about story assignments. When President Nixon made history by normalizing relations with China, Chung said she begged to go to China for CBS News, but more experienced reporters were sent. She said each news organization she's worked for since then has wanted her to go to China to do the "roots" story. This was after Alex Haley's phenomenally popular *Roots* TV series. She said she was "reluctant. . . . It would be so self-indulgent. It'd be I, me, my . . .

so self-centered." Finally, when she was at NBC, she agreed to do a story about her family in China.

Her transition from a reporter eager to cover the Nixon China break-through to one reluctant to examine China through her family wasn't made clear. Other Chinese American reporters would die to have Chung's access to network news power to tell interesting stories that link China and Chinese America.

Chung drew the old dichotomy of whether Asian American journal-ists are journalists first or Asian Americans first. (Here, she quoted from a column I did a year ago.) This question has been asked, and answered in numerous permutations, for years by Asian American and other non-white journalists. That Chung raises it now is anachronistic.

"I don't know—it's a tough question. I don't have an answer," was her answer. "I think you have to do what you want." She concluded, "Kudos to all of you who take the time and are willing to take the time to become activists. So the message is: We need to be unreasonable from time to time. Thanks to those of you who are willing to be activists and unreasonable, we can actually effect some change."

So where have you been, Connie Chung?

When someone in the audience asked her that, she said, "I don't have any—really a good answer for the fact I haven't been involved," Chung stumbled. "I've been terribly remiss, I made a terrible mistake." She said she's been busy pursuing her career.

She said after the New York convention fiasco, she and Jeanne Park began talking. "I made a terrible mistake in not joining earlier." She said she's never been an activist. "I've always been wishy washy. I never joined groups. For me, journalism was the perfect profession because I wouldn't take stands. It required a balance. It required objectivity. It required not taking a position on either side. And so for me, it was the perfect profes-sion."

Not all AAJA members were skeptical of Chung. Several fed Chung softball questions, and one, Kristen Sze, an aspiring TV news star, told Chung she had nothing to apologize for, that she's been her role model for years.

The most political thing Chung said was a brief answer to a final ques-tion about whether she sees a bias against Asian American men in TV or in society at large. "Yeah, I do," Chung said without elaborating.

Chung's studied neutrality, her ultimate "professionalism," will be applauded by many Asian American journalists. From the beginning of AAJA, and even preceding it, Asian American journalists have wrestled with the question of "activism" and "political stances." Some swallow whole the idea that one needs to be "objective" and not involved. Just do your job. Just climb the career ladder. Maybe you can become a star like Connie Chung, too.

Then why even have an AAJA? There are non-ethnic journalism professional groups that Asian American journalists can (and do) join. Presumably, AAJA formed to address specific needs of Asian American journalists who either don't feel welcome in non-ethnic journalism groups or who believe an ethnic-specific group can better articulate the needs of its members.

AAJA and groups like it are thought to be necessary now because journalism, like other American institutions, is struggling with its relative lack of diversity. But if by AAJA's tilt toward star power over substance, perhaps there is no need for AAJA, after all.

Disposable Commodities

Asian Week, June 2, 1995

The toppling of two Asian American media icons, Connie Chung and Margaret Cho, has Asian Americans abuzz. In a society that continues to be both racist and sexist, Chung and Cho benefited because they are Asian American women. Ironically, their temporary loss of status can be construed as "reverse sexism," especially in Chung's case.

The superstar TV news personality has occupied a special place in the Asian American iconography, not because she necessarily did anything special for Asian America other than be at the right place at the right time. As Lisa Chung (not related to Connie), executive director of the Asian American Journalists Association (AAJA), noted, Connie Chung has been an inspirational role model "just by being there."

Officially, AAJA protested Chung's dismissal in a letter to CBS. "We are just beginning to deal with the rise of anti-affirmative action and anti-immigrant sentiments in this country, and the way the media covers these issues will greatly affect race relations," the group's letter said. "There are far too few journalists of color on-air nationwide, and we can ill afford to lose the presence of someone like Chung."

That was a boilerplate response. It's a great leap for AAJA to defend Chung on implied racial grounds when she herself has never asserted her own ethnicity in an industry that needs to be educated about Asian Americans. And to wrap her dismissal with the anti-immigrant and anti–affirmative action movements is politically fraudulent.

Many Asian American media professionals know Chung has chosen to distance herself from her Chinese ethnicity, even though she has protested that she's proud to be Chinese. Other than looking at her, it is hard to tell.

I recall an anecdote related by three Chinese Americans who met with Chung and her CBS News boss, Eric Ober, last year over Chung's televised report about the Chinese government's using Chinese scholars and students in the United States as spies. The three Chinese Americans represented different organizations that objected to the facts and tone of Chung's report, which implied spying within the ranks of Chinese scholars and students in this country was commonplace.

At one point, Ginny Gong of the Organization of Chinese Americans referred to Asian American identity. According to Gong and two others in that meeting, Chung said she doesn't consider herself a hyphenated American, specifically an "Asian American." "I'm Chinese," Chung reportedly said. Gong thought, "Well, you could have fooled me."

Chung could have fooled a lot of people. When she reached the highest pinnacle in her business, co-anchoring a network evening news shows, neither she nor media critics mentioned a racial breakthrough. Instead, they ballyhooed the fact Chung was only the second woman to climb the network TV news summit. (Barbara Walters was the first twenty years ago when she was teamed with Harry Reasoner at ABC News.)

I and other Asian Americans wondered why she and national media critics never mentioned her being the first Asian American to reach that pop-cultural pedestal. Maybe it has to do with numbers. Asian Americans make up only about 3 percent of the U.S. population; women are 51 percent.

Then again, Asian American women have always been favored "twofers" in the insidious games played by American institutions to appear open minded about allowing more women and racial minorities to share power, whereas Asian American men are barely "one-fers," and not coveted ones at that.

In a statement following her dismissal, Chung alluded to gender inequities, but not to any possible racial discrimination. Chung is probably correct about being a victim of the "old boys network." She was the junior partner to Dan Rather, an entrenched media star. Rather has respectable journalistic credentials. Chung's journalistic credentials are much less weighty. Emerald Yeh, who has anchored the San Francisco NBC affiliate KRON's evening newscasts, offered an apt analogy of TV news and Chung's career.

"Connie reflects what's happened to TV news," Yeh told me. "She once was a serious White House correspondent. Then she became a celebrity. Now she's doing some tabloid-like shows [in addition to her news anchoring duties]."

Yeh was referring to *Eye to Eye with Connie Chung,* a CBS News magazine show that lopped off her name after her fall from grace. It often focused on celebrity journalism and Chung, being its anchor, was central to that emphasis. Indeed, her shadowing of bad-girl skater Tonya Harding brought Chung criticism, as did her "exclusive" interview with Faye Resnick, a close friend of the late Nicole Brown Simpson. Earlier in her career, she anchored another TV newsmagazine show that used reenactments of events, sullying her reputation.

The biggest ethical question mark for Chung was her infamous interview with the mother of House Speaker Newt Gingrich. Chung's "just between you and me" prelude to Gingrich's mother's whispered "She's a bitch" comment about Hillary Rodham Clinton set off thunderous criticism of both Chung and CBS News.

Even during the new Rather-Chung team's honeymoon, Chung's questionable worthiness to sit beside the great Dan Rather emerged. One Asian American woman TV-news veteran in San Francisco expressed ambivalence about Chung. This woman, who didn't want to be publicly identified, told me she recognizes Chung has been a "high-profile Asian" but "she didn't deserve to get that job [*CBS Evening News* co-anchor]. . . . I'm not confident of her journalistic abilities. She's telegenic and has chutzpah, but she's not good enough" to deserve the high-profile anchor position. My source recalls her anger at hearing Chung tell "cute, self-deprecating jokes" at the expense of her Chinese background in a speech to a Radio and Television News Directors Association convention a few years ago.

Margaret Cho's loss of her primetime network comedy series, *All American Girl,* shares some characteristics with Connie Chung's diminished status but also has distinctive aspects. That Cho is a woman undoubtedly made her less threatening to the TV (male) gods, but her race was a factor in her getting the show. Her comedic talent and fortuitous timing were probably the most important ingredients.

There has not been a primetime network TV entertainment program with an Asian emphasis (I don't count *Kung Fu*). Cho's talent was being recognized as she climbed the competitive stand-up comics' ladder. Her club routines were a combination of generational and Asian American cultural sensibilities.

When I saw Cho perform a few years back, she was funny and irreverent. She skillfully walked the tightrope between self-hatred and satiric self-examination. Ethnic jokes told by ethnic comedians often border on self-degradation. They can also be devastatingly funny and pointedly on target. In performances four years ago, Cho used her life as resource material. She was then 22 years old.

She did Asian-based and anti-racist jokes. She opened with, "Hi, I'm Margaret Cho and I drive very well," a jab at the stereotype that Asians are lousy drivers. She said she's been called "Chink," and her response was, "Hey, Chinks are Chinese. I'm Korean, so I'm a gook. If you're going to be a racist, at least get with the terminology."

In a phone interview with her then, I learned she had been doing comedy since she was 19. She was born in San Francisco and lived with her Korean immigrant parents in a predominantly white neighborhood. The source of her comedy, she said, was "anger." She was angry as a person "living in two worlds," one Asian, the other white American. Her anger was at white Americans who "make me feel I don't belong." Her goal, in performing to largely white audiences, was to "change people's attitudes" about Asians and Asian Americans.

So, at least for this observer, there was hope her TV show would be an important vehicle to convey a genuine sense of Asian America within an American TV comedy framework. Never happened.

All American Girl featured a mostly Asian American cast but its shtick was somewhere out of the Borscht Belt, only with yellow actors mouthing the lines. That should be no surprise since the show's producers and writers were mostly white. Network TV apparently can't tolerate an in-your-face racial message that Cho delivered in her club acts for fear of offending the majority white audience. Generational sensibilities, as a hip twentysomething California "Valley Girl," came through, however.

Her TV Asian family was mostly a joke, and not a funny one at that. The show wasted the talent of actor B. D. Wong. The show did not show America an emerging subculture, Asian America, other than mildly offensive or watered-down stereotypes.

Not unlike Connie Chung's singular role-model status, Margaret Cho's *All American Girl* became a lightning rod for Asian America's supreme angst over our shaky status in this society. The show turned off many Asian Americans while it won tight-lipped support from others who wanted it to survive not because of its artistic merit but because of the ephemeral tokenism of having a primetime network show that employed a lot of Asian American actors.

Some Asian Americans said they watched *All American Girl* for no other reason than to support the cast. This kind of "negative positive" support simply shows our lowly status in America, despite individual success stories and easy acceptance of us among some Americans. There are approximately ten million of us now. Some of us are accomplished in science, medicine, the law, the academy, and the arts and cultural life, and in business. Others of us reside in the vast middle ground, just like millions of other Americans. Then we have our unfortunates, people who are "victims" of racism, sexism, capitalism's excesses and cruelties, of political circumstances beyond their control.

Yet, we get very little respect, other than as America's favorite pet minority. Sure, Connie Chung won a place in American pop-cultural iconography. So has Margaret Cho. Somehow, we still don't matter in America, not yet anyway. That's why Chung and Cho have been so important to some of us. They represented "success" and "status" and "somebody-ness" in a society that disses us.

If you analyze their status through a prism of racism and sexism, they are disposable commodities who serve at the behest of the white-male cultural power structure. White men put them on a pedestal for their own purposes. Now they've brought them down. When you accept the rules of the game that elevate you, you've got to accept the rules that bring you down.

Chung and Cho weren't in control. They got pretty far allowing their female-ness to be exploited. They couldn't buck the tremendous odds of pervasive racism and sexism, but their demise, which I suspect will be temporary, doesn't mean that Asian America ought to despair. The pipeline is filling up with exemplary Asian Americans. A few more are bound to pop out into the public imagination. Let's hope the ones that do will carry the heavy burden of their racial identity better than Chung and Cho have been able or willing to.

[After her dismissal, Connie Chung took some time off. She and her husband Maury Povich adopted a child. Then Chung returned to network TV, co-anchoring one of the 20/20 shows on ABC. Cho fell into several years of relative anonymity and problems with alcohol and drugs but is back on the stand-up comedy circuit and is working on a book about her experiences on the TV show. A film about her one-woman comedy show, I'm the One That I Want, has won critical praise. Her routine includes an honest critique of her TV experience.]

Mercenaries

Asian Week, August 13, 1993

Every few years, a big commercial film causes the collective temperatures of some Asian Americans to boil. Rising Sun is the latest. Rising Sun offends on some of the same grounds that Year of the Dragon, directed by Michael Cimino, did—a white cop hero whose main squeeze is a gorgeous Asian (or half Asian) babe. Both movies also featured Asian bad guys.

These complaints are chicken feed, however. Year of the Dragon and Rising Sun differ in one important respect. The latter is based on a best-selling potboiler. The former was based on the true-life gang killings at a San Francisco Chinatown restaurant over Labor Day weekend in 1977. More than Dragon, Rising Sun is both the subject and expression of paranoia.

Protesting Asian Americans are concerned whether Rising Sun will inspire more anti-Asian sentiments in America. The movie's theme— unchanged fundamentally from the book—is American paranoia at Japan's economic prowess, not American self-criticism as its director and simpering critics claim.

Michael Crichton's book was an anti-Japan polemic wrapped around a murder mystery. Crichton synthesized a popular analysis that Japan is conspiring to dominate the American economy through product dumping, direct investment, and influence peddling with American politicians, academics, and media.

Other analysts, including Labor Secretary Robert Reich, recognize Japan's economic aggressiveness but emphasize home-grown reasons for American economic woes—mismanagement, the short-term greed of American investors, policies that have ballooned the national debt, a low savings rate, and bad public schools.

It boils down to who is to blame for the American economic malaise—Japan or the United States? The truth lies somewhere in between, but ambiguity makes for dull drama. Crichton sides with the Japan-bashers. He tries to balance the anti-Japan polemics with sympathetic statements from the main police character, John Connor (played by Sean Connery), who is steeped in Japanese culture and who some believe has been bought off by the Japanese.

Much has been made of director Philip Kaufman softening the book's anti-Japan tone by changing the murderer's race to white from Japanese and by muting or eliminating some of the book's anti-Japan rhetoric. Kaufman made one other significant alteration. The junior white cop in the book became an African American (Wesley Snipes). Why? According to press reports, the director said he wanted to heighten the tension between the two main cop characters.

What the director has inadvertently done is potentially heighten tensions between blacks and Asians and set up a conspiracy of whites and blacks against yellows. It's not that the Snipes character is overtly racist toward Japanese. But one scene that played on Snipes' ethnicity makes a mockery of four Japanese yakuza (gangsters).

The scene is gratuitous and never appeared in the book. It shows Snipes and Connery leading the yakuza (driving a snazzy pink Cadillac convertible) into South Central Los Angeles, the lair of black gangs. Snipes entices his homeboys to give the yakuza a bad time, which they do. They surround the Japanese-occupied Cadillac, snarl at the occupants, slash open the convertible's roof, and generally harass the Japanese, who look frightened and stupid. The scene is played for laughs. In the screening I attended, some in the audience hooted and hollered, and you can bet it wasn't in sympathy with the yakuza.

Not that there isn't some real-life tension between African Americans and Japanese (recall racist remarks made by a few Japanese officials about African Americans). But this subtext wasn't part of the book and wasn't necessary for the movie.

The movie has gotten mixed reviews. Vincent Canby of the *New York Times* called the film "insufferably smug. . . . It directs attention not to internal reasons for America's economic problems, but to inscrutable, generalized, unknown others from abroad, whose yellow skins and strange manners announce their evil purposes as much as their unfair trade practices."

San Francisco Bay Area critics were exceedingly kind. Edward Guthmann of the *San Francisco Chronicle* called the film a "classy, but confusing murder mystery." He said he didn't see anything in the film that justified complaints by Asian American groups. "There's a big difference between dramatizing prejudice and endorsing prejudice, and I think Kaufman understands the distinction quite well." Another *Chronicle* critic, Mick LaSalle, strenuously defends and reflects Crichton's view that his thesis is more anti-American than anti-Japanese. "All 'Rising Sun' does is assume the existence of a competition and then root for the Americans. . . . Just because some people are offended does not make 'Rising Sun' a Japan-bashing film."

Shorn of its racial and political controversies, the film was boring and confusing. The lauded "chemistry" between Connery and Snipes was forced and stilted. A major artistic problem was transforming Crichton's dialogue of lectures into snappy cinematic repartee. The lecture tone remains in the film, making the Snipes character look particularly stupid at times.

Sure, the kinky sex, high-speed chases, and obligatory kung-fu fight rivet an audience's attention, but these elements are so formulaic, so bereft of originality and surprise that they ultimately contribute to the film's mediocrity.

Critics who said there was more America-bashing than Japan-bashing must have been watching a different movie. Almost all the Japanese characters were cardboard cartoons. The yakuza looked menacing, wearing dark glasses even in the dark. The fleeting scenes of elder Japanese businessmen left the impression they were permanently attached to tall young blondes.

The two most interesting Japanese characters are Cary Horiyuki-Tagawa's Eddie Sakamura and Mako's Yoshida. Eddie is the playboy with a taste for young American blondes, but had more dimensions than standard Hollywoodized Asian Americans. Yoshida stays above the fray and has a knowing relationship with the Connery character.

There are dumb or compliant Americans—the U.S. senator who turns from Japan-basher to supporter after a dark secret of his was discovered; the *Los Angeles Times* reporter on the take; the white American advisor to the Japanese corporation; the racist cop who turns out to also be on the take. In the end, there is only one hero, Sean Connery, all knowing, a step or two ahead of everyone.

This tired Hollywood formula reminded me of *Black Rain,* the Ridley Scott film starring Michael Douglas as a cowboy New York cop who went to Japan to find the Japanese bad guy he had let escape in America. This film had some success examining values differences between America and Japan. It featured a strong Japanese character, a Tokyo cop, and changed the rough Douglas character slightly at the end to come to respect Japanese culture. Once again, the white guy, Douglas, was the hero. He solved the crime, cutting through Japanese cultural and bureaucratic barriers. As flawed as *Black Rain* was, it was more respectful of Japan than *Rising Sun* is.

About the protests: The passions of some Asian Americans against the book and film indicate a continuing level of alienation and marginalization that is difficult for non–Asian Americans to understand. These unsettled feelings reflect a frustration that "our" stories aren't being told on the big screen. The announced reason for the protests is that *Rising Sun* perpetuates negative stereotypes of Asian characters that can inspire anti-Asian feelings in America. The history of anti-Asian sentiments is the context for these protests.

But they also symbolize our enduring "otherness" in America. That won't change soon despite our growing numbers and purported increasing influence in various sectors of American society. Some have criticized the Asian American actors in the movie. Some Asian American actors didn't want to audition because they didn't like Crichton's book.

The dilemma here boils down to an issue between employment and artistic integrity. Actors act, and they say they need more opportunities to do so because there are relatively few good roles for Asian Americans.

The truth is, Hollywood still reflects a white majority America and answers to one god, colored green. If something will sell, then Hollywood will make a movie to exploit it. Thus, Asian Americans interested in a cinematic career face familiar choices: Take what's offered with a hope (maybe) of changing things once inside the system, or stay out with integrity intact. Some Asian American actors, directors, etc., may have no desire to artistically express their ethnic identities. They then become mercenaries, the way other Asian Americans have become mercenaries in business, the law, the social sciences, and the media.

The Politics of a Bond Film

Asian Week, January 8, 1998

Tomorrow Never Dies is a James Bond film that is updated to current gender sensibilities (even though they are quite confusing and not as clearcut as feminist orthodoxy would want them to be) while hewing closely to the classic male-dominance values of a bygone era. But the most refreshing aspect of this latest Bond epic is its elevation of two Asian-related elements. One is the introduction of a strong Asian woman equal to James Bond's famous derring-do. The other is a theme that is nothing less than a metaphor for harmonious East-West relations and an antidote to the virulent anti-China sentiments that has raged rampantly among certain political circles in the West.

Skeptics might at this point assert, "Surely you jest." A Bond film is simply male fantasy set against Cold War intrigues and other variations of world domination (by men, of course). Bond women have been objects, pure and simple. Along with the gadgetry and thrill-a-minute action and Bond's unfailing heroism, the women—gorgeous, alluring, one-dimensional appendages—have been part of the Bond mythology that has managed to endure despite the best efforts of the feminist sisterhood.

I am here to argue that it is not necessary to turn in one's Sensitivity Badge in order to appreciate *Tomorrow Never Dies*'s attempts at gender equality and its surprisingly kind-hearted treatment of an otherwise Evil China. There is still plenty of male-female imbalance in this latest Bond film that stars Pierce Brosnan as the British super-spy, Agent 007 James

Bond. Enter Michelle Yeoh, born in Malaysia, made famous in Hong Kong as a female action hero the equal of Jackie Chan.

Tomorrow Never Dies is Yeoh's breakthrough crossover film. And she does it with a kick-butt panache that lights up the screen. She's got, well, machisma. She plays a Chinese security agent who teams with Bond to combat a Rupert Murdoch–like global media mogul who wants to start a war between Great Britain and China, all for the sake of making his media properties indispensable reading and viewing, with book and movie tie-ins to boot. What a deliciously appropriate villain in our media global village!

Notice the two opposing nations in the movie—Britain and China. Could it be more than coincidence that this movie destined for a world-wide audience would fictionally portray potential conflict between two nations that barely six months ago amicably exchanged sovereignty rights over Hong Kong?

The idea of China being the next Evil Empire to the West has been percolating in international political and journalistic circles for quite some time. It has shown up in different guises, such as China as a leading human rights abuser, and China as unfair international trader. There are several anti-China pro-Tibet commercial films in release now (*Seven Years in Tibet*, *Kundun*) and an out-and-out anti-Chinese screed starring Hollywood's most vocal Tibet sympathizer, Richard Gere (*Red Corner*). China has also been cast as a worldwide environmental despoiler.

It is perhaps incidental that *Tomorrow Never Dies* treats China not as a pariah, but, along with Michelle Yeoh's prodigious screen charisma, it is enough in this period of growing China-bashing that a Western pop-cultural vehicle like a James Bond film can deliver an entertaining message debunking a negative Asian stereotype.

Money Talks

San Francisco Examiner, July 21, 1999

When the NAACP speaks, the TV networks listen. Or do they?

Kweisi Mfume, president of the National Association for the Advancement of Colored People, criticized the four major TV networks for not having enough African American lead characters in their shows.

Faster than you can say "Must-See TV," network bosses said, "Yeah, that's right," or words to that effect.

"Those of us in the entertainment industry need to make sure the characters on our screen reflect the diversity of our population as a whole," CBS said.

"Although we are proud of the minority representation in many of NBC's dramas . . . we realize that there is still work to be done," NBC added.

"We are making improvements in this area, and we understand the need to do more. We are very sensitive on this issue," echoed ABC.

Or, as Seinfeld might say, yada, yada, yada. In fact, this exchange is like a bad rerun, warmed over platitudes in the ongoing American cultural wars.

Mfume certainly has a point, but here's another perspective: The black representation on network TV shows, while pathetic in some respects, is a lot better than that of, say, Latino or Asian American representation.

What major TV cop drama, current or past, has not had a black lieutenant or captain in charge of a squad room? This character has become a cliché. Think *NYPD Blue*, *Law & Order*, *Martial Law*, and *Homicide*.

If not the top-billed star, these characters are at least among the top tier of the ensemble casts of these shows.

On network comedies, Mfume is right on. Comedies are much more segregated than dramas on TV.

Images on TV shows may seem a trivial matter—after all, it's just TV— but they carry symbolic weight in our nation's continuing psychodrama over racial and ethnic issues.

One theory holds that American culture should reflect the nation's variety of people. Whether we like it or not, TV is a major American cultural form. So if TV shows have all-white or almost all-white casts, that must mean that black, brown, red, and yellow Americans and multiple shades in between don't count.

A subtheory is that TV and the movies (another major cultural form) should reflect the reality of the nation's racial and ethnic diversity. If that were so, however, then I wonder whether having African Americans as high police officials truly reflects the reality of police hierarchies.

Following this line, then why don't major TV medical dramas like *ER* and *Chicago Hope* feature Asian American characters as doctors, nurses, and medical technicians? Neither of those shows does, when in fact if you walked into a Chicago hospital (the locale of both of those dramas) you could hardly avoid seeing an Asian American doctor, nurse, or technician.

Latinos have legitimate gripes as well. Jimmy Smits and Benjamin Bratt, two Latino stars, had leading roles in cop dramas but have gone on to other things. Few other shows have Latinos in lead parts.

The bottom line, of course, is the bottom line—money. TV shows aren't on the air for art's sake or to make us feel good about ourselves. They are vehicles to sell cars, computers, phone service, soft drinks, beer, and other goods of our materialistic system. TV advertisers shy away from shows that have too many racial minority characters because, they say, these shows aren't watched by affluent white suburban audiences.

I once asked an Asian American who held a prominent entertainment executive job about why TV cop dramas had to have a black lieutenant and why Asian Americans aren't depicted as regulars on medical shows. "Simple demographics," was his simple answer.

More than any civil rights group, money talks, especially on TV.

The News Media: Only Getting Part of It
Asian Week, July 29, 1994

This is an epic week for racial and ethnic minority American journalists, including Asian Americans. We are meeting, six thousand of us, in Atlanta, an unprecedented gathering of the four minority journalists' organizations—African Americans, Latinos, Asian Americans, and Native Americans.

In preparation for this convention, called Unity '94, representatives of each organization conducted a groundbreaking study of mainstream American journalism coverage of minority communities and issues, called "Newswatch." San Francisco State University's Center for Integration and Improvement of Journalism, under director Jon Funabiki, coordinated this effort.

I was one of four principal Newswatch writers. What follows is a synopsis of my findings on news media coverage of Asian Americans over the past year or two.

Not long ago, Asian Americans could rightly complain that mainstream news media either ignored us, or covered us in stereotypical ways. In the 1970s, Asian gang stories were popular. (They still are.) In the 1980s, the widely reported Asian American "model minority" story created a new stereotype.

Television coverage of Asian Americans remains spotty and sensation-alized, but print coverage, while retaining some of the polar good-and-bad images, has become increasingly nuanced, textured, and true to life, thanks in part to more Asian American journalists, some of whom are bringing more informed coverage.

American journalism has advanced by quantum leaps from the days when it was an active anti-Asian influence, such as in the 1870s when it helped create a political atmosphere that resulted in the Chinese Exclusion Act of 1882. The American press also helped shape public opinion that supported the unconstitutional World War II internment of Japanese Americans, most of them U.S. citizens.

Journalism eventually catches up with trends, and the Asian American growth pattern has been a story begging to be told in its many facets. The biggest reason for improved coverage is the phenomenal growth and complexity of the Asian American population itself. But covering Asian America today is complicated by its diversity. Different Asian ethnic groups speak different languages and have different traditions, customs, histories, and American experiences.

Distinguishing between and among the groups is important. The umbrella label of "Asian Americans" can be a useful shorthand tool to politically identify the diverse Asian ethnic groups, and some Asian Americans embrace the label as a mark of political empowerment. Using "Asian American" is appropriate when discussing discrimination or bias because individuals from different Asian ethnic groups experience subtle institutional discrimination. Occasionally, Asian Americans are targeted for bigoted attacks or are mistaken for one another ethnically. The idea of "foreign-ness" hangs over all Asian Americans, whether fifth-generation American or newly arrived refugee.

Basic journalistic principles apply when covering the burgeoning Asian American story: good reporting, precise writing, cultivation of credible sources, knowledge of cultural traditions, histories, and experiences. The assumption here is that journalism values the latter attributes, but shrinking newsroom resources and a tendency toward "tabloidization" steal time and personnel that could otherwise study complex communities like Asian ethnic groups.

Progress hasn't eliminated some coverage problems, including use of stereotypes and a general lack of knowledge. The lack of institutionalized Asian American analytical and commentary voices is a continuing hole. Varied African American syndicated columnists are heard, and even a few Latino columnists are emerging. Regular Asian American viewpoints on Asian American and national issues are inaudible in the mainstream press.

Some good reporting took place in the dramatic story of the smuggling of Chinese nationals into the United States. Major news outlets in New York and California gave that story much attention in 1993, especially after a ship carrying almost 300 Chinese illegal immigrants in shocking conditions ran aground in New York waters.

A number of news organizations covered this story thoroughly, from breaking news to human-interest features. But one reporting flaw showed up in some stories, the estimate of how many Chinese nationals were being smuggled into the United States. These stories quoted unnamed sources as saying "hundreds of thousands" of Chinese a year were being smuggled in. Ko-lin Chin, a Rutgers sociologist who has studied the smuggling trade, was then quoted in an Associated Press story this spring as saying he believes 10,000 Chinese a year are smuggled in.

Given official U.S. government estimates that 300,000 people enter the United States illegally each year, mostly from Mexico and Central America, a figure of "hundreds of thousands" of Chinese is unreliable on its face. Citing unnamed sources wildly guessing is irresponsible journalism. As good a story as this was, the numbers involved call into question the vast expenditure of resources on this one story alone.

Speaking of labeling, journalism contributes to a confusion of identity of Asian Americans. This was most apparent in articles about Chinese food. The *New York Times* said, on September 23, 1993, "the American customers had all but disappeared" from Chinese restaurants because of a study indicating Chinese food had a high fat content.

An October 27, 1993, story in the *Washington Post*'s Food section on the same subject noted the Chinese community was "outraged and insulted by [the] study." It added that the study's finding that Chinese food, "as ordered and eaten by Americans, may be higher in fat than one might have thought."

New York Times restaurant critic Ruth Reichl, on March 18, 1994, wrote, "Most Chinese restaurants are so wary of American customers they don't even bother to offer them their best regional specialties."

American? Chinese? What is an "American"? Is it a racial-ethnic group (white European)? Or is it a national identity under which even ethnic Chinese who are American citizens can be embraced?

Some writers couldn't avoid tiresome clichés or rhyming phrases. "Asian invasion" remains a sturdy favorite. This inflammatory phrase appeared regularly in different guises. Ironically, the "Asian invasion" imagery, which reinforces the idea Asians are hostile foreigners, detracted from what were otherwise balanced articles about the Asian American experience.

Cutesy phrases popped up in other articles. On October 20, 1993, New York Newsday wrote responsibly about the controversial study on fat in Chinese food. But the headlines and graphics were trivializing clichés: "Much Ado About Moo Shu," "The Hot & Sour News About Chinese Food," "Chinese Food: Rice and Wrongs," "Take One from Column A."

In an otherwise insightful profile of Nike chairman Phil Knight, Frank Deford (August 1993 Vanity Fair) resorted to stereotype. Example: "Even more, though, people who have studied him [Knight] say that his immersion in Japan and other places Asian has more particularly influenced him in his ability to be inscrutable and manipulative." Are Asians, as a racial group, the only people who are "inscrutable" and "manipulative"? Example: "he [Knight] replies without cracking even an Asian smile." Is there a European smile?

Asians as exotica was the theme in some stories about Chinese women distance runners breaking world records. USA Today sports columnist Tom Weir (September 17, 1993) loaded up on stereotypes: "In China, 1993 is the Year of the Monkey. Fitting, because the Chinese are trying to play the rest of the sports world for chimps. . . . Confucius say that if Chinese are telling the truth [about a diet including turtle blood being partially responsible for world records]. . . . So, now, hold off on that next order of Mao Tse-tongue."

Contrast Kenny Moore's precise reporting in Sports Illustrated (September 27, 1993). Moore quoted several experts who cited demographics,

youth, and a punishing training regimen as the main reasons for the astonishing results. Moore didn't duck allegations of drug usage either.

The "mysterious Orient" hasn't vanished from the vocabulary of American journalism. ABC-TV's *Good Morning America* spent an early 1994
week in Hong Kong. The white American hosts occasionally laced their
chatter with references to "strange" and "mysterious" things. Strange and
mysterious to whom?

Asian Americans remain invisible to some journalists. A recent *Sacramento Bee* article about the search for a new chancellor at the University
of California at Davis said, "And there are currently no members of ethnic minorities at the helm of a UC campus." Then who is Chang-lin Tien,
chancellor at the flagship Berkeley campus?

Recent stories about the U.S. Senate have called it a "98-percent white
male club." In a July 23, 1993, *New York Times* article about the only black
female senator, Carol Moseley-Braun, Ben Nighthorse Campbell, the new
senator from Colorado who happens to be a Northern Cheyenne Indian,
was said to be "the Senate's only other nonwhite." Then of what ethnic
background are Hawaii's two senators, Daniel Inouye and Daniel Akaka?

In many stories about American race relations, Asian Americans aren't
mentioned, while Latinos are beginning to gain some notice to alter the
old black-and-white paradigm. One example was in a *New York Times* story
about youth crime (May 18, 1994) that indirectly quoted a criminologist
as saying, "One reason white gang members are not studied more is that they
blend into the American mainstream more easily than their black and brown
counterparts." Did those once-favorite Asian gangs suddenly disappear?

Public opinion polls conducted by news organizations are notorious for
leaving out Asian American views. Difficulties in gathering a statistically
significant sampling of different Asian ethnic groups are a serious barrier
to reflecting more diverse opinions, but polls in regions of increasing Asian
American presence should deepen their efforts to include Asians.

Then there's just plain bad journalism. A *Santa Clarita (California) Signal* article last year, headlined "Getting Oriented" (done up in a fake
calligraphic font), quotes a non-Japanese teacher of Japanese foreign
students on Japanese marriage relationships. The teacher has culled "her
knowledge from her intimacy with Japanese students over the years." The
teacher said that a Japanese husband would slap his wife if she doesn't have
his dinner ready for him when he gets home and would slap her again if

she hasn't done the dishes. Those outrageous generalizations should have been checked with Japanese cultural experts.

There are still sharp qualitative differences between print and TV coverage of Asian Americans. Some Los Angeles Asian American community activists, for instance, have renewed complaints about how Los Angeles TV news shows ignore Asian Americans, except for sensational crimes, in a region with a high Asian presence.

Kathy Imahara, a civil rights attorney, said, "Los Angeles seems to have done a strange thing in [its] need to have an Asian woman anchor on all of the stations. I'm not sure where that's from. That hasn't, however, translated into any more stories about the Asian community."

American journalism need not expend extraordinary energy to further improve Asian American coverage. It needs to use good reporting and precise writing with an extra dose of curiosity—about apparent differences in cultures, real differences in languages.

Hiring more Asian American journalists would help, but editors should use more than an ethnic criteria. They should look for, cultivate, and encourage Asian American journalists who bring special language and cultural skills. Filling an unstated quota with someone who happens to be of Asian descent but who has little special knowledge or skill isn't going to help cover the Asian American communities better.

If applicable, news organizations should assign reporters to cover Asian newcomers. Cultivating sources can be difficult, but hardly impossible. Specialized language and cultural training for reporters would be money well spent. Showing respect for sources and learning about newcomers and not automatically imposing Western values on them should help eradicate false notions, ignorance, and insensitivity, without compromising journalistic values of fairness, balance, and skepticism.

Everybody's Child

San Francisco Examiner, April 24, 1997

Tiger Woods has become a Rorschach test, especially since his inspiring Master's victory earlier this month. Before winning at the hallowed Augusta, Georgia, course, Woods was already a rising star. Afterward, he's become a Supernova of the Michael Jordan class, a worldwide celebrity.

That has to do more with us than him. "Us" in this case is a lot of people with different agendas and perspectives. For the most part, sportswriters ran out of superlatives and apocalyptic metaphors to describe Woods' Masters win. Some insisted his emergence as the game's newest star is limited to the world of golf, which has never seen the likes of a Tiger Woods.

These minimalist sports scribes aren't buying Woods' impact on the big, wide world outside the well-manicured lawns of elitist (and overwhelmingly white) country clubs. They miss a huge point about the meaning of the Tiger Woods phenomenon, which has everything to do with race, class, culture, and, unfortunately, commercialism in America.

It is difficult for sportswriters and perhaps other white people to comprehend the effect Woods has had on non-white people in America. Much has been made of Woods' fascinating racial background. His mother is Thai, his father part African American, Chinese, Cherokee, and white European. Woods himself has coined a new label to embrace his many ethnicities—"Cablinasian," referring to his white European, African American, and Asian mixture.

For strange and intriguing reasons, most journalists persist in labeling Woods as black or African American. Some may add, as an afterthought, that he's also part Asian. For their own perfectly understandable reasons, many African Americans regard Woods as African American, ignoring his Asian and other parts. When Woods won the Master's, one of the most noteworthy aspects was the fact he was the first person of African heritage to come away with the sport's most prestigious tournament victory. Little was made of the fact he was the first person of Asian descent to break the Master's color barrier.

To me and other Asian Americans, Woods' Asian-ness makes him an object of our curiosity, admiration, respect, and envy. After all, there are so few prominent, nationally known Asian Americans that an athlete of such prodigious talents like Woods who has some Asian heritage is bound to arouse swelling ethnic pride.

As one can see, any number of us can claim a piece of Tiger Woods, regardless of how he regards himself.

What I am about to say is in no way an attempt to appropriate the preternaturally gifted Woods as an Asian American icon at the expense of African Americans and others. For all the troubled, tangled race relations in this country, African Americans have had—and continue to have—many national heroes, ranging from Colin Powell to comedian Bill Cosby to TV personality Oprah Winfrey to politician Jesse Jackson to basketball legend Michael Jordan.

Few Asian Americans come close to that kind of status. Within Asian American circles, in fact, there is an unspoken burning desire among some to capture the attention and respect of the American public. To do so would mean validation of one's worth in this society, which has had a history of excluding and disrespecting people of Asian descent.

That is why Tiger Woods' victory at the Master's meant so much to some Asian Americans who could look beyond his mixed-race heritage to claim at least a part of him. It meant someone who had even a partial Asian background had triumphed in an endeavor that had heretofore been the province of well-to-do white men, most of whom are so used to their station in life they figure it's a birthright.

Publication Credits

"American Dream, Chinatown Branch" was originally published as "Chinatown, My Chinatown" in *East Bay Express*, July 30, 1999.

"A 'Manong' with Magical Hands" was originally published as "Barber George Catambay: From Hair to Eternity" in *Filipinas*, October 1998, pp. 60–63. Reprinted with permission from *Filipinas* magazine.

"Traditions: Old and New" was originally published under Bill Wong's byline in *Asian Week*, February 26, 1993.

"'Rock On, Mr. President'" was originally published as "Rock on, Mr. President" in *San Francisco Examiner*, November 5, 1996.

"Conquering Frontiers and Barriers" was originally published as "Angel Island: For Chinese, it was misnamed" in *San Francisco Examiner*, May 7, 1998.

"Wong Is an American Name" was originally published as "Wong Kim Ark's Legacy" in *Asian Week*, April 30, 1998.

"The 'Forgotten Holocaust'" was originally published as "Remembering China's 'forgotten Holocaust'" in *San Francisco Examiner*, July 23, 1998.

"Healing Wounds, or Opening Them?" was originally published as "East is not always East" in *Salon.com* at http://www.Salon.com, August 3, 1999.

"The Price of Memories" was originally published as "Saving Our Heritage" in *Asian Week*, April 16, 1998.

"Still Searching for Gold Mountain" was originally published under Bill Wong's byline in *Asian Week*, June 18, 1993.

"Second-Class Citizenship" was originally published as "U.S. to huddled masses, yearning to breathe free: Get lost" in *San Francisco Examiner*, September 27, 1996.

"Downsize Your SUV" was originally published as "Environmentalists and Immigration" in *San Francisco Examiner*, March 11, 1998.

"*Se Habla* English" was originally published as "No reason to fear a multilingual society" in *San Francisco Examiner*, March 27, 1998.

"A State of Mind" was originally published as "Is There an Asian America?" in *Filipinas*, May 1999, pp. 25–27. Reprinted with permission from *Filipinas* Magazine.

"So That's Why I Can't Lose Weight" was originally published as "The hidden essence of being 'Oriental'" in *Oakland Tribune*, January 30, 1989.

"Yellow Chic" was originally published as "Exploit 'Asian chic' fad while it's hot" in *Oakland Tribune*, February 3, 1989.

"A Tumultuous World in Transition" was originally published as "The Seap family's tumultuous world" in *Oakland Tribune*, February 3, 1993.

"'We Lost a Country'" was originally published as "Missing in action in Vietnam retrospective: The Vietnamese themselves" in *Asian Week*, May 5, 1995.

"Who's a Bonehead Now?" was originally published as "How Prop. 227 May Hurt Families" in *Asian Week*, May 14, 1998.

"Paradise Lost" was originally published under Bill Wong's byline in *Asian Week*, January 15, 1993.

"Minnesota Chow Mein" was originally published as "The Search for the Perfect Chow Mein" in *East-West News*, July 21, 1988.

"Best Friend or Best Meal?" was originally published as "Controversy over man's best friend" in *Oakland Tribune*, March 24, 1989.

"Violating the Crustacean Creed" was originally published as "Crabs have feelings too" in *San Francisco Examiner*, May 8, 1997.

"Parenting, Chinese Style" was originally published under Bill Wong's byline in *Asian Week*, October 5, 1990.

"The American Nightmare" was originally published under Bill Wong's byline in *Asian Week*, July 15, 1994.

"'The Boat People Own Everything'" was originally published under Bill Wong's byline in *Asian Week*, October 18, 1989.

"Learning from the Vincent Chin Case" was originally published under Bill Wong's byline in *Asian Week*, October 6, 1989.

"Escaping Racism: No Way Out" was originally published as "Why do Asian Americans get racist comments when race isn't germane?" In *Asian Week*, April 21, 1995.

"The Golden State of Bigotry" was originally published under Bill Wong's byline in *Asian Week*, October 22, 1993.

"Swastikas in the Sunset" was originally published as "Swastikas shock Asian Americans" in *San Francisco Examiner*, March 28, 1997.

"Un-American Christians" was originally published as "Non-whites as 'targets of opportunity'" in *San Francisco Examiner*, August 24, 1999.

"I Am a Gook" was originally published as "Sen. McCain: I am a gook . . . ," in *San Francisco Examiner*, February 23, 2000.

"Picking on the Most Vulnerable" was originally published as "Asian-Americans and Welfare Reform" in *Nieman Reports*, Summer 1999, pp. 47–48.

"New Global Capitalists" was originally published as "Moneyed Interests: Class in the campaign finance controversy" in *Asian Week*, November 28, 1997.

"An Obnoxious Status Quest" was originally published as "Our Classroom Status" in *Asian Week*, September 10, 1998.

"The Rich Can Be Nice Too" was originally published as "Asian donors not in the headlines" in *San Francisco Examiner*, December 27, 1996.

"Exploiting Our Own" was originally published as "Sweatshop Fame: An old story gets new legs" in *Asian Week*, June 21, 1996.

"Between a Rock and a Hard Place" was originally published under Bill Wong's byline in *Asian Week*, October 9, 1992.

"Calling for Magician Administrators" was originally published as "University of California needs a magician for president" in *Oakland Tribune*, July 25, 1995.

"The Selfish Versus the Altruists" was originally published as "Asian split on affirmative action" in *Oakland Tribune*, July 26, 1995.

"When Values Collide" was originally published as "Lowell case: Multiple-choice questions" in *San Francisco Examiner*, March 3, 1999.

"The 'Hottest' Dating Trend" was originally published under Bill Wong's byline in *Asian Week*, December 14, 1990.

"Special Assets" was originally published as "Buying into stereotypical Image" in *Oakland Tribune*, December 7, 1990.

"Hiding Behind a Cultural Defense" was originally published under Bill Wong's byline in *Asian Week*, November 19, 1993.

"The Hero of Asian Men" was originally published under Bill Wong's byline in *Asian Week*, December 18, 1992.

"Just Who Is the Victim Here?" was originally published under Bill Wong's byline in *Asian Week*, September 21, 1990.

"Playing Together" was originally published as "On race, friendship and hoops" in *Oakland Tribune*, July 30, 1990.

"Plenty of Blame to Go Around" was originally published as "What do we make of this scene?" in *Oakland Tribune*, November 5, 1990.

"Middleman Myopia" was originally published as "The O. J. Simpson case: A metaphor for Asian American role in U.S. race relations" in *Asian Week*, March 10, 1995.

"Yellow Pride Versus Multiculturalism" was originally published under Bill Wong's byline in *Asian Week*, July 3, 1992.

"Beyond Black and White" was originally published as "Conversation Stopper: Multiculturalism vs. the black-white paradigm" in *Asian Week*, July 25, 1997.

"Right Man, Wrong Time" was originally published under Bill Wong's byline in *Asian Week*, November 20, 1992.

"Race and Ideology: Bumping into Each Other" was originally published as "Ted Dang's Mayoral Bid: An Object Lesson for Asian America" in *Asian Week*, October 21, 1994.

"An Asian American 'Mr. Fixit'" was originally published as "Great Aspirations" in *Asian Week*, October 25, 1996.

"Riding a Yellow Wave" was originally published as "Favorite son" in *Salon.com* at http://www.Salon.com, October 27, 1998.

"A Common Human Affliction" was originally published as "Fallout from the Lotus Fund debacle" in *San Francisco Examiner*, July 25, 1996.

"A Question of Loyalty" was originally published as "A Question of Loyalty" in *Asian Week*, April 4, 1997.

"Trolling for the Big Fish" was originally published as "More Scandalous Blame: Asian Americans' names surface—now let's hear the others" in *Asian Week*, July 23, 1998.

"Scientific Scapegoat" was originally published as "'Spy' shadow falls on Chinese" in *San Francisco Examiner*, March 17, 1999.

"'It Makes You Feel Special'" was originally published as "Why some kids choose the streets" in *Oakland Tribune*, May 15, 1994.

"The Model Minority Criminal" was originally published under Bill Wong's byline in *Asian Week*, January 29, 1993.

"*Born to Kill*" was originally published as "Book sheds light on Vietnamese-American experience" in *Oakland Tribune*, January 22, 1995.

"Boyish Appeal" was originally published under Bill Wong's byline in *Asian Week*, February 9, 1990.

"Colorblind Casting" was originally published under Bill Wong's byline in *Asian Week*, August 24, 1990.

"Forbidden in More Ways Than One" was originally published under Bill Wong's byline in *Asian Week*, January 26, 1990.

"The Connie Chung Syndrome" was originally published as "The Asian Male TV Anchor Issue—Wendy Tokuda Speaks Her Mind" in *East-West News*, November 26, 1987.

"Kowtowing to the Queen" was originally published under Bill Wong's byline in *Asian Week*, September 10, 1993.

"Disposable Commodities" was originally published as "The toppling of Chung and Cho: Why we shouldn't despair" in *Asian Week*, June 2, 1995.

"Mercenaries" was originally published under Bill Wong's byline in *Asian Week*, August 13, 1993.

"The Politics of a Bond Film" was originally published as "Hurrah for Bond" in *Asian Week*, January 8, 1998.

"Money Talks" was originally published as "TV that's black and white—and brown, red, and yellow" in *San Francisco Examiner*, July 21, 1999.

"The News Media: Only Getting Part of It" was originally published under Bill Wong's byline in *Asian Week*, July 29, 1994.

"Everybody's Child" was originally published as "Tiger Woods: The sharing of ethnic pride" in *San Francisco Examiner*, April 24, 1997.

Index